The Rehearsal, Becket, Eurydice, The Orchestra

The Rehearsal: 'This is the quintessential Anouilh: guests up at the château, the waiflike girl from the lower classes destroyed by the cynicism of her social superiors, love and innocence killed by class and betrayal.' *Herald Tribune*

Becket: 'A fluent, vivid play . . . What seemed to matter was not so much Anouilh's view that medieval England was an occupied nation, like France in the 1940s . . . It was not even Becket's moral self-discovery . . . It was the increasingly tortured rapport between him and Henry . . . riveting.' *The Times*

Eurydice: 'A fascinating piece . . . it wraps the myth of Orpheus and Eurydice around the familiar Anouilh themes of heroism and the refusal to compromise.' *Financial Times*

The volume also contains *The Orchestra*, 'A Play within a Concert', translated by Jeremy Sams, and an introduction by Ned Chaillet.

Jean Anouilh was born in Bordeaux in 1910. He studied law briefly at the Sorbonne and then became a copywriter for an advertising agency. In 1931 he became secretary to the actor-manager, Louis Jouvet, and his first play, *The Ermine*, was staged the following year. *Antigone* firmly established his popularity in France in 1944, and Peter Brook's 1950 production of *Ring Round the Moon* (1947) in Christopher Fry's translation made his name in England. His best-known plays are: *Restless Heart* (1934); *Dinner with the Family, Traveller without Luggage* (both 1937); *Thieves' Carnival* (1938); *Léocadia* (1939); *Point of Departure (Eurydice)* (1941); *Romeo and Jeannette* (1945); *Medea* (1946); *Ardèle* (1948); *The Rehearsal* (1950); *Colombe* (1951); *The Waltz of the Toreadors* (1952); *The Lark* (1953); *Ornifle* (1955); *Poor Bitos* (1956); *Becket* (1959); *The Fighting Cock* (1966); *Dear Antoine* (1971); *The Director of the Opera* (1973); *Number One* (1981). Twice married, he lived mainly in Switzerland for the last thirty years of his life. Anouilh died in 1987.

by the same author

Plays: One
(Antigone, The Lark, Poor Bitos, Léocadia,
The Waltz of the Toreadors)

JEAN ANOUILH

Plays: Two

The Rehearsal
translated by Jeremy Sams

Becket
translated by Jeremy Sams

Eurydice
translated by Peter Meyer

The Orchestra
translated by Jeremy Sams

with an introduction by Ned Chaillet

METHUEN DRAMA

METHUEN WORLD CLASSICS

This collection first published in Great Britain in 1997
by Methuen Drama
Random House, 20 Vauxhall Bridge Road, London SW1V 2SA
and Australia, New Zealand and South Africa
and distributed in the United States of America
by Heinemann, a division of Reed Elsevier Inc.
361 Hanover Street, Portsmouth, New Hampshire
NH 03801 3959

Random House UK Limited Reg. No. 954009

Typeset by Deltatype Ltd, Birkenhead, Merseyside
Printed and bound in Great Britain by
Cox & Wyman Ltd, Reading, Berks

Caution

Contents

Jean Anouilh:
Chronology

1910	23 June: born in Bordeaux to François Anouilh, a tailor, and Marie-Magdalene, a musician.
1919?	For a season, as his mother played violin in the orchestra of the Casino at Arcachon, near Bordeaux, he watched operetta night after night.
1928	Complaints officer, Grands Magasins du Louvre.
1929	Wrote the comedic curtain-raiser, *Humulus le Muet* (*Humulus the Mute*) and *Mandarine*.
1930	Noël Coward appears as Elyot Chase in his play *Private Lives* at the Phoenix Theatre, London.
1931	Wrote *L'Hermine* (*The Ermine*) (*Pièces noires*). Married for the first time, to Monelle Valentin.
1931–32	Secretary to Louis Jouvet's theatre company, Comédie des Champs-Elysées.
1932	His first produced play, *L'Hermine*, at Théâtre de l'Œuvre, Paris. Wrote *Le Bal des voleurs* (*Thieves' Carnival*) (*Pièces roses*).
1933	Production of *Mandarine*, Théâtre de l'Athénée, Paris.
1935	*Y avait un prisonnier* (*There Was a Prisoner*) performed at Théâtre des Ambassadeurs, Paris. It is sold to Hollywood.
1936	Wrote *Le Voyageur sans bagage* (*Traveller without Luggage*) (*Pièces noires*).
1937	*Le Voyageur sans bagage* produced at Théâtre des Mathurins, Paris. *Le Voyageur sans bagage* appeared on the London stage under the title *Identity Unknown*.
1938	*Le Bal des voleurs* produced at Théâtre des Arts, Paris; also produced at Theatre de Quatre Saisons, New York City.
1939	*Léocadia* (*Pièces roses*) produced at Théâtre de l'Atelier, Paris.
1941	*Eurydice* (*Pièces noires*) produced at Théâtre de l'Atelier.
1944	*Antigone* (*Nouvelles pièces noires*) produced at Théâtre de l'Atelier. Tennessee Williams's play *The Glass Menagerie* produced in Chicago; 1945 in New York.
1946	*Roméo et Jeannette* (*Nouvelles pièces noires*) produced at Théâtre de l'Atelier.
1947	*L'Invitation au château* (*Ring Round the Moon*) (*Pièces brillantes*) produced at Théâtre de l'Atelier.

1948   *Eurydice,* translated by Mel Ferrer, produced at the
Coronet Theater, Los Angeles.
Ardèle (Pièces grinçantes) produced at Comédie des Champs-
Elysées.
Arthur Miller's play *Death of a Salesman* produced in New
York.

1949   *Antigone* presented by the Old Vic Theatre Company at
the New Theatre, London, starring Sir Laurence Olivier
and Vivien Leigh.

1950   *La Répétition ou l'amour puni (The Rehearsal) (Pièces brillantes)*
produced at Théâtre Marigny, Paris.
Eurydice, under the title *Point of Departure,* produced in
Kitty Black's translation at the Lyric Theatre,
Hammersmith, with the actors Dirk Bogarde, Mai
Zetterling and Hugh Griffiths; transferring to the Globe
Theatre (now the Gielgud), London.
Ring Round the Moon, translated by Christopher Fry,
directed by Peter Brook, with Paul Scofield as twin hero
and villain, produced at the Globe Theatre.
Eugène Ionesco's play *La Cantatrice chauve (The Bald Prima
Donna)* produced at Les Noctambules, Paris.

1951   *Eurydice,* under the title *Legend of Lovers,* produced at the
Plymouth Theater, New York City.
Thieves' Carnival produced in London.
Colombe (Pièces brillantes) produced at Théâtre de l'Atelier.

1952   *The Rehearsal,* translated by Pamela Hansford Johnson
and Kitty Black, produced at the Ziegfeld Theater, New
York City.
First production of *La Valse de toréadors (Waltz of the
Toreadors) (Pièces grinçantes).*
Translated and edited *Trois Comédies de William Shakespeare:
As You Like It, The Winter's Tale, Twelfth Night.*

1953   30 July: married Nicole Lançon, his second marriage.
First production of *L'Alouette (The Lark) (Pièces costumées).*
Samuel Beckett's *En Attendant Godot (Waiting for Godot)*
produced by Roger Blin at Théâtre de Babylone.

1956   *Pauvre Bitos ou le dîner de têtes (Poor Bitos or the Dinner of Heads)
(Pièces grinçantes)* produced at Théâtre Montparnasse,
Paris.

1957   Writes *L'Orchestre (The Orchestra) (Pièces grinçantes).*

1958   Harold Pinter's play *The Birthday Party* produced in
London.

1959   *Becket ou l'honneur de Dieu (Becket, or The Honour of God) (Pièces
costumées)* produced at Théâtre Montparnasse.

Traveller without Luggage, translated by John Whiting, produced at the Arts Theatre, London.

1960 *Becket*, in the translation by Lucienne Hill, produced at the St James Theater, New York City.

1961 *Becket*, produced by the Royal Shakespeare Company at the Aldwych Theatre in the translation by Lucienne Hill, directed by Peter Hall, transferring to the Globe Theatre (now the Gielgud).

The Rehearsal opens at the Bristol Old Vic in April and transfers to London, where it plays at the Globe, the Queen's, the Globe again, and finally at the Apollo.

1962 *L'Orchestre* produced in Paris.

1963 *Becket* filmed with Peter O'Toole and Richard Burton.

1964 *Traveller without Luggage*, translated by Lucienne Hill, produced at ANTA Playhouse, New York City.

1967 *The Orchestra* performed at the Little Theatre, Bristol.

1969 *The Orchestra* produced at Studio Arena, Buffalo, New York, and Off Broadway.

First production of *Cher Antoine* (*Dear Antoine*) (*Pièces baroques*).

1981 *Le Nombril* (*The Navel*) produced in Paris.

1984 *Number One*, Michael Frayn's translation of *Le Nombril*, produced at the Queen's Theatre, London.

1987 Published the memoir *La Vicomtesse d'Eristal n'a pas reçu son balai mécanique* (*The Viscountess d'Eristal Has Not Received Her Mechanised Carpet Cleaner*).

3 October: died of a heart attack, aged 77, in Lausanne, Switzerland.

A note on categories

The published plays were divided by Anouilh into groups, after the model of Shaw's 'Plays Pleasant' and 'Unpleasant'. The plays discussed represent:

Pièces noires (Plays Black)
Pièces roses (Plays Pink)
Pièces brillantes (Plays Bright – Glittering Plays [Jeremy Sams])
Pièces grinçantes (Plays Grating – Plays that set your teeth on edge)
Pièces costumées (Plays in Costume)
Pièces baroques (Plays Baroque)

Introduction

Playwrights who have survived the full scrutiny of the twentieth century are few. A dozen years is usually sufficient to establish, consolidate and destroy a reputation. Dramatists are lucky if a single play continues to be produced ten years after its first performance. Jean Anouilh's first play was produced in 1932. After over sixty-five years of scrutiny, his plays in all their variety continue to be performed at the centre of the world repertoire: on Broadway, in London's West End, throughout European capitals, at major repertory theatres, at colleges and universities, and as a staple of the amateur stage. Quotations from his work litter sites on the Internet, particularly remarks on love, God and money which always appealed to his core constituency: the bourgeoisie. It is hard to say what he might have thought of an insurance company's display of the words, 'God is on everyone's side . . . And, in the last analysis, he is on the side of those with plenty of money and large armies'.

But Anouilh was himself an advertising copywriter for two years in his youth.

The new translations published here represent an Anouilh for the 1990s and a new century, freshly voiced by Jeremy Sams and Peter Meyer in versions that have been performed in London, New York and at the Chichester Festival Theatre, long an English stronghold of Anouilh productions. What they demonstrate with grace and sinew is Anouilh's mastery of theatrical form, his control of contrasting emotions and arguments, and his highly polished and painful wit. The durability of his dramatic *argument* is an achievement that puts him in the uneasy company of George Bernard Shaw and Bertolt Brecht, and while Shaw was an early model, Brecht's subjects are an ideological world removed from Anouilh's roasted middle classes. But Brecht, like Anouilh, was inclined to *show* his argument dramatically rather than leave it solely to explanation. (Interestingly, despite their differences, it was those three writers who best responded in their very different ways to Joan of Arc for the twentieth century.)

When Anouilh died in 1987, at the age of seventy-seven, the obituaries mourned the loss of a great entertainer. Some suggested he had fallen fatally out of fashion; that in his retreat to the shores of Lake Geneva in Switzerland, where he lived for most of the last thirty years of his life, he had removed himself from the metropolitan tussle and therefore from the forefront of French theatre.

It would be truer to say that his very durability removed him from fashion. Success, on the other hand, remained within his grasp until his death. Audiences who had known his work for over fifty years knew many of his tricks, and, more to the point, knew that there were likely to be tricks. They knew that there would increasingly be characters who would be the author's mouthpieces sounding off at the corruptions endemic in human society, particularly those in a politically left-leaning French society. They knew, too, of the author's contempt for audiences who flocked to obscure subsidised theatre productions and came away content to be left in bemused ignorance by their evening's entertainment. Those subsidised theatres left him to the mercy of the marketplace. But to the very end a new play dispatched to Paris would be an event. Not necessarily a welcome one to the French critics, who usually spluttered in intellectual fury at the continuing public regard for the dramatist – though even they had their moments of respect: notably with *Cher Antoine* in 1969, written when the playwright was fifty-nine, and which they hailed as 'a superb gift', as if it were a swan song and the triumphant summation of his waning powers.

In the English-speaking theatre, Anouilh was never to have glory days in his later years such as he had in the late 1940s, 1950s and early 1960s, but then few writers ever had such days and years.

Much of that had to do with the Second World War.

His first play to be produced, and the earliest that he allowed to be published, was *The Ermine* (*L'Hermine*), which appeared on the Paris stage in 1932 to the disdain of the theatrical director Louis Jouvet who employed him as a secretary to his company. 'You understand, little chap,' Jouvet said to him, 'your characters are not the sort one would wish to have lunch with.'

The Ermine was not a particular success, and it had a specific grimness that Anouilh later identified as a *Pièce noir*, or Play Black, but it gained enough respect to confirm him in his dedication to the theatre. Three years later his play *There Was a Prisoner* (*Y avait un prisonnier*) appeared briefly on the Paris stage, and was sold to Hollywood. The money from that sale, and from scenarios he wrote for films in following years, allowed him to dedicate his art to the theatre and he was rewarded in 1937 with a hit production of his 1936 play *Traveller without Luggage* (*Le Voyageur sans bagage*).

Although an obscure adaptation of the play was performed in London under the title *Identity Unknown* in the year of the Paris production, Anouilh had to wait for the war in Europe to end before he was to make a real impact on British audiences and critics. By the time he was ready for assaults on Britain and the United States, he had an army of extraordinary characters already

written, in plays such as *Antigone*, *Eurydice*, *Léocadia* and *Thieves'
Carnival* (*Le Bal des voleurs*) which had been performed in France
during the Occupation. In the post-war years, he would turn out a
major new play a year.

Between 1946 and 1953 he was to write *Roméo et Jeannette* (*Falling
Mansion* in its first English production), *Ring Round the Moon*
(*L'Invitation au château*), *Ardèle*, *The Rehearsal* (*La Répétition ou l'amour
puni*), *Colombe*, *The Waltz of the Toreadors* and *The Lark. Poor Bitos* and
Becket were to come before the end of the decade. The Globe
Theatre on London's Shaftesbury Avenue, now the Gielgud,
became a receiving house for play after play by Anouilh.

Death and M. Anouilh
From *Eurydice*:

M. Henri Why do you hate death? Death is beautiful, only
death provides the real climate for love.

In 1951, *The Times* reflected on 'The Vogue of M. Jean Anouilh –
A Theatrical Phenomenon':

The most prolific source of theatrical animation in this country
is a Frenchman. *Colombe*, which comes to the New Theatre on
December 13, is the eighth of M. Jean Anouilh's plays to be
presented here. None of them, except *Ring Round the Moon*, Mr
Christopher Fry's adaptation of *L'Invitation au château*, has run
for very long, but together they have earned the author a bigger
reputation with us than any other foreign dramatist has
managed to make in recent years. What is the secret of this
extraordinary vogue?
It is hard to believe that M. Anouilh's ideas are sympathetic
to English audiences. Whether applied to contemporary material or to classical legend they are on friendlier terms with
death than with life. Since life denies the human spirit the
serenity which it altogether never loses hope of knowing, death
will perhaps be kinder ... Death at least is pitiful, offering a
profound repose ...'

After musing on Anouilh's pessimistic view of the fate of innocence,
and the advantages that death might bring in preserving purity, the
writer goes on:

But if M. Anouilh is a pessimist, he is the most exhilarating of
pessimists. Neither Pirandello nor M. Jean-Jacques Bernard,
other foreign dramatists who have had notable success on the

London stage, roused, as he has roused, both coterie and
popular enthusiasm . . .

The writer's thoughtful consideration of Anouilh's impact on
British audiences demonstrates just how different the theatre of
Anouilh was, not only from Continental writers, but even more
radically from British contemporaries who, in those days, were
drifting from Shavian talk to elaborate poetry. That the plays
endure, and remain distinct, may reflect Anouilh's acknowledged
debt to a range of writers who have proved somewhat indigestible
to British authors. His admired Shaw was difficult enough for
British authors, but few indeed had absorbed the naturalism of
August Strindberg or found anything at all to do with the self-
referential theatricality of Luigi Pirandello. Finally, perhaps the
most difficult ingredient is that of his beloved Molière who
acknowledged that tragedy was comic.

The Times did well to recognise in 1951 the phenomenon of
Anouilh's popularity. *Ring Round the Moon* was to run for 682
performances, *The Waltz of the Toreadors* would run for 700 and
even the difficult *Poor Bitos*, with its star-making role for Donald
Pleasance, would run for 336.

With storming great parts for actors, it was no surprise that Sir
Laurence Olivier and Vivien Leigh were among the first British
theatre people to see the potential of performing in his plays, even
starting the translating career of the actress Lucienne Hill when
they asked her to translate his play *Ardèle* so they might understand
it better. The first production of that play, in her translation,
attracted the rising stars Paul Daneman and Eric Porter. Other
actors who leapt at the opportunity to work in his dramas included
Paul Scofield, Maggie Smith, Rex Harrison and Dirk Bogarde.
Becket, with its roistering King Henry II and transforming
Archbishop Becket, has attracted such actors as Olivier, Richard
Burton, Anthony Quinn, Christopher Plummer, Eric Porter and
Peter O'Toole. Robert Lindsay and Derek Jacobi tackled the
freshly minted language of Jeremy Sams's translation in its
premiere.

With actors of such calibre continuing to be drawn to Anouilh's
plays, it may not be such a surprise that a writer sometimes
dismissed as a boulevard magician should still attract enthusiastic
audiences. But actors alone would not be enough to overcome the
sometimes morbid conclusions of even his *Pièces roses*, Plays Pink, so
adroitly identified in *The Times*.

The pure theatricality of his work is perhaps one answer. In the
two or three hours of traffic on the stage, his worlds are intact and
self-sufficient in their artificiality. Packing up meaning and taking it

home is an option, but despite a gloomy final prognosis, a debate roused by many of his plays would be hard-stretched to go beyond a late after-show dinner. The later plays in particular seem to put all their cards on the table. This is not true, of course (and I would say so, wouldn't I), of *The Rehearsal*, *Becket*, *Eurydice*, or even, in its more specialised way, *The Orchestra*, all of which have caused debate for decades.

Taking aboard his ability to amuse, however, should he be considered a perfect boulevard writer as his cruellest apologists might have it? It is hard to limit him thus, when other works simmer with implication and repressed expression, as if his theatrical coming of age under the Nazi occupation of France had confirmed his instinct to hide his personal philosophy at all costs. For such works, however literal they may appear, there is a universality to be found and hidden agendas to explore.

Becket, a tremendous international success with rollicking royal energy, is a case in point. The casual history of England that he provides allows him to present England under Henry II as if it were occupied France under the Germans. Literary critics who seize on the title and subtitle of the play, *Becket, or the Honour of God*, and despair at Thomas à Becket's unclear actions in accepting his own death in defence of 'God's honour', and not in defence of a God he may not love, or even believe in, will not have travelled the theatrical journey of the play. As the King's playmate, as the man who quietly allows the King to diminish him in the face of royal presumption and royal prerogative by taking a woman he cares for and later elevating him to Archbishop when he is not even a priest, Becket is a man without honour. Anouilh's play allows the audience to travel with Becket emotionally and intellectually, and in ambiguity, to his discovery of that lack of honour.

Anouilh's command of theatre is such that when an audience journeys with Becket to that conclusion, they must also journey with his friend, the King. When Becket acknowledges to Henry that he loved him 'inasmuch as [he] was capable of love', they also experience Henry's pang of jealousy as he demands to know if Becket then started to love God.

'I started to love God's honour' is the best answer that the King, the audience or the critics will receive about the saint's embrace of his fate.

Uneasiness comes when critics consider Anouilh's recommendation of death as a solution to the corruption of innocence, and death as a solution to the decay of love. Becket's acceptance of death in defence of God's honour is not death in defence of God. Something more complicated is happening.

Death, however, is not an absolute prescription by the play-wright, and is not the only ending in the play. Henry chooses a different path. By uttering the words that rid him of his turbulent priest, he condemns his friend to die. In doing so, he chooses a life of solitude rather than the pain of love and its rejection; a solitude which Anouilh sees as the natural condition of man. The Queen Mother tells Henry that if he loves Becket so much he should 're-call him, pardon him ... Do something!'

The King replies: 'I am. I'm learning to be alone again. It seems a trick you never forget.'

Prescriptions are not something Anouilh is willing to dispense, perhaps having seen too many during the war years, but he is happy to offer opinions through the characters that represented him more or less directly from the first appearance of General Saint-Pé in *Ardèle* (1948) to Léon Saint-Pé in *Le Nombril* (1981). These characters are domestic blusterers, disappointed husbands, witnesses of decay, manipulators and *authors*. Such autobiographi-cal figures often echo the more fictional characters, including those from the classical sources. They have opinions on the virtue of death, but the tragedy of individuals is being swayed by arias on death from characters who continue to live.

When, in *Eurydice*, the mysterious figure of M. Henri advises Orpheus that 'only death provides the real climate for love', Anouilh has taken us through a dark and bitter modern retelling of the classic Orpheus myth, with flashing moments of enviable tenderness. It is a *Pièce noir* after all. In legend, Orpheus is a great musician who loves and is loved by Eurydice, a woman he pursues into Hades to bring back to life when she dies. He is granted his desire and told not to look at her until they have safely emerged from Hades into the light. He looks back and she fades away to die for ever.

The Orpheus of *Eurydice* is a busker, a violinist of some shy charm and a small talent who travels with his father playing in cafés for cash. The Eurydice he meets is an actress who becomes for him an idealised image of love, an encapsulation of purity that is impossible for her to sustain. When the repulsive Dulac, the company manager who has been sleeping with her, sends her a note demanding her return, she flees from them both and is killed in a motor accident.

Before he is given the chance to bring her back from the dead, he hears a highly partial story about her relationship with the company manager and, in his tormented jealousy, he demands that she look him in the eyes, thus condemning her to eternal death. As she is fading back into death, more and more of the story emerges from characters who come forward, including minor characters glimpsed briefly in their few hours of uncorrupted love.

While Orpheus laments the loss of his love, once again purified in his eyes, M. Henri paints a picture of the corruption that life would have brought to their love. With the presence of his failed and decaying father asleep in front of him in a hotel room, Orpheus accepts M. Henri's suggestion and follows Eurydice into death. (The stagecraft in the writing of that single scene is extraordinary.)

General Saint-Pé, Anouilh's prototype mouthpiece in *Ardèle*, offers the same advice to the star-crossed lovers in that play, one of whom happens to be his middle-aged sister, both of whom happen to be hunchbacks, telling them life is the enemy of love. They take their own lives.

In *The Rehearsal*, too, true love exists for a day, until it is ruthlessly destroyed by those around it who feel their barely adequate existence is threatened. A particular agent of the destruction in the play is given the name Hero. Sodden with alcohol, he cannot finally escape his self-loathing and engineers his own death by forcing a suicidal duel.

A choice for death is the driving machine in each of these very different plays, but the layers of classical and historical reference are more than convenient borrowings. In different guises, Anouilh holds up modern mirrors to the human past, and shows us a race continuous in its degradation of youthful promise.

The Rehearsal includes an elaborate staging of Marivaux's play *The Double Inconstancy*, which the staff and guests of the Duchess and Duke (Tiger) are rehearsing as a kind of guerrilla theatre for a ball. Double inconstancy is also on the menu in the household, with the Duke and Duchess and their lovers in a tolerant domestic compromise that is threatened when the Duke falls in love with Lucile, the temporary governess to the twelve wards of the ménage.

Ingenious interweaving of Marivaux's text and the modern story once again demonstrates Anouilh's sophisticated stagecraft – Alan Ayckbourn and Tom Stoppard have set themselves similar challenges in recent years – and always takes forward character and plot development. (The translation of the two eras into English is a similar challenge, and adroitly accomplished here.) As in his use of legend, and in his enduring retelling of classic drama, *Antigone*, Anouilh is intent on demonstrating a continuity of human frailty. And human frailty is drama.

In *The Rehearsal*, it is not so much desire, possessiveness, or even jealousy that motivates wives and lovers to unite against the happiness of the Duke's first moment of love with the innocent young woman who will be ruthlessly soiled; it is their contentment with discontent that drives them. Happiness is manipulated into misery, and corruption is codified as civilised behaviour. It was always thus, says the play, and everything that was charming and comical resolves itself in despair.

Or does it? The play is placed among Anouilh's *Pièces brillantes*, or Plays Glittering. While Hero has determined to die, Tiger is in his car searching for Lucile; if he does not find her, the Duchess expects him to accept his social responsibility and entertain his guests – she expects him to start having fun again in two months' time. Life goes on, even for a prophet of death.

Separate from the mainstream of Anouilh's major plays are a number of smaller but no less ambitious works. *The Orchestra* is one such, populated by 'an all-female orchestra on a bandstand, in the restaurant in a spa-town'. With the exception of the Pianist, who is a man, the musicians we meet are women whose lives are revealed in hurried conversations between musical numbers.

What we first hear of their lives is mundane: what they cook, how they knit, what lotions to use. Their relationships with men begin to creep in, and particularly the relationship one of the women has with the Pianist. In the course of the concert, as we meet them during their breaks from the music, we encounter her despair. By the end, she, too, has made a gesture to death.

The effect is limited: 'What's the point of shooting yourself if not to annoy other people.'

As life has always gone on, it goes on again: a gavotte plays, the musicians grin beneath their silly hats, swaying gracefully until the curtain.

It is a drama that gathers women together under the gaze of a weak man, much as did Ingmar Bergman's film *Now About All These Women*, or Federico Fellini's $8\frac{1}{2}$. As such, its view of women is coloured by the weak man's view, and leaves itself open to charges of misogyny which can only be countered by performance. For once, however, Anouilh's technical challenge proved itself to be beyond the skill of easy realisation.

For the piece to work to its best effect the concert must also take place, played by the characters we meet. It is 'a play within a concert', and few producers have found solutions to its demands. They were demands worth making.

Anouilh famously spent three months watching his mother playing violin in the orchestra of the Casino at Arcachon, near

Bordeaux, and both *Eurydice* and *The Orchestra* are dramas constructed from a knowledge of the lives of working musicians. Apart from the fact of those three months, and a paragraph-worth of detail, little else of Anouilh's life and influences was verified by the author in his lifetime, until near the end.

A man without history

Life is something that happens in chronological order. Or, as John Lennon put it in a song: 'Life is what happens to you while you're busy making other plans.' Artistic intentions are an attempt to make sense of that inevitable clock.

Many of the best artists cloak their private lives in obscurity in the hope that during their lifetime their artistic work will be judged as separate from the artist's life.

Jean Anouilh threw out a phrase that gave him artistic space for decades. *'Je n'ai pas de biographie . . .'* – 'I have no biography and I am very glad of it,' he wrote to the critic Hubert Gignoux in 1946. He did not seem to begrudge M. Ginoux the basic facts of his life: that he was born in Bordeaux on 23 June 1910, and that he came to Paris when he was very young. His education was listed simply, at the Colbert Primary School and Chaptal College, and he mentioned a year and a half studying law in Paris, and two years' work with an advertising agency. 'The rest is my life, and I shall keep the details to myself,' he concluded.

In the year of his death, 1987, he was still a man without a biography, or at least without a biography that he would put his name to, but in that year he became a man with an *autobiography*, or, rather, Memories of a Young Man, a trawl of illuminating anecdotage that gave the French world his charming recollection of the events that turned him into a playwright of the highest international standing.

The Viscountess d'Eristal Has Not Received Her Mechanised Carpet Cleaner (*La Vicomtesse d'Eristal n'a pas reçu son balai mécanique*), was his belated public display of the life of the young Anouilh, the title referring to his first job in a Paris department store, and the first complaint he had to handle in that job.

With invention and an odd diplomacy, he made a success of that work, but quickly left to join an advertising agency as a copywriter. He had already decided that he wanted to become a playwright, and found advertising a big step closer to his dream. In the buccaneering days of early advertising, he found the work a field for adventurers, including Jacques Prévert, the surrealist poet, and the young screenwriter Jean Aurenche, who was to give Anouilh the idea for his first play, *Humulus le Muet* (*Humulus the Mute*).

In his time as a copywriter, he won prizes for the best campaigns of various months and, indeed, when he left the department store his boss told him: 'It is a pity, Anouilh, you would have made a good complaints officer.' But his destination was clear to him and he found an opening to the world of theatre in a job as script-reader and secretary in Louis Jouvet's theatre company.

With no help from Jouvet, he none the less found himself moving in important theatrical circles, and married to a young actress, Monelle Valentin, whose life was to provide him with a hatred of poverty that drew him to the works of Bernard Shaw. It was the theatrical producers George Pitoëff and his wife Ludmilla who gave him support, and provided him with the theatrical model of Pirandello with his influential themes of plays within plays and loss of memory which were to colour his own work for years to come.

It was Pitöeff, also, who directed and starred in *Traveller without Luggage* and gave Anouilh the success he craved.

The war followed, and Anouilh's war years include his story of his capture by the Germans when France fell, and his escape (with a wife-murderer, had he but known it) back to Paris. It was there that the Anouilh of later English and American success flourished during the Occupation.

He joined the director André Barsacq at the Théâtre de l'Atelier and revived his play *Thieves' Carnival*, which they had to submit to German censors. The performance was allowed, with the stipulation that the first night would be reserved for German officers. The officers failed to arrive, so the company began the performance anyway. Well into the first act of the performance, the French secretaries of the Germans arrived and demanded that the play begin again for them. Barsacq refused, and the public in Paris gave their support to the Atelier and Anouilh for the rest of the war.

Antigone premiered at the Atelier towards the end of the war, attracting audiences from the Resistance and the Occupation, both of which assumed the play was in support of their position. Ambiguity, *Antigone*, and a body of exceptional work which dazzled postwar theatre audiences are illuminated in his reminiscences, not presently available in English.

But audiences everywhere have the plays, and the prejudices of various Saint-Pé's, to reveal the workings of Anouilh's mind and the culmination of his experience. Theatrically brilliant, the plays are designed to leave indelible images in the mind from their staging, but reading the plays can be memorable in itself. With his dialogue rendered into potent English, the reader should also take the time to note the delicately placed stage directions which give advice on how to read, and how to act, the subtly varied emotions of the action.

If someone is 'smiling quietly', that has impact on their character. If words are uttered 'brusquely', the temperature of a scene will change. Something said 'stiffly' is a character note.

Comedian and tragedian at once, Anouilh remains accessible across generations. If his biography is not all there in his writing, much of Europe in the twentieth century is.

Ned Chaillet, 1997

The Rehearsal

or Love Punished

translated by Jeremy Sams

Translator's Note

I've always had rather a soft spot for Anouilh. *Ring Round the Moon* was one of the first plays I ever saw – it was, still is, a great 'am-dram' favourite. And, coincidentally, it was also the first play I worked on professionally as a composer. It was only when I started reading his works in French – in Anouilh's wonderfully colour-coded collections, *Pièces noires, Pièces roses*, and of course *Pièces brillantes* ('glittering plays', I suppose), in which we find *The Rehearsal* – that I realised I had misjudged my man.

Let me explain. A proper translation can never falsify a play any more than a lighting designer can misrepresent a stage set. But he can shine bright and seductive light on certain areas while leaving others in comparative obscurity. The translations of Anouilh which the West End came to know and admire were mostly written in the 1950s, when the theatre was enjoying a surfeit of poetic whimsy. There was Ealing and Pinewood in the cinema, the ghosts of Barrie and Priestley still stalked the boards, verse drama proliferated. Until the kitchen sink washed it all away.

These translations, as every translation properly should, reflected their age. Down, even, to the titles. *Ring Round the Moon* and *Time Remembered* are the invention of Christopher Fry and Patricia Moyes respectively – giving a poetic and nostalgic tinge which Anouilh's *L'Invitation au château* and *Léocadia* hardly imply. Kitty Black's *Eurydice* became *Point of Departure* (with Dirk Bogarde) and then *Legend of Lovers* (with Richard Burton).

Fry's *Ring Round the Moon* is a very handy dipstick for the theatre of the day. It's a marvellous translation, such as only a leading playwright could compose. But he's forever adding whimsical asides of his own, out-cuting Anouilh step for step. The vital scene in which a Jewish financier describes the trains to the camps – brave and necessary for Paris in 1947 – is omitted in its entirety. Funnily enough, this clean-up extends to France. My first draft of *The Rehearsal* was translated from the Larousse edition. Its notes were jolly handy, but they didn't mention that several passages had been expunged, being considered likely, I presume, to bring a blush to the French teenager's cheek – if you can imagine that.

Don't get me wrong. Anouilh is first and foremost an entertainer, reared and steeped in Boulevard theatrical tradition. But these plays are not mere confections. There is a darker, tougher side, a hard centre to all the fluff and froth and periwigs. He writes about cynical people, but in turn casts a cynical eye upon them. *The Rehearsal*, like the Marivaux play it contains, is 'the elegant anatomy of a crime'. Stylish, yes, but brutal. In a sterile world, love flowers briefly, before it is systematically trampled to death.

My eye, as translator, has focused more on the wood than the trees, more on the skeleton than the rather rococo closet. Which is not to say that I haven't tried to make it witty and stylish; I have, probably rather too strenuously – but I have striven not to over-embellish and where cuts have been made they have been of curlicues and peristyles rather than structural columns.

Having said that, the text as published here is fuller than the performing version. Future actors and directors may find it over long, in which case they must give the script a good firm shake and see what drops off. They may find, as I did, that the Count's dissertations on modern acting or detective stories, for example, or the Countess's thumbnail biography of her 'poor dear aunt' read rather better than they play. For the rest, I had only one intention, which only readers and audiences can judge, to make *The Rehearsal* look and sound like a play written in English.

To achieve this, one has to translate not only the words but also the metaphors, the grammar, and even the punctuation. Parisians have an endearing habit of dressing in blazers and English tweeds and somehow looking more French than ever. Similarly, translations often sound like a foreign language – 'translatorese'. You know the sort of thing: 'Oh you are a silly goose!' 'Father, father, today is my name-day!' It's almost unavoidable, and I am sure a lot remains in this script, despite many rewrites, many, many coats of paint. I've tried to lay the ghost somewhat by attempting a discrete parody of the style when the characters are acting Marivaux. It's come out like a rather bizarre hybrid, a sort of prose blank verse.

Jeremy Sams
January, 1991

This translation of *The Rehearsal* was first performed at the Almeida Theatre, London on 13 September 1990 with the following cast:

The Countess	Nicola Pagett
Damiens	Donald Pelmear
The Count	Jonathan Hyde
Hortensia	Christine Kavanagh
Hero	Jonathan Kent
Villebosse	Harry Burton
Lucile	Julia Ormond
A Valet	Andrew Jenner

Directed by Ian McDiarmid
Set Anthony Ward
Costumes Jasper Conran
Lighting Nick Chelton
Sound John Leonard

The action takes place in France, in 1950, over three days.

Act One

An elegant room. Enter **Countess** *and* **M. Damiens**. *Louis XV costumes.*

Countess Monsieur Damiens, I do want to thank you for lending us your god-daughter.

Damiens Obliging you, madame, is not only a duty but a pleasure.

Countess Where would we have been without her? My poor dear aunt, the marquise, was a creature of infinite whimsy. This notion of hers, to leave us 'Ferbroques' on the condition that we spend a month here every year, was very touching, I must say. The place is a complete desert. She herself could never stick it for more than a week. She'd spend all winter in Paris, pining for 'Ferbroques', but come the first cuckoo, she'd make a bee-line for the nearest resort. Poor darling, she was at the mercy of several eminent doctors. Despite being in perfect health, no summer was ever long enough to complete her various cures. She sploshed her way through every spa in Europe, caked in mud from top to toe, only to emerge just in time to dash back to Paris for the autumn collections, swearing blind on everything she held most dear – meaning us, probably – that next year would see her at 'Ferbroques' without fail. But come the spring the doctors would lead her off to waters new. So when she finally escaped these miracle cures – by dying – she wanted us to keep her promises on her behalf.

Damiens Most thoughtful of her.

Countess Yes. A month in the country, if you give a ball or two, passes quickly enough. And how could we refuse a place like this? It's a jewel. But as for the clause in her will which stipulated that we should bring up twelve small orphans in the west wing . . . Well, she must have laughed when she wrote that.

Damiens Perhaps a regard for Christian charity . . . ?

Countess My aunt was a rationalist from birth. Any parting gesture she might make to the Deity would only be from a sense of politeness. She loathed children. She had a footman – he died a few months after she did – probably couldn't stand the peace and quiet. His sole task was to precede her in the street, sweeping children from her path. She'd developed an allergy to them since being hit on the head by a diabolo while out walking in the park.

Damiens Perhaps she was prompted by a sense of remorse . . .

Countess You obviously didn't know my aunt. No, there can only have been one reason for founding this orphanage – the desire to play a practical joke on the Count and myself from beyond the grave. Good old Tiger took it remarkably well. 'Fine', he said when they'd finished reading the will, 'She plainly wants us to be deafened by twelve screaming brats four weeks every year. Very well, we'll take up the gauntlet, my darling. We'll take a dozen deaf-mutes.'

Damiens But perhaps you abandoned that idea. I'm sure I heard the sound of children playing, as I came through the grounds.

Countess Yes. The will did unfortunately specify orphans. Try laying your hands on a dozen of the deaf and dumb variety at short notice. You'll find it a little tricky. So we mustered twelve common or garden orphans, sound in limb and vocal chord, and took refuge in the east wing. 'Ferbroques' is enormous, thank God. All that remained was to organise the Grand Charity Ball that Tiger and I were to give to inaugurate the orphanage. Tiger's quite marvellous at that sort of thing. One of the last men of our time to understand that triviality has to be taken totally seriously. In one night, he'd thought up the theme. Within hours, an army of decorators had arrived from Paris. It was complete turmoil. Pins, paper and paste all over the place. We all mucked in of course – perched up on our ladders all day long. They had to ferry sandwiches up to us at meal times – Tiger excelled himself. Every minute a fresh idea. The workmen were dropping like flies. Anyhow, it was all going terribly well – the great day was approaching – when suddenly, out of the blue – the orphans turned up. We'd forgotten all about them! That's when I sent you my telegram and you were sweet enough to lend us your god-daughter. Is she happy here?

Damiens She adores children.

Countess Well, that's her job, isn't it?

Damiens Yes. When her mother died, she had to earn her living.

Countess I suppose it's like looking after anything else. Frankly, I prefer my roses. They don't make so much noise. Have you visited our greenhouses?

Damiens I haven't seen a thing. Since I arrived yesterday evening, I've only had time to try on my costume and attempt to learn my lines.

Countess It's so good of you to join the cast at a moment's notice.

Losing Gontaut-Biron, who was supposed to be playing the part of Trivelin, plunged Tiger into the depths of despair. I feared the worst.

Damiens Really?

Countess Really. He has this surprising way of suddenly finding certain things terribly serious. It seems that he acquitted himself wonderfully well in 1940, holding out all alone on the Loire – when everyone else had decamped to Toulouse. Five hours after the cease fire, he was still popping away with a makeshift little cannon against a horde of Pomeranian fusiliers. They kept waving white flags and telling him through a loudhailer that we'd surrendered and to stop being silly. But to no avail. The fall of France was a fact that did not concern him in the slightest. But when he'd fired off his last shell, he asked the Germans if he could have a bath. He shaved, had his nails done – his batman, the only other survivor, happened to be a manicurist – and never referred to the defeat again. But a ball put in jeopardy, well that's a different matter. He'd be quite capable of killing himself.

Damiens I'm happy to spare him that obligation, by taking on this small part. In my youth I had some talent as an amateur.

Countess I'm sure you still have. A lawyer never stops acting, we all know that.

The **Count** *enters similarly costumed.*

Count Well, are we rehearsing or not? The play is by Marivaux – so we can't make it up as we go along. Where is your god-daughter, Monsieur Damiens? It's too bad of those orphans to keep her to themselves. We need her too.

Damiens She's just putting them to bed. She'll be joining us in a minute.

Count Be a good fellow will you and go and extricate her from their clutches. We can't start without her.

Damiens *goes.* **Count** *sits down next to his wife.*

Darling, it's all shaping up rather well. Doing the play during dinner is a brilliant idea. One character gets up from the table, calls out to another. They start to talk. People listen – they think it's a real conversation. The turn of phrase may seem a bit odd to begin with, but I'll have taken care – as will you, at your end of the table – that our conversation should have taken on an eighteenth-century flavour. People will hardly notice the transition. Just as they start to think, 'God, they're going on a bit', enter a new character, a valet, who gives them both a piece of his mind. General astonishment. People think, 'Dear God, the servant problem'. Then they *get* it – it's a play. Too late – it has begun. And we'll have sidestepped that ghastly moment of panic which always grips a sophisticated audience when confronted by an evening of amateur theatricals.

Countess One snag. It's by Marivaux. Most people have never read any.

Count So much the better – they'll all think I wrote it. And we mustn't be too hard on these people. They're a bit dim, certainly, but no one expects our sort to produce geniuses. There are simply not enough of us to guarantee the supply. We leave that to the people. All that's demanded of our class is to be consistent – and to endure. That is our talent. We do what we can.

Countess Another snag. If they listen to the play, the food will get cold.

Count Too bad. We always feed them far too well. You do seem a little negative this evening, darling. And anyway the menu can be planned round the action of the play. When attention starts to wander, I'll bring on lobsters and champagne – and for the poetic passages, toothpicks. Nothing makes people seem more pensive than digging away at a stubborn bit of meat stuck between the molars. At least that will make them look as if they're thinking – and if they make the right faces – who knows – thought may follow. I think this girl will be charming as Sylvia.

Countess I think she lacks sparkle. I can't imagine why you made all this fuss about giving her the part.

Count Precisely for that reason. She'll stand out against your dazzling friends. She burns with an inner fire, contained by a natural reserve.

Countess You're not in love with her are you?

Count Not remotely.

Countess Good. She's not for you.

Count The real bore is the Louis XV costumes and the wigs. It's all too 'chocolate-boxy'. But 'Ferbroques' is an eighteenth-century chateau – there's no getting round that. Now in a Renaissance house like yours at Grandlieu, we could have laid on something truly extraordinary.

Countess Well, it's too late now.

Count Yes. Too late. But I shan't sleep a wink until I can think of some way of making the period more amusing. I thought of giving all the men beards, but that's an easy option. Of updating it to this century . . . But no one would get it. We mustn't overtax our audience must we?

Countess How old is she?

Count Just twenty. Come on, help me think.

Countess What about?

Count The costumes! The whole thing's teetering on the edge of banality. I'm seriously worried.

Countess What if we asked them all to turn up without wigs?

Count (*observing himself in a mirror*) You're absolutely right! That girl's hair is such an extraordinary colour. It would be a crime to cover it up.

Countess I think she's rather plain.

Count Oh, so do I. I was talking about her hair.

Countess Tiger. You know that you are free to do as you please. You must give me the credit for never having stood in the way of your affairs. But don't go fluttering round her too much. Damiens has been my family solicitor for more than thirty years and I would hate to give him any cause for complaint.

Count My dear, what do you take me for? I have my faults, I admit. Considerable ones. But no one's ever questioned the fact that I'm a gentleman. That, my title and my name – are about the only things I can lay claim to – not counting 'Ferbroques' and a dozen orphans.

Countess What's that got to do with it?

Count You will excuse me; it has a great deal to do with it. My father, who was a splendid man, took particular pains to apprise me of this very point on his deathbed. I was quite young but I have never forgotten his advice – actually it's the only piece of advice he'd ever felt obliged to give me. It was a few hours before his death. The bishop was hovering in the ante-room, with his entire clergy standing by, ready to administer extreme unction. Father summoned me in. 'My boy,' he said, 'it's all a bit late now but I realise that I've never taken that much notice of you. Time's running out. As far as the family honour is concerned, I have

complete faith in you. One thing, though. You're young, you'll
want to have your bit of fun. So, do whatever you like – but only
with women of your own class. With others, things always turn out
badly. You either end up marrying a chambermaid or an actress –
penal servitude without remission – or you beget bastards by some
seamstress and they grow up resentful and start revolutions. Have
your grubby little flings by all means, we're none of us angels, but
only with your own kind.

A brief silence.

My father was a considerable man. I never saw that much of him
but at that moment I knew that I loved him. With all my heart.

Countess (*also after a brief silence*) This isn't a reproach Tiger, but
sometimes I feel that you really *did* give him your heart. Certainly
no one has seen any sign of it since.

Count (*pulling himself together*) Your conversation's a little on the
gloomy side today, my love. Let's not get carried away. You know
how fond I am of you. I've never really cared for anyone *but* you.
But for God's sake don't tell Hortensia or I'll never hear the end of
it!

Countess Do you tell all your mistresses that you're in love with
them?

Count Well, one has to really. Women are such sticklers for
etiquette. I honestly believe you're the only woman I've *never* said it
to.

Countess What an honour! Do you expect me to be grateful?

Count I can't lie to you. What we have is too delicate and too
precious for that. Come on, Eliane, let's pull ourselves together.
We'll be talking all sorts of nonsense in a minute. Love is the
consolation of the poor. At this stage of the game, it's a little
unbecoming for us to stand here surrounded by luxury, lamenting
the fact that we've never experienced it. There are thousands of
things in the world more worthy of our attention. I ask no more
than that my life should be a perfect party, which is as much of an
achievement as beating your breast and boring everyone else to
death. Anyway, at the risk of being indiscreet, my love, if that's
what you fancy, you do have Villebosse. Villebosse – or anyone
else, how should I know? The world is full of roaring boys.

Countess Villebosse gets on my nerves.

Count Oh really? I think he's charming. He's young, he's handsome. Always ready to dive off a cliff or walk through fire on request. But you're surely not going to make me stand here and sing his praises?

Countess Don't be rude, Tiger. He does happen to be my lover.

Count (*a bit more brusquely*) Let's drop it, Eliane. There are some conversations I'd rather not have. You're free – I'm free. We're very fond of each other and we are here to give our friends a party, which in this God-forsaken place is quite a challenge, I'm sure you'll agree. Believe me, there are infinitely more important things than indulging our emotions. Our guests never get bored, that's the important thing, and if we let things slip now that's fifteen years' reputation down the drain overnight. (*Looks in the mirror.*) Do you really think it would be better without the wigs? Yes, perhaps you're right. It lends a sort of unfinished quality. The human face of the eighteenth century. I'll issue fresh instructions.

He kisses her hand.

You're always right, Eliane. I do adore you.

He exits. **Hortensia** *enters, similarly attired.*

Hortensia Oh, I'm sorry. They told me Tiger was with you.

Countess You've just missed him.

Hortensia He's obsessed by this party. We hardly ever see him.

Countess My dear Hortensia, I'm long past the stage of getting jealous of Tiger's parties.

Hortensia Oh I'm not suffering unduly. Are we going to rehearse this play? I'm not a hundred per cent sure of what I'm doing.

Countess That's the first time I've ever heard you say that.

Hortensia Acting isn't really my thing.

Countess You astonish me. We're waiting for that girl who's playing Sylvia.

Hortensia Why was he so keen on casting her?

Countess She's charming.

Hortensia I think she lacks sparkle.

Countess That's where you're wrong. She burns with an inner fire contained by a natural reserve.

Hortensia I hear he's even given his valet a part. I just hope that when the whole thing's over, he'll send them back where they belong.

Countess Wrong again, I'm afraid. If she's even half way decent in the play, if I know Tiger, he'll be dancing with her all night.

Hortensia That would be extremely unpleasant. Till now, yours was one of the few houses where one could be absolutely sure of only meeting one's own sort.

Countess My dear Hortensia, it has taken Tiger fifteen years of hard work and painstaking attention to detail to become the uncontested arbiter of what constitutes good taste. So now he can do exactly what he wants. If he decides that Monsieur Damiens' god-daughter is socially acceptable, then socially acceptable she is.

Hortensia It's grotesque. Isn't she some sort of nursemaid?

Countess If the children had been ours, Tiger would probably never have dared. She's here to look after the orphans. Tiger has a genius for exploiting social niceties, and, to be brutally frank, I think he wants to have her.

Hortensia There is a distinct edge to your voice, Eliane.

Countess Not a bit of it. I look on your affair with Tiger entirely amicably. Look, since we're being frank with each other, I think you're perfect for him. He's very much in love with you, you know.

Hortensia Is he?

Countess So he says. You just have to decide whether everything he says is true. I stopped checking up long ago.

Hortensia Well, I can promise you that he will not be dancing with her all night.

Countess No scenes, though, that's the surest way to drive him into her arms.

Hortensia Thanks for the advice, Eliane, but I think I know him quite well too.

Countess Your dress is absolutely stunning.

Hortensia And you look gorgeous!

Countess You've no idea what a relief it is that you're so beautiful. I would have been mortified if Tiger had got mixed up with just anybody. Turn around. My God, the design is so witty. Jacquot is a total genius.

Hortensia Do you still go to Léonore? It's amazing how she's managed to keep the Louis XV while still being bang up to date. Is she coming?

Countess Who?

Hortensia Léonore. Oh, she's bound to be. She's invited everywhere nowadays, even by Tiger.

Countess Especially by Tiger!

Hortensia Why, 'especially'? It's long been accepted that Léonore – even though she used to work in a hat shop – is now a considerable social figure. He's just following fashion.

Countess Tiger will never follow a fashion that he hasn't started himself. One must give him credit for that.

Hortensia So why is she invited? Because of her genius?

Countess Tiger doesn't think genius is that much of a social asset. No, it's just the royal prerogative, my dear. He's so sure of himself he feels he can ennoble her. And I invite her because four years ago he was after her, and she said no.

Hortensia How sweet of you to tell me!

Countess My dear, it's ancient history. And actually turning Tiger down is such a rare distinction, it's almost a guarantee of social acceptability.

Hortensia Eliane, you're losing your sting. I've decided I'm not going to suffer; not with Tiger, not with anybody.

Countess I think that's precisely why he's so fond of you – and so am I. (*They embrace.*) Darling Hortensia, when all's said and done, one has so few friends.

Hero *enters – holding his wig.*

Countess Ah, here he is. Hero, Hero, I do adore you.

Hero I couldn't have put it better myself, Eliane. Are we going to rehearse? What a tyrant Tiger is to make us work in costume three whole days ahead of time. I don't know how to act in this thing.

Countess That's exactly why he wants us to rehearse in them. He thinks the reason costume balls are so slow to get off the ground is that people spend the first few hours wondering if their breeches are going to stay up.

Hero The breeches are fine. The waistcoat's the problem – miles too tight. And he's just told me we can do without the wigs.

Hortensia Yes, that's the tyrant's latest whim.

Hero Pity. That was my favourite bit – I'm starting to lose my hair.

Countess You're thirty-seven, Hero . . .

Hero Yes and I'll be bald by forty – my doctor says it's because I have too much sex. He's as hairy as a yak, which doesn't say a lot for his private life. I told him as much – he got his own back by reminding me that anyway, cirrhosis would finish me off before very long. Two thousand francs, just to find out you're going to die.

Countess I still think you should get married.

Hero Fine, if you can find a woman who'll make me forget all the others – otherwise it'd be just one more to please, and I don't think I've got the stamina.

Countess Hero, you play the cynic, but you couldn't be more soft-hearted. One only has to look at you.

Hero Your taste for paradox is leading you astray, Eliane. This deep soulful look is caused by drink. It's true I'm soft-hearted but I like to cause pain.

Countess I never met anyone truly wicked who actually admitted it.

Hero I'm not wicked. I just like breaking things. It's a taste that most little boys grow out of. I've kept it.

Hortensia When are you going to make me suffer, Hero? I can't wait.

Hero Whenever you like, my love. But I don't think it would amuse either of us very much. We're too alike.

Enter **Villebosse**.

Villebosse Have you heard the news?

Hero Bound to have done. We always hear everything before you do.

Villebosse Apparently we are to play without wigs. We'll all look ridiculous.

Hero I don't think a wig would have saved you, Villebosse. (*He goes to the drinks.*) May I?

Countess Hero! We're about to rehearse.

Hero Eliane, you know perfectly well that my talent lies at the bottom of a glass. Sadly, I can never remember which one.

Villebosse (*to the* **Countess**) This man is infuriating. I can't bear him hovering about you.

Countess You're being boring, Villebosse. What's the point in taking a lover if he's going to be more critical than your husband?

Villebosse Tiger is a cynic, he doesn't love you. I do. I don't want to provoke a scandal under your roof, but if that pathetic drunk so much as lays a finger on you, I'll strike him publicly, without the least hesitation.

Countess Hero is quite capable of striking you back – then refusing to fight.

Villebosse Then his refusal will be made public. He will die of shame.

Countess Whatever Hero dies of, I don't think it will be that. He swallowed his pride years ago – along with everything else.

Villebosse But don't you despise him?

Countess I don't know that I do.

Villebosse For heaven's sake Eliane, I want you to say you despise him. This minute. If you don't, I'll pack my bags and go. And I won't be acting in the play.

Countess If you do that to Tiger, you'll never see me again.

Villebosse Tiger's little indulgences are the least of my concerns. He'll find someone to replace me. I love you Eliane. I am your lover. That has to count for something.

Countess I'm beginning to see that it counts for rather a lot. My dear Villebosse, I don't know how, but you manage to make vice seem considerably more tedious than virtue.

Villebosse Very well. In that case, I'll pretend to have forgotten my lines. I'll ruin the performance. I'm fed up with being the only one to suffer.

Hero What's he on about?

Countess He says he's suffering.

Hero Fascinating. Hortensia, you've got a hard little heart. Come and observe this interesting natural phenomenon. Man suffering for love. One should never miss an opportunity for self-improvement.

Villebosse Sir, I am not talking to you.

Enter **Tiger**, *holding* **Lucile** *by the hand. Followed by* **M. Damiens** *and a* **Valet**, *both in costume.*

Count With scant regard for personal safety, I have liberated Lucile from those twelve little monsters. (*Sucks his finger.*) I bleed. One of them tried to savage me. Right. We're all here. Let us begin. 'The Double Inconstancy' is a merciless play. I would ask you not to forget that. Sylvia and Harlequin are really in love. The Prince desires Sylvia. Perhaps he even loves her. What law forbids a prince to love as deeply and as simply as Harlequin? The whole court will conspire to drive the young lovers apart, in such a way that Sylvia will fall in love with the Prince and Harlequin will fall in love with Flaminia. It's the elegant anatomy of a crime. Villebosse: Harlequin is tender and good but shallow, greedy and naive. Flaminia and her sister are both so lovely . . . they smell so good. Don't forget, even when he's rejecting them and thinking noble thoughts about Sylvia, he can still smell them. The sweet smell of silk on a scented skin – what a trap for a poor boy. Flaminia and Lisette are impetuous, flirtatious and as hard as nails; the poor little country boy probably smells quite good to them too. They toy with him, tease him with their claws. What is desire if not curiosity? Why refuse pleasure without obligation? And anyway, they're a breed apart and know it. To them, Harlequin's just a boisterous little puppy who likes licking people. They let the puppy lick them all over their nice pearls . . . It's a new game and, no harm done. Eliane, Hortensia, it would be pointless of me to give you any direction. You'll both be excellent. Tirvelin is dull, fastidious and too eager to please. As for Sylvia . . . (*He turns to* **Lucile**.) what can I say about Sylvia? She's not romantic, she's kind. She's not naive, she's good. She's not hard, she's frank. She's not overawed by the ladies of the court . . . not even by the Prince. She seems to know everything without ever having been taught. In this worthless world of taffeta and treachery – there she stands alone, guileless, naked under her simple cotton frock, watching, silent and true, as they whirl and scheme about her. And then Sylvia – a small unknowable creature, a million miles away, looks at him and troubles his soul. There was always something in this world besides pleasure and he never knew it.

His voice has changed in spite of himself. **Hortensia, Countess** *and* **Hero,** *behind his glass, look at him in surprise. He finishes as if suddenly embarrassed.*

But I don't need to explain that part to you, mademoiselle. You have only to be yourself.

Everybody looks at them, motionless.

Curtain.

Act Two

Same décor. **Lucile** *and the* **Count**, *in costume.*

Count Look, I know I shouldn't talk to you like this. But I'm half way through life and still am incapable of denying myself a pleasure. (*He looks at her, checks himself.*) Sorry. I've uttered the forbidden word. You'll have to be patient with me. I will learn your vocabulary. Incidentally, what joyless conspiracy of bigots and old maids managed to discredit the word 'pleasure' over the last two centuries? It is one of the sweetest and noblest words in the language. Good and evil must originally have been defined as that which gives pleasure and that which doesn't – as simple as that. And what about love? Isn't it simply the pleasure of the heart? God knows one has time enough to suffer for it afterwards. (*Looks at her.*) Anyway, it's so fulfilling to be in love with a mute. It encourages meditation and soliloquy. Ah, the delights of talking to oneself. And one is the perfect audience. Totally enthralled, yet quick in riposte. I haven't had a good chat with myself in years. I've underestimated myself; I'm actually rather good company. How ready we are to judge by appearances. I find I'm really quite sensitive, with hidden depths.

Lucile You know we're supposed to be rehearsing. They're sure to be listening at the door.

Count She speaks! Fascinating. A talking mute. And – *mirabile dictu* – She doesn't tell me to shut up – just to keep my voice down.

Lucile If I'd really wanted to shut you up, I could have done that when I came here a week ago. Or I could have just let you talk and not have listened. It's the truth. I'm worried they might be eavesdropping.

Count Why do you never want to see me except at rehearsals? And if it's true that I don't annoy you, then why are you playing games?

Lucile I'm not, I promise you. When I fall in love with a man – the minute I'm sure of it – I'll do everything in my power to give him pleasure, as you put it. Straight away – no games.

Count Now what special qualifications or virtues must a man possess to deserve such an honour?

Lucile None whatsoever. I will be his even if he is penniless or homeless, or on the run, or even married with children and we could only meet for an hour a week in a café somewhere. . . .

Count (*ironically*) Women. You shroud yourselves in mystery but you're all alike. *Particularly* if he's penniless. *Especially* if he's on the run. You refuse to be taken by force, but a modicum of pity always does the trick.

Lucile (*softly*) Even if he's rich and happy, it would be just the same.

Count Well, then. I'm rich. I'm happy. I want you to love me.

Lucile That's just how little children ask for the moon. It's part of my job to tell them that 'I want doesn't get'. Do you really think I wouldn't want to love you? You or anybody else? It must be so good to give everything.

Count Yes, mustn't it? And luckily, I'm a born taker. I'm sure we can work something out!

Lucile Monsieur, one can only give to the rich.

Count You'll have to explain. I always came bottom in Bible Studies. Interpreting parables was never my strong point.

Lucile The boy who loves me as I wish to be loved will not have to ask.

Count But how will you know he loves you, you silly thing? Because he says so?

Lucile No, he would never dream of saying so. Certainly not as wittily as you do.

Count So what'll he do, then? Talk about the moon in June? Sigh a bit? Throw himself at your feet while beating his hollow breast? The hypocrite!

Lucile I imagine he'll be embarrassed, tongue-tied perhaps. He may not even be able to look into my eyes. He will ask some other girl to dance but I'll know I'm the one he loves.

Count (*after a slight pause*) The rules are a bit complicated but I'm sure I'll get the hang of it. I'm good at games.

Lucile I'm afraid this is a game that can't be taught.

Count You see, when I'm in love, I want to be lovable. I want to be funny. I want to shine. Peacocks spread their tails. That seems perfectly natural to me.

Lucile Above all, I hope he won't be able to tell me in detail what he is like when he is in love. I hope he will be as surprised as I am . . .

But, please let's rehearse. It would be dreadful if we didn't know our lines.

Count Very well. And thank you for putting me in my place so sweetly. I'm an idiot. I've been rather spoilt most of my life. I've picked up some bad habits. You're absolutely right. Let's forget the whole thing and rehearse. 'But Sylvia, you do not look at me . . .' Just one thing. Look, I'm pathetic, I admit it. I know it would be wonderful to be uncomplicated; to give yourself completely and all that. It's just a gift I don't possess, that's all. You are the most wonderful girl hidden away behind that misty veil. You've been here a week and ever since you arrived – I don't know why – I've thought only of you. I've said so in the only way I know – by trying to be amusing – and you've made it plain that either the subject or my way of broaching it displeases you. Okay, I've been well brought up. I'm not going to pounce on you or chase you up and down the corridors. Nor am I going to throw myself in the moat. There is a more moderate middle course . . . merely to regret the passing of what might have been. So. There we go. Let us rehearse, mademoiselle. They probably are eavesdropping. I've made enough of a fool of myself for one evening. I've no desire to advertise the fact. 'Sylvia, you do not look at me. I find you strangely sad when I address you. I fear you think me importunate.'

Lucile (*smiling at him*) You are sweet though.

Count What do you mean 'sweet'?

Lucile You're still that dashing young man, with his white gloves, his cane, and his brand new bowler hat, strutting up and down the Avenue du Bois.

Count Who told you that? When I was wearing my first bowler hat, you were still in your cradle.

Lucile That's not the point. I see you as you are. It's hard to grow up, isn't it? . . . But please, let's rehearse.

Count This is very disconcerting. The first time you look on me kindly, it's to smother me in pity. No one's ever tried that trick on me before. All right, I did have a bowler hat and okay, I might have been a bit young for it but it was the fashion at the time. But I didn't look that ridiculous, not as far as I can recall . . . At least girls of your age didn't seem to think so at the time. And I don't see what it is about my manner that makes you think that you can treat me like a little boy.

Lucile Don't be angry. There's nothing wrong with being a little boy.

Count I am not a little boy. I fought in the war. I fired a cannon, a great big cannon. They gave me a lovely shiny medal – yes, I know that is a bit childish – but I never wear it. For the last fifteen years I've thrown the best parties in Paris. Parties for grown-ups. I can drive a car. I've even raced one. I was a diplomat for a while and if I'd stuck with it, I'd probably be Ambassador or something by now. Apart from that – I don't know – I'm just a man like any other. Perhaps more brilliant than some. Or so I'm told. But I've had enough of listening to you and your siren song. Let's rehearse. 'But Sylvia, you do not look at me . . .'

Lucile (*returning to her place, ready to rehearse*) It really doesn't matter what I say. You won't get far by listening to the idle thoughts of young girls. Just accept me for what I am. I won't be offended.

Count I'm not even listening. I'm just astonished that you . . . anyway, come on, we must rehearse. I'm ridiculous and you – whatever you say – are playing games and with considerably more skill than I. I've learnt to be a good loser. That was part of my excellent education. Just don't go boasting about it, that's all.

Lucile Boast? Who to?

Count I don't know. Your godfather. Some girlfriend.

Lucile I never talk to my godfather. You must have noticed we're far from close. And I have no friends.

Count Good. Well, don't tell the orphans then.

Lucile No, no. I will tell them. Definitely. They're always clamouring for unlikely bedtime stories – and my stock of fairy tales is running low. But I'll change it a bit. I'll set it in the middle ages. The Prince and the Serving Maid. Anyway, they never understand my stories. Or perhaps they do; they always seem to fall asleep before the end.

Count Good. Let's rehearse. 'But Sylvia, you do not look at me. I find you strangely sad when I address you. I fear you think me importunate.'

Lucile 'Yes, you are importunate. I was only just saying so.'

Count 'You were talking about me? And what were you saying, pretty Sylvia?'

Lucile 'Oh, all sorts of things. I was saying that you don't yet know what I'm thinking.'

Count 'I know you are resolved not to give me your heart. In that respect I know what you are thinking.'

Lucile 'You aren't as wise as you would like to think. Be less boastful. And tell me, you know how things stand with Harlequin and me – suppose I wanted to love you, only suppose it, and suppose that I gave in to my desire. Would I do right, would I do wrong? Come tell me your advice, and in confidence.'

Count 'Since man is not the master of his heart, if you desire to love me it is right that you should satisfy your heart's desire. That is my advice.'

Lucile 'Are you speaking as a friend?'

Count 'As a friend and as an honest man.'

Lucile 'I agree, I have reached the same decision and I think we are both right. So – I will love you, and will have no compunction about loving you – should I so desire.'

Count 'But you do not desire – so I am no better off!'

Lucile 'Do not attempt to guess what . . .'

Count (*interrupting her*) That's it. I've got it. It's obvious. You've been lying to me. You've got someone already. Some nice young man no doubt also not unconnected with education. You write him four-page letters every night in your little room.

Lucile That doesn't sound like Marivaux to me.

Count I'm asking you a question. Answer me quickly. They're coming back in.

Lucile (*seriously*) No. I am not in love. I have never been in love.

The others enter.

Countess How's your scene coming along?

Count I think we're both rather gifted.

Countess Perhaps those of us who are less so might get to rehearse a bit as well.

Count Do you think we should do the whole thing from the beginning? Damiens says he's a bit nervous about it.

Countess What Monsieur Damiens needs is an audience. In any case we haven't got time for a whole run-through before dinner. We'll see how we feel this evening.

Count Very well, let's take it from Act Two. We'll take Sylvia's big speeches as read. Hortensia, darling, we need to rehearse your bits. I can't help feeling you're a little too waspish in your scene with Sylvia. It feels too obvious. Be charming. You can do it. Don't forget, she's not supposed to be able to see through you.

Hortensia If you think I'm not up to the part, Tiger, just say so.

Count Hortensia, the part could have been written for you. I'm only talking about fine-tuning. Actors, they're quite impossible. As soon as they open their mouths, they fall head over heels in love with the sound of their own voices. And they expect us to share in their delight. No, seriously, they do. There's nothing less natural on earth than what passes for naturalism on stage. Don't go thinking it's enough to be life-like. For a start, in real life one has to work with such terrible material. We live in a world that has completely forgotten the correct use of the semi-colon; we never finish a sentence properly, it always goes dot, dot, dot . . . because the *mot juste* always escapes us. And then that 'naturalistic' way of speaking which actors are always claiming to have. All that stammering, hesitating, 'umm'ing and 'ah'ing . . . why ask five or six hundred people to pay good money to sit through that? But they turn up and they love it. They recognise themselves. But the point is that theatre has got to do better than that. Life's all very well but it lacks form. Art must use every trick in the book to lend it one. To be more real than real life. But I'm boring you. I'm starting to take myself seriously. Come on, let's have a bash at Act Two. Sylvia, the stage is yours.

Lucile (*to* **Hortensia**) 'Yes, I believe you – it seems you wish me no ill. You're the only one that I can stand. I look on all the others as my foes. But where is Harlequin?'

Hortensia 'He will be here soon – he is down in the dining room.'

Hero (*into his glass. Looking at* **Villebosse**, *sulking in a corner*) No he's not – he's over there – down in the dumps.

Villebosse Sir, I've already told you, I'm not speaking to you – and I must warn you my patience has its limits.

Count Come on, Hero, do try and be serious for once.

Hero I'm sorry, old chap, it can't be done, I'm still too sober to be serious. Try me later.

Lucile 'That's the worst thing about this country. I've scarcely seen such civil women, such well-bred men. They have such perfect manners, so full of politeness and friendly advice that you'd think they were the finest people in the world, with the purest hearts and the clearest consciences. And you'd be wrong.' (*To the* **Count**.) Shall I skip this bit?

Count Yes, do. You're doing awfully well, though.

Lucile '. . . to cheat your neighbour, to break your promises, to be disloyal, untruthful and shallow, such are the noble aspirations of the fine people of the horrible place. And who are they? Where do they come from, what are they made of?'

Hortensia 'Of the same clay as the rest of mankind, Sylvie. That fact should not astonish you at all. They think that marriage to the Prince would bring you happiness.'

Lucile 'But am I not obliged to be faithful? That should be my desire and my duty. And how could I be happy if I could not do my duty? In any case, is not my constancy a part of my charm?' (*To the* **Count**.) Shall I skip this bit as well?

Count No, it's lovely, keep going.

Lucile 'And they have the impertinence to say "Go on, do yourself a really bad turn, which will only cause you sorrow, and compromise your self-esteem". And because I have no desire to, people think me stubborn.'

Hortensia 'One cannot change the way that people think. They simply want their Prince to be happy.'

Count Very good, Hortensia.

Lucile 'But why does he not want someone who will come to him of her own free will? What whim is this of his to want someone who could never want him? What pleasure would he possibly find in that?' (*She is looking at the* **Count** *by now.*)

Countess Tiger. Tell her the Prince isn't actually on stage. She's supposed to be looking at Hortensia.

Lucile 'And he does everything to such ludicrous excess. All those concerts, plays, enormous meals, more like wedding banquets – the jewels he sends me – it must cost him a fortune. It is mad, it will ruin him. A whole draper's shop from him is as nothing compared to the little ball of wool which Harlequin gave me.'

Hortensia 'I don't doubt it, for such is love – and I too have loved in that fashion – even down to the ball of wool.' . . . I'm sorry, does she really mean that? Because I don't think I'm playing it right. Could she really prefer one tiny ball of wool to all the Prince's jewels?

Count Could you?

Hortensia Tiger, it's nothing to do with me . . . and if this is your idea of a game it's not very entertaining! Anyway you just said we're not supposed to be playing ourselves . . .

Count Forgive me. But when I cast this play I knew exactly what I was doing. And you spoke that line to perfection.

Hortensia I was trying to make it sincere.

Count And since you've never valued the smallest thing higher than your own personal gratification then in making it sincere you made it come across as completely phoney. Which was perfect and just what I was after. On?

Hortensia You're playing clever little games with us. And quite soon we're going to get heartily sick of it.

Count All the best directors do that. You're lucky I'm not screaming at you or throwing scripts around the room. You can't have a production of brilliance without the odd nervous breakdown. Genius is seldom polite. No. This is good. Sylvia, let's pick it up from 'Ah well, then he must try to forget me'.

Lucile 'Ah well, then he must try to forget me, or send me hence, or talk to other girls. There are those who already have a lover, as I do, but none the less seem prepared to take on the whole of mankind. It does not seem to worry them at all. I only know that it would worry me.'

Hortensia 'So my child, you feel you have yet to find your equal here.'

Count Now that was perfect. The hint of acid behind the smile. You must have been rehearsing it all night.

Lucile 'There are prettier girls than me here. But even if they were half as pretty, they would still be making better use of their looks than I. Certainly there are ugly women here – but they put on such airs you would hardly notice.'

Countess You're supposed to look at Flaminia when you say that bit. I'm not actually on stage yet. My moment has yet to come.

Hortensia 'That is true. But your beauty is obviously entirely natural – and entirely charming.'

Lucile 'It is, it is indeed. I do not practise to deceive. I am all of a piece – content to be what I am. The other women here – their beauty is bounteous and brazen – and quite clear in its intention. So they are deemed more comely than a shy thing like myself – I am as afraid to look a man in the eyes as I am embarrassed that he should find me beautiful.'

Countess Don't you think she should try and say that more modestly, Tiger. People will think she's giving as good as she gets.

Count But she is, my love, she is – and we all want her to.

Countess Yes but, you see, although mademoiselle is absolutely ravishing – I think we're all agreed on that – and particularly well cast, I still don't feel (and I'm sure she's too clever to mind me saying this) that she doesn't quite possess the radiant beauty which would justify her character's complete self-confidence. So I think on the whole she should try and do it a bit more simply.

Count I disagree – I think she's doing very well. Hortensia, can we continue?

Hortensia 'And this is what touches the Prince the most. Your *naiveté*, your unadorned beauty. Your natural grace. But do not praise the other women here too much. They do not waste much time on praising you.'

Lucile 'Oh, what do they say?'

Hortensia 'Oh, various impertinences. They dare to make fun of you, and of the Prince. "Have you seen a more ordinary face", they were asking only the other day – nasty jealous creatures – "or a more awkward figure?". None of the men claimed to find you all that attractive either. I was furious, as you can imagine.'

Lucile 'You see how men, in flattering shallow women, are forced to betray their own true feelings.'

Count She's so witty – no, I think she puts that really neatly. She's completely adorable.

Hortensia 'Hardly "forced" my dear.' Tiger, I do wish you wouldn't keep butting in all the time. It's infuriating. 'Hardly "forced" . . .'

Lucile 'How I hate those women. But if they find me so unattractive, how do they account for the fact that the Prince loves me and turns his back on them?'

Hortensia 'Oh, they're convinced that it will never last, that you are just a toy and he'll abandon you sooner or later.'

Count Wonderful. You said that really well, Hortensia. You've got it now, you've absolutely got it. Just settle into it and see where it takes you. We'll take the rest as read, shall we, and cut to my entrance with Eliane. It's extremely important. (*Taking her by the arm.*) Come on Eliane, we're entering now . . .

Lucile 'Ah, Sir, why have you come? Did you not know that I was here?'

Count 'I did, mademoiselle, I knew. You told me I would not see you again. Nor would I have ventured into your presence without madame who begged me to accompany her to allow her to pay her respects to you.'

Lucile 'I am not angry to see you again; I fear you will find me sad. As far as this lady is concerned, I am flattered that she wishes to pay me her compliments. I hardly deserve them, but let her proceed if such is her desire. I will return them as best I can – she must excuse me if I cannot match her skill.'

Countess 'Of course I will excuse you, my child. I would not demand the impossible.'

Lucile '(*aside*) "Demand the impossible" . . . How dare she speak like that?'

Countess 'How old are you, my child?'

Lucile 'I've quite forgotten, mother!'

Hortensia (*to* **Lucile**) 'Well said.'

Countess 'I think she's getting angry.'

Count 'Madam, this discourse is getting out of hand. Under the pretext of paying your respects you insult Sylvia.'

Countess 'That was never my intention. I was merely curious to meet this little girl who seems to have occasioned such an excess of passion and desire and to find out what it is about her that is so irresistible. They tell me she is *naive* – I suppose that lends a rustic charm which some might find amusing. Let her give us a few instances of this *naiveté*. Let us see her wit.'

Lucile 'No, no, madame, it is hardly worth the trouble. It is no match for yours.'

Countess 'Well, it was *naiveté* we wanted – and that was rather good.'

Count 'Madame, you must leave.'

Countess 'This grows tedious – and if she will not leave then I will.'

Count (*to* **Countess**) 'I am responsible for your behaviour.'

Countess 'Farewell then. If such a girl is the object of your affection – then I feel I need seek no further revenge . . .'

Count Perfect. Right, on to Act Three.

Countess No, that will do for now. I'm tired, Tiger, and I need to talk to you. Will you come up to my room?

Hortensia She's right; let's have a bit of a break. I can see it's all great fun for Tiger. Less so for the rest of us perhaps. I think we need a breather, my love.

Count Fine. Break. The rehearsal will continue in fifteen minutes.

Hortensia *exits*.

Hero. Women never really understand the theatre. When they're not playing themselves, they lose interest.

Hero They should take up drinking. All games seem fun when you're drunk. You should try it too, Villebosse.

Villebosse (*turns on him, angrily*) Sir, one day I'll suggest a different game, which will be anything but fun, I promise you.

Countess (*from the doorway*) Are you coming, Tiger?

Villebosse (*suspiciously*) Where shall I find you, Eliane?

Countess I've no idea. You're being boring, Villebosse.

Exeunt omnes, except **Hero**, **Lucile**, **Damiens**.

Hero (*to* **Lucile**) Mademoiselle, you play your part to perfection. I drank in your every word. And a drunkard can't say fairer than that. In fact, I quite forgot to drink anything else. I'll let my doctor know tomorrow. I'm sure he'll be writing to thank you. I'm now going to step out of the eighteenth century. This waistcoast is far too tight. As indeed I am. I seem to have gallons of water swelling up in my belly, although I never touch the stuff. Funny that. Life's full of contradictions. But you know that, don't you, little thing. You back away. My smell, perhaps? I smell of alcohol. What do you expect me to smell of, for God's sake? It's not a bad smell. It's funny, they use alcohol to preserve the livers of the great alcoholics of history. To frighten the nice little boys and girls. Do I frighten you? That's because you can't see my liver. Apparently, it's in a quite spectacular state of disrepair. A tropical forest, bursting with flowers of every hue. Oh, I see. You don't like flowers. That's fine. No doubt I disgust you. (*Smiling.*) That's fine too. I have to be a *bit* disgusting. It's part of my role. Not the one in the Marivaux . . . The one I play in real life.

He passes **Damiens** *on the way out.*

Monsieur Damiens, your god-daughter is charming. And I tell you, if instead of Hero de – I won't bother you with my name, it's far too long – I was just called M. Damiens, pure and simple, I swear I'd get her away from here. Drunk's honour. (*Exit.*)

Lucile *gives a little shudder. Makes as if to leave.* **Damiens** *stops her.*

Damiens I must talk to you, Lucile.

Lucile (*unwillingly*) I'm listening.

Damiens You're young. You know little of the world and its ways. When your poor mother died, you wished to work for your living, to be independent and of course that is a highly laudable sentiment. Although, as you know, you were in no way obliged to . . .

Lucile Not obliged? Mother lived on her widow's pension. What choice did I have?

Damiens I was there . . .

Lucile You are my godfather, that's true. And it was very good of you to take an interest in me, but I didn't want to be beholden to you in any way.

Damiens (*gently*) But why, Lucile?

Lucile You know why.

Damiens The offer I made you may have seemed monstrous at the time. God knows what dreams girls cherish at eighteen. That is why I left you to yourself. I wanted the reality of life and hard work to teach you the sad truth. I know these past two years have not been easy for you.

Lucile Have I ever complained?

Damiens No, never. You are too proud. But do you think I've enjoyed watching you struggle to make ends meet? You are a pretty girl. I know that at your age, pretty girls like pretty things. I would have liked to make your life a little easier.

Lucile Believe me, I'm not cut out to be a heroine. I would have liked that too. But not from you.

Damiens You have no one in the world. I think I had the right, the duty even . . .

Lucile You know I find this sort of conversation painful. Please let's not go through it all over again. You gave me dolls and the odd sewing box when I was a little girl. And then you found me this job. You have amply discharged any duty you may have had. I can manage very well on my own, from now on.

Damiens Why won't you allow me to give you the security, the protection you need?

Lucile (*to his face*) And if I accepted, who would you be protecting me against? Other men making the same proposal as you?

Damiens (*bitterly*) Against worthless men, men who don't love you and respect you as I do. Men who would only want you for one night's pleasure.

Lucile Can't you see that I'm quite capable of protecting myself?

Damiens Against me, perhaps. But that's only because I'm honest enough to make my intentions quite clear. But not against someone younger, someone more brilliant, someone who'd lie to you.

Lucile If he were younger and more brilliant that would make it less shameful even if it were short lived. Or especially if it were short lived. Shame is easier to bear in small doses. Compared to that, one night's pleasure would be preferable. You never know, it might even be mutual . . .

Damiens I hate to hear you talking so cynically. I wish I'd never brought you here.

Lucile Why? Because they doll me up and force me to act in their plays for free? In my position, there are certain things you learn to accept. The Governess of the first children's home I worked in made that quite clear, believe me. And in a rather more sordid way. Yes, I've had my share of humiliations, in order to earn my crust. I know the score. And if that's the lesson you wanted me to learn from life – well, I've learnt it.

Damiens My dear girl. This man desires you and he won't let go until he gets what he wants. And everyone here knows what he's up to. Didn't you notice what was going on during rehearsals just now? The Countess is a clever woman. She vets his mistresses and he does the same for her lovers. But the game's got to be played by the rules. In other words, the cards have to be marked. No outsiders. No surprises. His courtship of you is therefore completely unacceptable. She will cover you with humiliation. Then she'll get rid of you.

Lucile Is that what you're afraid of? That I'll lose my job? I'll go to another children's home. You'll never understand how rich you are when you have nothing to lose. All children are more or less the same, anyway. They all make the same racket, have the same little accidents. And they all demand to be smothered with kisses at bedtime, by a little girl who's only slightly older than they are and who is paid to pretend to be their mother.

Damiens You will not become this man's mistress.

Lucile No. I won't. You needn't worry. But for different reasons. For my own reasons.

Enter the **Count**. *Brusquely. He is somewhat pale.*

Count I'm so sorry, M. Damiens, but I'm going to have to kidnap your god-daughter again. Bit of a tricky scene needs some detailed work before the evening rehearsal. Do you mind?

Damiens (*stiffly*) I leave her in your hands. I was just putting her on her guard against the temptations of a milieu which is not her own. It was a charming idea to have her take part in this play and I thank you and Mme la Comtesse for being so good as to treat her as your equal. But I would urge her not to forget that she is here to earn her living. She is here to look after the children.

Count On the contrary, my dear Damiens, I'm doing everything in my power to make her forget that fact. No, Mademoiselle Lucile is my guest. And if she consents, not only to do us the honour of acting in our play with, I may add, considerably more talent than most of us can boast – but is also brave enough to take on the twelve monsters of the west wing, instead of getting up at the crack of noon and staring balefully into a mirror for a few hours like the rest of us, then that is all the more reason for her to earn our respect and our admiration. It is my intention to make that clear to everybody here.

Damiens If you are so good as to undertake to see to the matter yourself, Monsieur le Comte, I take my leave of you completely reassured.

He exits.

Count No, don't say a word. First I must ask your forgiveness. I've been surrounded by over-bred louts for so long that I seem to have become one myself. Obviously nothing can be done before the performance. A party's a party. It's there to be given. They'll all make life unbearable for you, but I know you're brave. I've just had a conversation with my wife. I thought I knew everything but I have just discovered how low a woman of intelligence and taste can sink, when she sniffs danger in the air. They've all seen that I'm in love with you and that it's not a passing fancy. Now this is what I suggest . . . No, don't say a word until I've finished – You must see that I can't go on with my jolly little life of pleasure, while somewhere else in this wide world, you are busy mopping up after a bunch of snotty kids that aren't even your own. You're worth more than that. You're worth more than anything I can offer you. (*He stops her interrupting him.*) I haven't much money so you need have no reservations on that score. My inheritance was frittered away long ago. But by selling the few odds and ends I have left, I could raise enough to send you abroad. You could resume your education. You'd be free. And in a few years, a few months who knows, I hope with all my heart, you'll find some lad of your own age, who'll be worthy of you and with whom you can build a real life. I will never see you again.

A short pause.

All right, I think you're embarrassed about the money. But it's necessary and what is money to a free spirit? No, one must never be middle class about money. I humbly beg you to share the little I have. You can leave here the morning after the party.

A short pause.

It's a selfish proposal from a selfish man, who hasn't yet held you in his arms – not even once – and who is not happy. (*Humbly.*) Do you accept?

Lucile No. Of course not. I'd rather stay now.

He looks at her hesitantly for a moment. Then takes her in his arms.

Count My child . . .

Lucile (*holds him tight and murmurs*) This is so good. So warm. So easy. I thought all this came much later.

Count So did I. We must have skipped a bit.

Lucile Well, I'm glad we did. This is perfect. (*Suddenly.*) I'm afraid.

Count Of what?

Lucile Of not amusing you for very long. I'm not beautiful.

Count You are.

Lucile Not like Hortensia.

Count Thank God.

Lucile I'm not intelligent.

Count Don't be stupid.

Lucile Anyway, I could never be witty on demand.

Count I should hope not!

Lucile I'm poor. The condition isn't serious. It's the habit. I dress badly and if I had lots of money, I'd probably dress even worse. What is there about me you could still love, once the novelty had worn off?

Count The very fact that you're not beautiful in the way the others are, that you're gauche, that you're poor.

Lucile (*quietly*) If I thought it was a taste for chambermaids that attracted you to me, a 'droit de seigneur', I'd die of shame.

Count Why won't you understand? You who understand everything. In fairy tales, it's always the poor girl who releases the Prince from the spell. The trouble is there are so many. There's not a shop-girl in the world who wouldn't fall in love with a Prince.

Lucile And everyone will think that's why I fell in love with you.

Count And they'll use that to drive us apart. But do you believe it?

Lucile No.

Count Nor do I. So don't be silly. I don't believe it. You don't believe it. Who else is there?

Lucile (*indicating the others, who are entering*) Here they are.

Count Bit players. Walk-on parts in our play. (*Aloud.*) 'Yes, Sylvia, up to now I have concealed my rank, so that I may earn your affection on my own account. I didn't wish to diminish any of the pleasure your love would afford me. Now you know me as I am, you are free to accept my hand, my heart – or if you wish, refuse them both, etc, etc.' Oh there you all are. I see you're on time. Thank you for that. I hope you're all rested. If you don't mind, before we resume our work on the play, we're going to do what real actors always do the evening before their first dress rehearsal. They'll always spend a proper amount of time on it, even if, strictly speaking, they should still be working on the text. I suggest the following sequence . . . which seems entirely logical to me . . . I give my hand to Lucile . . . Eliane on my right . . . Then, Hero . . . Lastly, you Hortensia . . . Then on the other side . . . Damiens . . . and Villebosse . . . Where is Villebosse?

Villebosse (*enters. As furious as ever*) They told me we were rehearsing on the terrace. It's four o'clock. Are we rehearsing or not?

Count Just hang on, Villebosse. For the moment we're doing something even more important. The curtain call.

And, indeed, in the order suggested by the **Count**, *they bow. The curtain falls quickly.*

Act Three

Same décor. **Hortensia** *seated. The* **Countess** *pacing nervously. Enter* **Villebosse**.

Villebosse Are we rehearsing or not?

Countess You're disturbing us, Villebosse.

Hortensia Tiger insisted that we should be ready and in costume by four. We're still waiting for him.

Villebosse Look, what exactly has been going on since yesterday? We haven't been rehearsing. We've just been going through the motions, not investing the words with any particular meaning . . . or rather certain lines suddenly have too much meaning and seem to be bristling with all sorts of subtexts and resonances . . . which are going completely over my head. Then everyone starts giggling like idiots for no apparent reason. The insults start flying, that little girl bursts into tears. Tiger goes all red and walks out . . . Today we're a whole hour behind schedule. We open in three days. I've got an extremely demanding part. And I have no intention of looking ridiculous.

Countess You can run along now, Villebosse. I have to speak to Hortensia.

Villebosse Eliane, I don't understand you any more either. Your attitude to me is completely baffling. After all, what have I done to deserve this?

Countess Nothing. Absolutely nothing. Which may well be the trouble. Now, toddle along, do.

Villebosse But Eliane, I am suffering.

Countess Well, go and suffer in the garden. I've got to talk to Hortensia. We'll give you a shout.

Villebosse I can't see how I've managed to upset you since yesterday.

Countess You poor boy, it's nothing to do with you. I just want you to leave us alone for a bit, that's all.

Villebosse Very well, I will go. But, I'm nearing the end of my tether. I'll wait on the terrace, until you call. You owe me an explanation.

Countess You'll get one. We'll all get one.

Villebosse *exits*.

Now, my dear Hortensia. I don't understand you. This won't do at all. He's wooing that girl quite openly. He's besotted by her. Anyone can see that. He's even forgotten about his party. It's the first time he's ever done that. And you sit there and do absolutely nothing.

Hortensia I find the whole thing utterly disgusting.

Countess Yes, but what's the point of finding it disgusting if you don't do anything about it? You have to fight back. If I were Tiger's mistress, I certainly wouldn't allow myself to be treated like this. You disappoint me, you really do.

Hortensia You know as well as I do that a show-down would do absolutely no good whatsoever.

Countess You surely don't expect me to have one on your behalf. I didn't have one over you and I'm damned if I'm going to over this little girl.

Hortensia So let's leave him to it. He'll end up in her room tonight. And tomorrow he'll have forgotten all about her.

Countess Are you blind? Tiger isn't the same man. Something has touched him . . . deep inside . . . probably for the first time. I was watching him during dinner last night. He looked like he did in a snapshot a friend took of him during the war, on the morning of the German offensive. A perfectly happy, serious little boy, standing proudly by his cannon. I never thought anything but death could bring that look back to his face. I tell you Hortensia, he's in love with her.

Hortensia He doesn't know what love is.

Countess He's learning fast, believe me. You can do whatever you like, but I will not stand for it. Anyway, are things still going smoothly between you? I mean, physically.

Hortensia Eliane, you're embarrassing me . . .

Countess Hortensia, this is no time for social niceties. We have to defend ourselves. Is he still attentive?

Hortensia Tiger is a magnificent lover.

Countess So I'm told. But there are degrees of success in the area. Tiger has only to spot a trim little figure and he's aflame with desire. I've seen him in the streets. He'll spend hours on end following gypsy women who reek of goats and cheap cigarettes . . . girls who walk barefoot in the muck, girls who work the fairgrounds. He'll claim that they're princesses – the only women who really know how to walk. The only reason I'm telling you all this is to show you that Tiger is a man of strong desires. I know him. He's not a man to be overly troubled by aesthetic considerations. So, cards on the table, Hortensia. How are things between you in that department?

Hortensia My dear Eliane, do you want details?

Countess Thank you, no. I have about as much interest in that side of Tiger's life as I do in his passion for polo. But at least when he comes back from a game, I can always ask him, quite frankly, if he was satisfied with his horse. Up till now, where that side of his life is concerned, I've restricted myself to vague conjecture. Today I have to know.

Hortensia I think I can safely say that he's quite satisfied with his horse.

Countess Good. It's important. He hasn't laid a finger on her yet. And she's still a virgin – that's obvious . . . probably clumsy, certainly without any particular skill. You're right. If he does decide to make a *sortie* into the west wing he may well come back with his tail between his legs. He has a pathological hatred of failure.

Hortensia Now you're oversimplifying, Eliane. Love, even when reduced to its lowest common denominator, is an infinitely more subtle pursuit than polo. The heart tends to get messed up in the pleasures of the flesh – often to rather surprising effect. This is pure speculation on my part but I imagine that a sentimental attachment to a simple soul who gives herself inexpertly may turn out to be a new and titillating experience for Tiger. Over and above pure lust, that is – or rather, subtly intermingled with it.

Countess I don't like a woman having such a clear idea of what her lover may or may not experience with someone else. I find it rather unhealthy, Hortensia. On my own territory, where I have remained Tiger's wife – the common ground of a shared intelligence, a mutual enjoyment of life – I feel I'm in danger of losing him. And that's enough for me. I will act, with or without you.

Hortensia With me, of course. What do you take me for? At the moment I have only one concern; to win him back. Even if I decide to leave him the day after.

Countess Do both, my dear. You'd be doing me a favour. In the gaps between mistresses Tiger is the perfect husband. He usually feels obliged to take me off somewhere nice and to embark on a discreet courtship. Entirely platonic of course – but then I've never felt the need for that sort of thing. I'd even take the opportunity to get rid of Villebosse – he's starting to bore me. It'd be heaven.

Hortensia Delighted to help out in my own modest way. Enjoy your honeymoon. Where will you go? Italy?

Countess It's a bit hackneyed nowadays. That's where he took me first time round – when he offered the moon, and I believed him. He's dying to go to China. He says it's the only country he's remotely curious about.

Hortensia Oh, China's lovely. Yes, let's work on a trip to China for you, Eliane. How shall we go about it?

Countess Darling, Hortensia. I'm going to have to kiss you. (*Does so.*) But tell me this. If you care so little for him, how do I know you won't encourage him to make a fool of himself over that girl? That wouldn't suit me at all. I feel that by being frank with you, I've rather lowered my guard . . .

Hortensia My dear Eliane, as a rule I'd be only too delighted to stir things up between you and Tiger. I've never really forgiven you for remaining his best friend while he was still my lover. But pride forbids it. I won't allow him to leave me for some little mouse. I want to leave him myself. I'll save you for another time.

Countess How kind she is and how divine she smells! Are you still wearing 'Plaisir d'une nuit'? I used to think it smelt just like Turkish Delight. But I'm now beginning to find it almost bearable. Come up to my room. I've had an idea. Simple, but I hope, effective. I'm sure the little ninny's stuffed to the gills with all sorts of complexes – not to mention highly woundable pride. I'll say that one of my rings has been stolen. I'll insist the servants' rooms be searched – hers included. Afterwards, we'll find it somewhere or other, in the garden perhaps, tucked under a cushion . . . the place is immaterial. That should be enough to scare her off. You know my dear, it's amazing how sensitive the poor can be . . .

They exit. **Tiger** *and* **Hero** *enter by another door.*

Hero Are we rehearsing or not, to quote Villebosse? I can manage three acts stuck in this waistcoat – no more. Thank God classical plays are so short. If we'd been doing something by Victor Hugo, I would have simply exploded before the end, splattering my liver like poisoned flowers all over the astonished guests. What an exit for a drunk.

Count (*sits down*) Hero, it isn't fun any more . . .

Hero You're not going to switch to another play, are you? I'm delighted with my part. I'm playing a lord. 'What are you playing, Hero?' 'Oh, I'm playing a lord!' Aloof, mysterious, not too many lines to learn . . .

Count It's no fun having fun any more.

Hero You took your time finding that out. I discovered that twenty years ago. So have a drink.

Count Being drunk wouldn't be any fun either.

Hero Do you think we get drunk for fun? Drinking is a serious occupation. If you only knew the perseverance and application it requires. Forever having to fill up all those glasses – then having to empty them. It's like being a washer-up in a café . . . There's a thought: why don't you get a job?

Count I don't think that would be much fun either.

Hero Do what I do. Make love. It's not that entertaining but it keeps hope alive.

Count I've done all that. Admittedly on a less grand scale than yourself, but I've done it. And I can tell you this. All things considered, it's no job for a grown man.

Hero You're getting depressed. How old are you now?

Count A year older than you, as you very well know. When I first met you in the third form, I'd missed a year. We owe our friendship to scarlet fever.

Hero Surely you don't nurse a secret desire to do something worthwhile?

Count Certainly not.

Hero Or to buckle down and earn some money? What with Eliane's fortune, that would be positively immoral and worse still – in appalling taste.

Count I hate money!

Hero Beware of overstatement. 'I mistrust money' is quite strong enough. So there's only one other possibility – have a nervous breakdown. A job in itself. That would be a whole year taken care of.

Count Just imagine this, Hero. Imagine everything suddenly falls into place. Everything is suddenly simple and calm. But at the same time out of reach, inaccessible.

Hero I'm not that imaginative. Let me translate. Alcohol is suddenly discovered to be the elixir of life. But all the bars I know have shut down.

Count That's it. No, not quite. There's one bar still open. Just one – a little provincial café, one you'd never dream of going into.

Hero There's no such thing as a little provincial café I'd never dream of going into.

Count All right, but say you do go in, by accident, for no reason at all. And once inside you discover that life was always much simpler, much more serious . . . just better . . . than you'd ever imagined.

Hero Your analogies are rather obscure and in dubious taste. What's more, they're making me thirsty. Enough of these parables. You're desperately in love.

Count Yes, I am.

Hero Good then, it's not serious. That's the eleventh time you've told me that.

Count That's true. All right, I'm not desperately in love.

Hero So, it's 'the real thing', then? You've told me that at least three times. Twice with tears in your eyes.

Count All right, then. I can't be desperately in love and it can't be 'the real thing'. Because it's like nothing I've ever known before.

Hero (*pouring himself another drink. In a new, darker tone*) You disgust me.

Count Why?

Hero (*softly*) The way you look.

Count Am I that ugly?

Hero No. That's the point. You're beautiful. You've become beautiful again. You look like you did at school, at St. Barge, when we were fifteen, the day we jumped the walls to go to a brothel, do you remember? You look like you used to in winter – both of us coming back from football, caked in mud, making fun of all the girls. You look like you did the night we swore eternal friendship, cutting ourselves with a rusty little penknife so we could mingle our blood . . . Don't do this to me, Tiger. I'll never forgive you.

Count It took a good hour to make the incision. In spite of our heady idealism, we were complete cowards. But we did it. Do you remember what we said? Do you remember the oath?

Hero (*brutally*) No!

Count I do – it suddenly came back to me yesterday evening.

Hero No, I don't want to know. You mustn't do this to me, Tiger. Look, my hand's shaking. I'm a wreck. In a couple of years, they'll be pushing me around in a wheelchair – or I'll be dead. I can't bear the thought of your becoming him again. It's too easy.

Count Who?

Hero You know!

He grips the glass. It shatters in his hand. They both look at it.

Sorry, old man. I like breaking things.

Count You're mad. You're bleeding. Here, take my handkerchief. The wine's depressed you today.

Hero Wine is always depressing. Take it from me. (*He offers a piece of glass.*) Come on. Cut yourself and swear.

Count Swear what?

Hero That we're happy as we are. That we'll keep on having fun and brave it out till the bitter end. If you're bored with Hortensia, find someone else. If you're short of money, I'll give you some of mine. If you want to forget, I'll teach you how to drink. But just have fun, like I do, I beg you. And stop looking like that.

Count That's the way I look now. I can't help it . . .

Hero One has to make a choice. We've made ours. There's no turning back. It would hurt me to see you look ridiculous . . . And then, it would hurt me even more to see you happy . . . in that way.

Count (*after a pause*) You still haven't forgiven me for Evangeline, have you?

Hero No.

Count It wasn't the marriage for you . . . You were nineteen. You were going to bury yourself alive. You . . . (*He stops.*) Forgive me. Today, for the first time, I see that perhaps I was wrong to stop you marrying that girl.

Hero What's done is done. You weren't wrong. And we've both had a lot of fun since. No regrets. Even if I had a wife, six kids and a house in the country, I'd still probably have come to the same sticky end. Just rather less spectacularly, that's all. Anyway, being a drunk is a great tradition in our family – glasses have been handed down from father to son. But one piece of advice deserves another. Leave what they call love alone. It's not for the likes of us.

Count If you care for me, you should want me to be happy.

Hero Not now. Not like that anyway. We should neither of us have any illusions. Our love for each other came to an end twenty years ago, when we both started wearing long trousers. Which doesn't, of course, stop us from being great friends. (*Pours himself a drink.*) Let's drink to that, Tiger. Have your fun. You're free, after all – but don't go telling me your secrets . . . and don't set your hopes too high. Life has a way of sorting things out and leaving them in some kind of order. It's very ordered, life.

Count We shall see.

Hero We *shall* see. One always does. That's what's so wonderful about the human condition. Five minutes before you die, you shout 'Eureka' and on that cheery note, down comes the curtain.

The **Countess** *and* **Hortensia** *enter.*

Eliane.

Countess Hero. Tiger. I'm very upset. I have to talk to you. My emerald ring has disappeared.

Count Ask your maid to look for it, my dear. Not me. I hate all that.

Countess We've been searching high and low since this morning. I had it yesterday. I had it here. I left it in the cloakroom where we put our costumes because I thought the green didn't go with my dress. I'm very upset. I just hope someone hasn't behaved badly.

Count Have them search the cloakroom again.

Countess Of course. But if I don't find it there, I'll have to get in touch with the insurance people. They'll have to send someone to make enquiries. It'll be ghastly.

Count After the ball is over, my love, after the break of day. I've no intention of dressing the local constabulary up in eighteenth-century costume. After the ball, I beg of you.

Countess I'm sorry, Tiger, but the insurance people have to be notified within a day. I'm going to keep looking. Will you come and help, Hero?

Hero Delighted to be of some use. First time in thirty years.

Count (*to the* **Countess**, *as she exits with* **Hero**) But no dramas, I beg of you. (*To* **Hortensia**.) My love, one can make one's life a complete misery, worrying about burglaries and shipwrecks, but ask anyone, anyone you know and you'll find that no one's ever been burgled and ships don't sink. And haven't you noticed that life, I mean 'real life' – grisly murders, mad passions, earth-shattering disasters and fabulous inheritances – all seems to take place exclusively in the newspapers.

Hortensia This ring business is a bore.

Count Eliane has enough jewels to lose the odd one now and again.

Hortensia She isn't taking it quite so lightheartedly. It was a beautiful stone. She intends to have all the servants searched.

Count They've been with the family for twenty years. So you must admit they've been biding their time. Her maid is somewhat younger it's true, but she is her god-daughter and she was born in the kitchen. Like kittens are. She spends all her time at mass. Short of selling the loot to buy more candles, I can't see why she'd want to embark on a career of crime.

Hortensia Be that as it may, Eliane has decided to search everywhere. It seems to me to be an elementary precaution. Now, let's think, who is there here apart from the servants . . . Villebosse, Hero, Damiens, myself . . .

Count (*interrupting*) My darling, I loathe detective stories. They've always struck me – in a strong field – as the world's most fatuous literary form. Tying a story into the most ridiculous and unlikely knots, to produce the spurious elegance of being unable to unravel them in the last few pages, strikes me as the work of a half-wit. Certainly not of a serious writer. If I'm ever depressed enough to pick one up, last thing at night, I'm always fast asleep before I find out 'who done it'. As a result I've a huge backlog of unsolved crimes in my brain and I neither know, nor care, who the culprits were. You must never try to discover the culprits in real life either. It's the most senseless activity imaginable. Everybody is guilty . . . or nobody is.

Hortensia Eliane's taste for paradox isn't as highly developed as yours. If I know her, she'll be searching those rooms, just as she said she would.

Count If she has the west wing searched then I'll demand that they search the east wing too. I'll suddenly mislay my watch and hide it in your room. Did you concoct this little fantasy together? Brilliant!

Hortensia (*suddenly completely transparent*) I don't know what you mean, Tiger.

Count (*taking her by the arms*) My dear little Hortensia, I have loved you. You know that. 'Love' is a big word but there are so many feelings and so few words to describe them that we often have to lump them all together under one heading. So let us say that my hands have loved you. And that at each of our encounters, I have experienced a sort of joy – very pure, that's the funny thing, a very pure, almost complete happiness when I touched you.

Hortensia Thank you.

Count Don't thank me. It's none of your doing. Look, I'll pay you a compliment. Probably the first, possibly the last. You are very beautiful. I don't mean your face, charming as it is. I don't much believe in faces. Anyway with the amount of make-up they wear nowadays, as long as they're not terminally ugly, most women's faces look pretty much alike. But your body is beautiful. And beauty, true beauty is a very serious matter. If there is a God, that must be part of him too.

Hortensia Heavens.

Count I know. Those words sound funny coming from me. And I do feel a bit of a fraud.

Hortensia I'm not used to you talking so seriously. Is this some new game, Tiger? It frightens me.

Count (*releases her. Lights up a cigar*) It frightens me a bit, too. I'm not used to going down to these depths. I'll have to come up for air in a minute.

Hortensia Tiger. This girl's not even pretty. She's delicate, I suppose, and slim enough but she has no poise. The first time you go anywhere together you'll be ashamed of her, in her little schoolma'am's frock. And if you try dressing her for the part, you'll be even more ashamed. I know you.

Count Yes, I'm probably enough of a fool to be ashamed. But it's not remotely important . . .

Hortensia You belong to a different race, Tiger. And although your heart or your head can make all sorts of stupid mistakes, your hands will always know the truth – that you still desire me . . .

Count (*looks at her gently, and with a smile*) Yes, I know. I'm capable of anything. But the fact is – I love her, and there it is . . .

Hortensia But it's completely ridiculous. She's the opposite of anything you could possibly love.

Count The opposite. Yes exactly. And yet I love her. Do you find that funny?

Hortensia (*who is laughing*) I find it ridiculous. Utterly ridiculous. I'm sorry, but it's just so bloody ridiculous . . .

Count I know it is. And it's wonderful. I'm glad to have the chance to be ridiculous at last.

Damiens *enters.*

Damiens Monsieur le Comte . . . Madame la Comtesse has discovered the loss of a valuable jewel and has instigated a search of all the rooms in the west wing. You assured me just now of the particular respect with which you would wish my god-daughter to be treated while she was in this house. Do you therefore allow her room to be searched?

Count Certainly not. Follow me. We'll put an end to this charade once and for all.

They exit. **Villebosse** *enters.*

Villebosse So. Are we rehearsing or not? We've been in costume for two hours.

Hortensia Villebosse, we're acting now. We've been acting our little socks off for quite some time. Surely you must have noticed. (*She goes out.*)

Villebosse My God, I'm being made a fool of. (*To* **Hero**, *who has entered.*) Sir!

Hero Sir?

Villebosse I am being made a fool of in this house.

Hero That's entirely possible.

Villebosse And I have the feeling you are responsible.

Hero That's equally possible.

Villebosse What would you say if I demanded reparation?

Hero Sir, I like breaking things. I never repair them. (*He goes out.*)

Villebosse (*following*) Sir, you have refused my challenge. I will shame you . . . publicly.

Countess (*entering, distraught*) Villebosse!

Villebosse Eliane, my love . . . You look distraught.

Countess I am distraught. Tiger has just insulted me unforgivably. My emerald ring has been stolen and when I asked Fourcault and Jasmin to search the west wing, he forbade them to go into that girl's room. He's been inflicting her on us all week and now he says that no one should enter her room, until mine has been searched first. He claims that I haven't lost the ring but have hidden it somewhere. Which is completely insulting.

Villebosse I will not tolerate this, Eliane. Permit me to seek the man out and challenge him.

Countess Don't you understand anything about anything? There's no point in challenging Tiger for his lack of respect for me. After all, I am his wife. No, he has to learn that he cannot make a fool of me with this tuppenny-ha'penny nobody of a nursemaid. Let him have his mistresses for God's sake. Hortensia's a good friend of mine and eminently suitable. But what will everyone say if my husband makes a fool of himself over this little . . . snake? If he takes her to Paris, I won't dare show my face. I promise you, I'm not leaving the house all winter.

Villebosse It's quite inexcusable. I will settle everything. You can rely on me, Eliane.

He exits. **Lucile** *enters.*

Lucile I have come to bring you the key to my room, madame. I want it to be searched like the others. And, who knows, perhaps they'll even find the ring there. Then everyone will be happy.

Countess I don't know what on earth you mean, my child. My maid is still looking in my room with my husband. It's entirely possible that I may have put the ring away somewhere, and forgotten all about it.

Lucile That would be good news indeed.

Countess Yes, it would; suspicion is always an unpleasant business for all concerned. I'm sorry if you're hurt. It was merely a general precaution that applied to all the servants. I assume you've come to tell me that you feel you have to give up your part in the play. And perhaps that you don't feel that you can look after the little ones any longer, poor mites, they were so fond of you . . . or so I was told. It'll break their tiny hearts. But, if your mind is made up, then I think the best way would be to cut yourself off from them as quickly, as brutally, as possible. For their sakes. Where children are concerned – as I surely don't need to tell you – it's important to take firm decisions. They'll cry all night, but, come the next morning, they won't be giving it another thought. They'll simply fall in love with the next young lady who comes along. I think the train leaves in an hour. The car can take you down to the station just as soon as you're packed. Naturally, although the decision was your own, I'll be happy, in view of your straitened circumstances, to pay you six months' wages.

The **Count** *has entered. The* **Countess** *turns calmly to him.*

Mademoiselle has said that she is going to leave us. I'm very sorry about your play of course, Tiger. But in three days I'm sure you'll have found somebody else. I was just saying to her that as far as the children are concerned, if her mind is made up, as it does seem to be, it would be best to go quickly. Very quickly. And not to see them again. They were attached to her – as indeed we all were – but we do want to avoid any public manifestation of grief.

Count Here is your emerald, Eliane.

Countess (*putting it back on her finger*) Oh, thank heavens for that. Where had it got to?

Count It was in your room. Under one of the candlesticks.

Countess Really? Now what can have possessed me to put it there?

Count Now I am going to ask you to apologise to this young lady.

Countess Apologise? What on earth for? I will, gladly . . . Mademoiselle, you must excuse me for being so absent-minded. I trust you will forgive me and that you won't think too badly of us, when you've gone. You agree, don't you, Tiger, that Fourcault should remit her six months' wages? I know it was her own decision but I do blame myself a bit. If I hadn't lost that ring she would never have dreamt of leaving us.

Count My dear Eliane, you know full well that I never allow one of my parties to be compromised in any way, whatever the circumstances. We cannot possibly cut or recast that part in three days. I would therefore beg you, if you possibly can, to prevail on her to reconsider.

Countess Honestly, I've done all I can. But she's hurt. She is adamant. I must admit I understand how she feels.

Count I'm sure you can do more. I insist that you win this small diplomatic victory, Eliane, or I will be terribly disappointed. I'll leave you together. We rehearse again in half an hour.

He exits. **Lucile** *is still silent. The* **Countess** *sits down. Very relaxed.*

Countess Well, here we are then. It seems I now have to talk you into staying, in order to make my life with Tiger worth living. It is a bit ironic, you must agree. I am a weak woman underneath, and Tiger's merest whim is my command. Don't whatever you do fall in love with a capricious man.

Lucile (*quietly*) Do you love him?

Countess What a question. He's my husband.

Lucile Do you think having fun all the time really makes him happy?

Countess My dear young lady, if we are going to have this conversation, and it seems that we must, you will forgive me if I do not allow it to assume too personal a tone. I loathe personal questions. Tiger wants me to ask you to stay – so I'm asking you. He'll have a fit if we have to cancel the performance. Anyway, why leave? We all admire your considerable efforts on behalf of those poor children and we certainly have no particular reason to prolong our stay in 'Ferbroques'. Tiger gets bored witless in the country. Once the party's over, we'll be whizzing back to Paris for the season. Then everything will be just as it was, won't it? So let's part friends, shall we? And once again, do please forgive that little episode. Tiger's quite capable of going into a sulk – for anything up to a week. And he would, if he thought you bore me any sort of grudge. We hardly know each other of course, but you must be aware of how much I value your godfather, M. Damiens. *A propos*, we were talking about you only this morning. You know he has an enormous affection for you?

Lucile Yes, he has told me.

Countess A man, I can't help feeling, who has had his fair share of suffering. He's lived apart from his wife for some years now, hasn't he? And she doesn't seem in their married life, how shall I put it, to have afforded him all the attention he might have deserved. Behind a rather forbidding exterior, he's actually a man of surprising sensitivity. Yes, he talked about you at some length.

Lucile Really?

Countess Yes, really. My child, I did get a little bit irritated just now, I'll admit it. All things considered, I'm really very fond of you. You're so young. You have this disarming way of seeming to know everything. But I'm sure that deep down under that Quaker seriousness, there's a doomed little moth dying to singe its wings in the first flame it can find. You think . . . oh, yes, it will be gorgeous . . . it will be everything you've ever dreamed of . . . So you live out the dream for a week, perhaps two. Then your eyes are open. Wide open and weeping. Damiens told me that you were proud; proud and poor. A great quality coupled with a great disadvantage. Of course, you may well meet someone from your own walk of life. But that won't last all that long either. The Prince Charming of the Young Farmers' Ball – blushing – picking you violets. I'll give him two years to turn into a sulky, petty-minded little tyrant. You're worth much more than that. It's always a great temptation for a girl just to go mad. But, believe me, the temptation to be totally sane is just as great and twice as dangerous. If you're pretty, intelligent and penniless, let's face it, you'll always be a bit déclassé. You have to take what you can. Damiens, who is a friend of mine, and I were very worried about you this morning. (*A beat. She gets up. Wanders nonchalantly to a table.*) Briefly, it's like this. His wife is barking mad, of course, and lives out in the country. She's ill. She's older than he is. She won't live long. Damiens is a man of honour and still very handsome. I remember fifteen or twenty years ago when he used to come to visit my mother – I wonder if I should be telling you all this? Of course I was just a girl, but I was madly in love with him for a whole winter . . . At least think about it. I'm talking to you as a woman who understands life, who is quite a bit older than you and who would be unhappy, really unhappy to see you squandering your youth on some mad escapade that has no future. When you have no status, when you're alone in the world, you have to look to the future. My God, I know it's no fun. It's not what you expect or want when you're twenty. But it's the way of the world, my dear. And there's not much either of us can do about it. (*A pause. She looks at* **Lucile**.) Listen to me, Damiens has served us so faithfully, and

for such a long time. As far as I am concerned, you would be as good
as his wife. This emerald will be my wedding present to you.
(*Offering it.*)

Lucile (*examines it briefly – then gives it back*) It would be too fine a gift
for such a sordid ceremony. But, thank you, madame.

Countess You're making a mistake. It was sincerely meant.

Lucile In any case, I have sworn that I will never marry – in that
way or any other.

Countess How on earth can you know that at your age? When did
you make that rash promise?

Lucile Last night.

Countess (*brusque*) Very well. When you see Tiger I'd be obliged if
you tell him I did all I could.

Lucile I'll tell him. Thank you, madame. (*She goes.*)

*The **Countess** paces up and down nervously, fanning herself distractedly.
For all the world like an actress in a play by Marivaux.*

Countess (*calling out of the window*) Hero! No, not you Villebosse.
Hero, come here at once. I need to speak to you.

*More nervous pacing. More fanning. Then **Hero** enters.*

Hero. We have to stop Tiger doing something foolish. He's in love
with that girl. She's been his mistress since last night. She's told
him that she loves him. It's insane and it's ridiculous. I don't know
if you've noticed him over the past few days . . . ?

Hero Yes, I have.

Countess It's disgusting.

Hero Disgusting. I told him so.

Countess But, are you on my side, Hero? Do something. You're
the only one who can, I'm sure of that.

Hero You mean to him? His good-nature is unassailable.

Countess Then to her, perhaps.

Hero (*à la Comédie Française*) 'My lord, is this the deed you'd have
me do, to woo this maid and be her lover too?'

Countess Victor Hugo. Very good. You can do it if you want to.
This girl's just a little romantic, a mad thing, an infatuated

shopgirl. All Paris knows you're irresistible. Seduce her. You know it's a shame we're not doing *Ruy Blas*. When I was fifteen, it was my favourite play.

Hero There's only one problem. This girl doesn't know I'm irresistible. Which robs me of my tactical advantage.

Countess Nonsense. In two days' time, with both Tiger and you in hot pursuit her head will be in a complete whirl. She'll be so smug she'll burst. Imagine, the two most brilliant men in the chateau only have eyes for her. I know all this 'Don't touch me, sir' saintliness. I was a bit like that before I married Tiger. But women are women, my love. Even when they're pretending to be angels. I don't have to teach you any tricks, Hero. Get a few drinks in her. Swear you love her. A little moonlight, a little music, and the little ninny will believe you. Or at least enough to abandon herself for one night. After which Tiger will either agree to break it off or to share her; either way, the danger will be past.

Hero You do me a considerable honour, Eliane – imagining no one can resist me. Normally, I'd say yes – if it was just another woman. After all, I have my professional reputation to consider. But not innocent young girls. They're unpredictable creatures and I try to have as little to do with them as possible.

Countess But I'm telling you she's not innocent any more. She's his mistress.

Hero Only since last night. I have a feeling she'll retain her state of grace a little while yet.

Countess Are you going to let Tiger get completely besotted? Make himself totally ridiculous? Hero, he's in love with her, I'm sure of it. And you don't care that he's in love . . . like a teenager.

Hero (*suddenly hard*) You're wrong. I do care.

Countess Are you afraid of hurting him? Of breaking their hearts, perhaps?

Hero No. I told you. I like breaking things.

A pause.

Countess Hero, she sleeps on her own at the far end of the west wing. If she really does love him, you may not be certain of success. But, you're a brute. We all know that. You're crazy about her. You've been drinking – as usual. You force her door. The lock doesn't work – I'll see to that. She'll cry out of course, but it's like the end of the world down there. And after all what can one little girl do with her little fists and her tearful entreaties against the full force of a grown man's desire? If she loves him, the pure shame of it will have driven her away by morning.

Hero (*very soft*) Evangéline.

Countess What did you say?

Hero Just a girl's name. Evangéline, Mme Blumenstein . . . you must have met her. She married a Jewish banker. It wasn't a happy marriage. She died a few years ago.

Countess A slim blonde thing, with marvellous great eyes, like a sacrificial lamb? Of course I remember her. We were introduced at the Rothschilds'. What's the connection?

Hero A vague, rather distant one. But I'm glad you remember her . . . Let's go and rehearse, Eliane. They're waiting for us. And this play has got to be well done. Like all things trivial, it's a serious matter. Her husband was a swine. They say he used to beat her.

Countess I've an idea. I'll have someone send Tiger a telegram this evening, calling him away. Gontaut-Biron owes me a favour . . .

Act Four

Lucile's *attic room. She is in her night-dress. Crouched, staring dreamily into the fire. The door opens gently. She looks up, surprised.*

Hero *enters, slightly dishevelled, with a bottle and two glasses.*

Hero (*charmingly*) Don't be afraid. Tiger has just telephoned to say he won't be coming back till very late tonight. He sent me to tell you the news and to keep you company for a bit. May I sit down?

Lucile (*indicating the only chair*) Yes.

Hero Thanks. You sit on the bed, my love. You'll be more comfy. Have a little drink?

Lucile No.

Hero You don't mind if I do? It would be unwise for me to stop now, having got this far. If I did, I would get drunk immediately and start behaving badly. While others sleep I embark on my long solitary struggle until dawn, when I can close my eyes at last. My bloody eyes. They will look. Everything bores them, but there they still are, stubbornly open and staring. Daytime I can cope with. I drink a bit. I talk . . . any old nonsense, as long as it stops me from thinking. Would you be so good as to stop me thinking for a while? Actually, it's an order from Tiger. He said 'Pop up and tell her I won't be coming back and keep her company for a bit.' (*A pause.*) I think he hoped you might chip in from time to time.

Lucile What would you like me to say?

Hero I've no idea. Something nice. Say that it's all been a ghastly mistake. That it's not Tiger you really love, it's me . . .

Lucile *smiles.*

All right tell me it's Tiger. It's not quite such fun but I suppose it's better than nothing.

Lucile I can't believe he would want us to talk about that. I can't believe he's talked to you about me.

Hero Oh my dear child. You don't know men. Compulsive gossips. We tell each other everything.

Lucile Are you very fond of him?

Hero We were chucking stink bombs at girls long before you took it into your pretty head to be born. We even mingled our blood one

night in the dormitory! 'In life as in death.' The opportunity to die
for each other didn't however present itself straight away, so since
then we've had to live. You know, like Castor and Pollux. It doesn't
matter. It's a sort of fable . . . anyway we've always been very close.
Certainly no woman has succeeded in coming between us.

Lucile (*like a little girl*) Has he had lots of women then?

Hero Little baby. Of course, he adores you, that goes without
saying. But it would have been a bit of a risk to have waited for you
to come along. Does that hurt you – that he's lived a bit?

Lucile That is my secret.

Hero You keep it, my angel. Wrap it up in your hanky and put it
somewhere safe. I've never been all that interested in secrets
myself. They're always more or less the same and they're only
really of interest to those who divulge them. You're young. Love is
an undiscovered country and you're just off the boat. You must feel
like some pioneer, the prospect of a whole brave new world before
you . . . No, it's very sweet. You'll soon learn that the play is only
written for two or three parts, with two or three scenes endlessly
repeated. And the words that seem to spring new minted and
irrepressible from one's heart in moments of ecstasy are in fact the
same old banalities which have been regurgitated since the
beginning of time. Nothing is new. Even our vices are duplicated in
the same dismal, desperate way. A proper catalogue, with the
prices in the right-hand column. Because everything has to be paid
for. Drink, gout and cirrhosis, sodomy – solitude and social
diseases. The price of passion – exhaustion. True love – a poor little
broken heart. There's no escape.

Lucile (*gently*) I have been in love with Tiger since yesterday and I
am twenty years old. So your tirade is a complete waste of time.

Hero Touché! There was only one reply to my drunken cynicism
and you found it. Tiger's a lucky devil. He wins at everything.

Lucile What is it that he's won?

Hero You. I must admit I underestimated you. It's nothing short
of miraculous how you managed to make everyone think you were
just an insignificant little hypocrite.

Lucile I am insignificant. I could hardly say a word. The wonder is
that he managed to bring me out of my shell.

Hero Tiger can do anything. I'll bet you were a cast-iron virgin. I'll bet no one's ever laid a finger on you. Oh dear, oh dear, I've hurt her feelings. Come on, have a drink with me. If I'm the only one who's doing the drinking, we'll never get to have a proper conversation.

Lucile No, thank you, monsieur.

Hero No, thank you, monsieur . . . so polite. Nice and neat. Nice and clean. A shiny little pebble his lordship happened to find on the beach. When he wasn't even looking. It's infuriating, but it so happens that I love him. Not in the same way as you do but still quite a lot. So I can forgive him everything. Yes, let's talk about him. That'll be nice. And perhaps it'll help me get to sleep . . . just a drop? No? Never mind. It's not often two people can get together and talk about a third whom they both love . . . and share a drink into the bargain. God knows there's so little love in this barren world . . . So tell me, how were you able to give yourself like that, I mean straight away . . . for the first time? After all, you hardly knew him yesterday. I'm not trying to steal your secrets. It's just that it's all so sweet; so unlike anything I've ever known that it could almost convert me! No? You don't want to tell me? Am I doomed never to know, even at second hand, how love is born?

Lucile (*softly as if to herself*) I'd never been able to bear anyone touching me. But when he took me in his arms, I felt I'd arrived at last. I was no longer that frightened little girl, clutching her suitcase, tossed hither and thither by everything and everybody. At last I had somewhere of my own, a haven, somewhere to be . . . And what more could I ask?

Hero And what if he'd just wanted a bit of fun?

Lucile All girls run that risk. And you can't waste much sympathy on the silly ones who get it wrong.

Hero All the same, I know the nature of the beast, when it wants to be loved. Go on, admit it. He almost tried too hard to be fascinating.

Lucile (*smiling now*) Yes, that's true. But I made allowances.

Hero But what could you have hoped for when you first clapped eyes on him?

Lucile Simply to be in his arms – as indeed I soon was.

Hero And after that?

Lucile After that . . . well, if I have to carry on my other life, my real life where you have to earn your living . . . well, there's no shortage of orphans in the world. It's not important. I will have had my share.

Hero (*lifts his arms in mock astonishment*) Not even a clinging vine. Clever old Tiger. Here he is, marooned in the middle of a life of party-giving; washed-up, worthless, sick at heart. He lifts his little finger and hey-presto – enter an angel who offers herself straight away and forever. Because it is forever with you isn't it?

Lucile Of course.

Hero And if he gets killed coming back in the car, then you'll probably die tomorrow. Daphnis and Chloë, Dido and Aeneas, and Tristan and Isolde, without even King Mark and his boring old sword to come between you. Amazing, m'sieur feels like a romantic idyll one day and . . . abracadabra . . . hey diddle diddle, here comes your idyll, a beautiful girl on a plate. A secret girl, elusive, untouchable, carefully preserved, just for you. She was waiting for you . . .

Lucile It's true. I was waiting for him . . .

Hero And all he had to do was turn up. It's guaranteed. Spotless and everlasting. So let the others make do with their women. The sort who are yours at midnight but everyone else's during the day. I'm sure you'll never take to any of that. You'll remain your own unassuming self even when he buys you nice dresses and everyone says how pretty you look.

Lucile He'll never buy me dresses. I promise you that.

Hero Why not?

Lucile Because I don't want any. I've acquired the habit of buying the odd dress for myself from time to time. It's a habit I intend to keep.

Hero I don't believe it; he's got the lot! Intelligence, wisdom, and to cap it all complete unselfishness. I bet you'll insist on looking after those orphans like the good girl that you are, content to stay up in your little room, the door carefully on the latch every night.

Lucile Not at all. But I will find another children's home not too far from Paris and he can visit me there whenever he wants.

Hero Won't that be lovely? I can see him asking politely for you in the front parlour, both of you terrified in case Matron gives you a ticking off. He'll be blushing like a teenager. A whole new life stretches before him. A second chance. But what's this? A dark cloud on the horizon? He is a fine French gentleman, the distillate of centuries of good breeding. He'll never allow you to work.

Lucile I'll have to. Weren't you ever taught that one must earn one's daily bread by the sweat of one's brow?

Hero No. We were sent to rather exclusive schools. That wasn't part of the curriculum. But go ahead if you want. Tiger will die of shame that's all. I know him.

Lucile It's not that easy to die of shame, believe me. And work isn't that boring. Certainly no more boring than doing nothing. And it demands considerably less imagination. When I think of the lengths you both go to just to kill time.

Hero That's absolutely true. We've sweated and slaved over it all our lives. It takes considerable guts and determination. Look at the poor. What do they do with their Sundays? They trudge round the streets, yawning. Poor things – it's as much as they can do to make it through to Monday. And we've always had seven Sundays a week, ever since we were little, so we weren't exactly spoiled, were we? We've just had to knuckle down and make the best of it. Now, thank God, the worst is behind us. Tiger has acquired the skill of amusing himself for up to fifteen hours a day without flagging. You ought to give it a go. He'll show you the ropes.

Lucile No.

Hero But if you spend your whole life at a children's home, and he spends his at the races, it'll be like a charlady marrying a night-porter – you'll never meet. You have to be a bit reasonable for God's sake.

Lucile I don't want to be reasonable. It's the first word people use when they want to do something wicked.

Hero 'Something wicked.' Now that's rather hard to define. In any case, little girl, it's better than doing something stupid.

Lucile But I want to be stupid. That's my way of loving him. Imagine me set up in some beautiful apartment, with him coming to call with a little parcel all done up in ribbons. I'd hate it. It'd last about a week. And that *would* be stupid.

Hero You know everything. You're going to save him from a terrible blunder. And he'll be only too pleased to play the game, the hypocrite. He'll have a nice little suit made, somewhere not too expensive, and wait outside your office every evening at six, with a tuppenny bunch of violets. And he'll be twenty again. With all the innocence of youth and a whole new future ahead of him. To be offered all that at forty! (*He rises. Shouts.*) No. It's too much, I tell you. Much too much.

Lucile What's wrong?

Hero (*pulls himself together. Explains slowly, with a smile*) It's just too good to be true, that's all. It's a fairy story.

Lucile (*rises*) Sir, we have talked a little as he wanted. Perhaps it would be better if you let me get to bed now. I've got to be up early to see to the children.

Hero (*still seated*) We haven't been talking for five minutes. Sit down – grant me a little more of your time. I don't sleep too well and I'm only keeping you up because I'm terrified of being on my own. Won't you pity me a little, mademoiselle?

She sits on the edge of the bed. He pours himself a drink.

Anyhow, I'm not exactly compromising you, am I? A young girl can entertain me in her room till quite late without being in the slightest danger. Not very alluring, am I? Bit of a wreck and I'm a year younger than Tiger. So much for a life of pleasure . . .

Lucile (*gently*) Why don't you try drinking less?

Hero Why should I? I'd have to meet an angel like his lordship. One who would take me under her wing. Angels are so rare.

Lucile (*again, gently*) Perhaps you'll meet one some day.

Hero With a glass in my hand? Looking like this, smelling like this. If it had been me who was in search of conversion, would you have been quite so angelic? (*He looks at her, smiling.*) Yet another indiscreet question . . . a little heavy handed, I know . . . but, anyway . . . When you turned up a few days ago; that first evening at dinner . . . with the exception of Villebosse who doesn't count, none of the men could take his eyes off you.

Lucile (*astonished, flattered even*) None of the men?

Hero How sweet. She didn't even notice. Yes, my dear, there were three of us. The butler's a bit old for that sort of thing but Tiger's valet got all the cutlery mixed up. He was burning to be converted just like the rest of us.

Lucile That's enough.

Hero Why? Am I upsetting you? Surely you're not a snob? That boy sleeps in the west wing too. If I were you, I'd bolt your door at night. He was a paratrooper in the war. That sort of experience can make a boy forget his place. What if the paratrooper decided to drop in? Now, my question is, what if it had been him – or me – instead of Tiger . . .?

Lucile (*simply*) But he's the one I love.

A pause.

Hero And what more is there to say?

Lucile (*gently*) Nothing.

Hero You're no fun. Try and play the game a bit. Just to get me through the night. Let's imagine that Tiger has never spoken to you. You don't love him. I've been staring at you over the dinner table for a week and this evening I've come up to your room on some pretext, to tell you that, like him, I need you.

He rises heavily. **Lucile** *gets up too.*

Lucile That's not a game I want to play. It's ugly. Why can't you see that? You're his friend. If he knew how you've been amusing yourself this evening, what would he think?

Hero We've begged, borrowed, stolen each other's mistresses before now, as all good friends do. And in any case, it would only be tit for tat. I was lying. There was an angel in my life, mademoiselle. It was a long time ago. I was nineteen and I'd hardly drunk a drop.

Lucile And he . . .

Hero No, he didn't steal her. But he made me leave her. For reasons which seemed valid at the time. She married someone else. He made her miserable. And now she's dead. And it's thanks to that banal little episode that I am what I am today.

Lucile (*kindly*) That's awful . . .

Hero Yes. Awful . . . as you say . . . and now Tiger owes me a young girl in return. And that's why I am in your room this evening.

Lucile (*backs off. Pale*) Get out or I'll call for help.

Hero There's no one on this floor. But you needn't worry. I don't want to touch you. I just want to talk to you.

Lucile I won't listen. I'll stop my ears.

Hero I'll scream at you. And you'll hear.

Lucile I'm not interested in the neurotic ravings of a drunk. You're wasting your time. You will only be ashamed tomorrow. So go back to your room.

Hero I'm never ashamed.

Lucile Are you doing all this for his wife? You know she doesn't love him. I'm not asking him to marry me, not even to keep me. I'll be invisible. I'll work and he can go on leading his own life in his own world if that's what frightens you all so much.

Hero His world, his life. Come off it. You must realise that I couldn't give a blind damn one way or the other.

Lucile Then why have you talked of nothing else? Do you think I haven't understood what's behind every word you've spoken since you've entered the room? Even when you've been pretending to love him, or to be sorry for me. Why go to so much trouble to spoil something that may be true and good and asks only to be left alone? Is it because you hate him?

Hero Not even that.

Lucile Why then?

Hero (*softly*) I like breaking things.

She looks directly at him. He turns away. Pours a drink.

Lucile Poor Hero. Poor little monster. I'm not afraid of you any more. How unhappy you must be.

Hero If I am unhappy that's entirely my affair. Be so good as to mind your own business.

Lucile It is my business. You're trying to harm me. I have only pity for you.

Hero (*screams in disgust*) I forbid you to pity me. You pathetic little nursemaid. Little Miss Mouse with her nice clean hands and feet, her cheap little dress, with her smug little principles – her measly thrift. You are everything I hate most in this world. Give me a whore who spreads her legs, some bitch who takes your money and still betrays you every time. Or some hag who stuffs powder up her nose. Some drunken slut lying on her back in her own filth. I hate you. And I forbid you to look at me like that.

He pours a drink and downs it in one.

(*With sadistic glee.*) You know where Tiger really is this evening? Do you know what was in that telegram, the one that called him away so suddenly? Do you know what he told me to tell you?

Lucile It's not true!

Hero What's not true, you little idiot? I haven't said anything yet. A bit of a coward are we? I bet you scream like that at the dentist's . . . even before he's reached for the drill. She looks down on you from her Olympian heights. She plays Joan of Arc, Antigone and all the rest of them rolled into one – all that stuff she's got out of her schoolbooks. But then, when it comes to the crunch, out comes the hanky and it's tears and sniffles just like anyone else. And this is the girl who sees fit to stand in judgement. To pity me.

Lucile You are a monster.

Hero You see, you try to be polite, observe all the niceties. Do your best to win their confidence. Wear yourself out saying she's attractive, desirable even, and you're quite prepared to offer a little consolation, you or the paratrooper . . . and this is how they reward you. (*He shouts suddenly.*) Right! Let's have the breakdown! Come on. Let's have it! It's long overdue. I shan't interrupt.

Lucile (*draws herself up*) I'm not going to cry.

Hero Good. Contempt. I prefer that. I hate tears. They disgust me. Now you're beautiful. Very hard, very taut. A little animal forced into a corner. Our little fly in the ointment. The intruder who has to be ejected. Our little spoilsport.

Lucile Say what you have to say.

Hero Now you're getting impatient. We've got plenty of time . . . We're quite alone on this floor and I sent the paratrooper off to the village and the others have shut themselves in their rooms in the other wing, wondering how it's all going to turn out. I can see them tossing and turning in their beds. M. Damiens black and shaggy like an old crow, who's been robbed of his piece of cheese. Hortensia and the Countess, in lace, with their detective stories and their sleeping pills within reach . . . But sleep won't come because there's still that little schemer, holed up in the attic, hatching up God knows what plans to pollute, to destroy the sanctity of the family. She's up there in the west wing, top floor, end of the corridor, you can't miss it . . . Who will rid us of this turbulent nursemaid? You see, my dear, Tiger has realised, a bit late, that he's made a mistake. A mistake as big and as stupid as he is. If he'd seen fit to seek my advice, I would have told him to spare you all this. You were a virgin. That was your only asset. He shouldn't have stripped you of it. You mustn't be too hard on him. He's not wicked. He's a romantic that's all, an incurable romantic and things go to his head. Of course he's got every excuse. It's irresistible having someone new, someone sweet who snuggles up to you and tells you she loves you and she's yours forever. Forever meaning tonight – now – this minute. It is a new pleasure, hitherto untasted. You would have to be some kind of saint to tear yourself from her arms and say 'No'. The bore is that the next day the girl's still in love with you and as far as she's concerned 'forever' began at breakfast. And you're saddled with her now. And straight away she's telling you all her secrets. There she is with her pretty little head on her shoulders, prattling on about her poor old mama who's all on her own now. And all about her cooking and what would be a good name for the baby. You can forget the forbidden delights and the sacrificial lamb of the night before. You can see yourself pushing the pram – I'm speaking metaphorically, of course – I'm sure you've been sensible and discreet. 'I'll keep working. I'll never let him buy me anything. We'll be free. Love will provide . . .' So you want to know the truth my love? Yes, you're strong enough now. That's what frightened Tiger away. He would rather you had asked for a few furs and a tastefully furnished apartment. A life like his can easily accommodate a mistress. But a great selfless love – that's way beyond his means, so in spite of having a certain fondness for you, he thought – and put yourself in his shoes – that it would be better to make a clean break so there could be no misunderstanding . . .

Lucile But why didn't he tell me this himself?

Hero What do you expect? He's charming. He throws parties. Why should he be a hero as well? He knows like everyone else that ever since Napoleon there is only one remedy for sudden love. Flight. And he flew. He just didn't feel up to getting embroiled in the whole business. Too sticky, too messy. I fear you've been endowing a sweet-natured clown with all sorts of imaginary qualities, my love . . .

Lucile Then why did he tell me he loved me?

Hero Excitement. Emotion – the heat of the moment. That sort of thing can be infectious. Love is as catching as 'flu. Also a certain way with words . . . You're young. You'll meet plenty of other men. But beware of sentimentalists. They're the worst.

Lucile (*after a pause. Stiffly*) Is this all he asked you to tell me?

Hero No, of course not. He's a gentleman. First of all there's the cheque . . . which naturally you'll refuse. In this respect, I have to admit, I do find him a wee bit heavy-handed. I wouldn't normally have mentioned it, but you see I'm only acting as a go-between. Then, as I told you, he said, 'Go and talk to her. Try to console her.'

Lucile *resists for a moment. Then breaks down into helpless sobbing.*

Hero That's it. Let yourself go . . . It's better if you can cry. Look. Already she's steeling herself. She's putting on a proud face. She wants to behave like a real grown-up lady; and just think, only yesterday, she was playing with dolls and hiding in her Mummy's skirts at the first sign of trouble. Except Mummy's not there any more. She's a big girl now and all on her own. There's only the big bad godfather who smells of dusty old law books and who's put nice Grandmamma's bonnet on over his ugly wolf's head . . . All the better to gobble you up, my dear. How alone you can be in the world, can't you, little kitten. I know all about that. You were feeling just a little bit sorry for me earlier on, weren't you? Now you understand. Here. She's going to have a nice little drink. That's a good girl.

He helps her drink.

And then she'll have another . . . and then another . . . and then she will have understood. (*He is now crying too. He murmurs.*) Evangéline . . .

A silence. He holds her close and strokes her softly. Looking into the distance, he murmurs.

My poor little thing. My poor little thing. Isn't life ugly? She was so impatient. She believed in everything. And suddenly she was all alone. Life opening up in front of her like an abyss. She says nothing. She hides herself away so that she can cry discreetly and then she marries some vile banker forced on her by the family, who have got tired of waiting. That brute in her bed at night. Slavery by day. Covered in jewels. On display. So she weeps silently for two or three more years. And then one day she's just too tired. So she dies, that's all. Without a word. Leaving no more trace on this earth than the shadow of a passing bird.

He weeps and caresses her. His face is bathed in tears. He murmurs.

My child. My sweet child. My poor little lost child.

He takes her in his arms. She does not resist.

Curtain.

Act Five

As Act One. **Villebosse** *is alone, in costume, furious and determined. Enter the* **Count** *putting on his stage waistcoat.*

Count Ah, you're here already, Villebosse. I know, I'm late. I got back in the middle of the night. Do excuse me for calling a morning rehearsal but we open the day after tomorrow and this afternoon I'm up to here with the orchestra.

Villebosse Sir. I've already been waiting for an hour. It was impossible to speak to you alone yesterday, and we must have a serious talk. You seem very cheerful this morning, sir, very happy.

Count Very cheerful, yes. And happier than I've ever been.

Villebosse Then you are fortunate, sir. There are others here who are unable to share your reasons for rejoicing.

Count I should hope so. My reasons are rather personal. Up till now, I have only been able to enjoy myself in company. Now I see that happiness is properly a solitary pursuit.

Villebosse Is there some hidden meaning, sir, behind your words?

Count Ever since the invention of language, Villebosse, there has been a hidden meaning behind everything we say. That's why words were invented in the first place.

Villebosse If there was a hidden meaning, sir, then it was out of place. Our situation is very delicate. You should not forget that.

Count My dear chap, to be perfectly honest, I've never lost that much sleep over it. But, since the morning, I'm afraid you're out of luck. I've decided to forget it altogether.

Villebosse What do you mean by that, sir?

Count That I'm delighted you're my wife's lover. I think you're an exceptional young man.

Villebosse (*leaps at him*) I absolutely forbid you to make light of the Countess's honour. Take that back, sir. Take that back or you will be answerable to me!

Count Take what back?

Villebosse What you just said. Your cynicism is a repellent affectation. I will not allow it to besmirch a creature who has an absolute right to our respect. The Countess, sir, is above suspicion.

Count Villebosse, you are adorable. I will never tire of listening to you and watching you tie yourself in knots. You are, without doubt, the funniest man I have ever met.

Villebosse (*climbing down from his high horse*) I'm suffering, sir, that's all. I say what I mean.

Count I can see that.

Villebosse Try as I may I can't get used to the corruption of the degenerate little world you live in. I come from Carcasonne. My family is not particularly grand. We are farmers. But our home has kept its drawbridge and its moat since the thirteenth century. We have never moved. We have never put in central heating. And we have never joked about a woman's honour. When I fell in love with the Countess, I came to you and proposed that we should fight to the death. My course seemed entirely clear. I would either marry the widow or perish in the attempt. You refused.

Count I had no wish to die that day. Or to kill you either. I'm very fond of you, Villebosse.

Villebosse So you wanted to prolong this complicated and degrading situation.

Count I wanted to live. That's always complicated and degrading.

Villebosse It's too late now. The honour and happiness of the Countess are my personal concern. And I must tell you this; I will not allow you to be unfaithful to your wife.

Count What?

Villebosse You understand me. I will not allow you to ridicule her. You will behave yourself, sir, from now on. You will behave correctly or you will have me to deal with.

Count What exactly are you demanding, Villebosse?

Villebosse That you break off your relationship with that young woman immediately. The Countess agrees to draw a veil over the whole unsavoury episode. She will forget it ever happened.

Count Oh, do I have to leave Hortensia, too?

Villebosse That she will tolerate. A weakness on her part. She has always been indulgent towards you – in a manner I find hard to understand. But be sure you are discreet and always give the Countess precedence. For God's sake, it's hardly my place to remind you of your duty. After all, she is your wife, sir.

Count I like you more and more, Villebosse. Let me embrace you.

Villebosse No.

Count Why not? I'm sure that deep down you like me too.

Villebosse It would not be fitting. Let us keep our distance, sir. Our situation is too delicate. But don't forget that I'll be watching you.

The **Countess** *enters.*

Countess To think, Tiger, that you've succeeded in getting us up at ten o'clock . . . Oh, look, dawn . . . gorgeous. We really should try and get up earlier. What a lovely morning. Did you have a good night?

Count Yes, Eliane. I've a couple of things I want to say to you.

Countess Villebosse?

Villebosse (*running to her*) Eliane?

Countess Do you want to make yourself useful?

Villebosse (*devotedly*) Always.

Countess Then run round the bedrooms and see if you can drum up the late-comers. We start rehearsing in ten minutes.

Villebosse You can count on me, Eliane. In ten minutes, everyone will be here.

He exits.

Countess You're looking so serious.

Count Yes. I'm in love with that girl.

Countess Fine.

Count We've always lived our lives intelligently, Eliane. With a mutual dislike of ugly scenes. It's not that we're afraid of them – it's just that they've always seemed in such bad taste. You have allowed me my mistresses and I've never questioned you too closely about who you've been off taking tea with. And we've thrown some good parties in our time. Our home is one that people are pleased to visit and considering how most marriages turn out, ours, on the whole, has been a delight.

Countess Thank you, Tiger.

Count I should thank you. Our success is entirely due to your wonderful understanding of life. In this increasingly strident and sex-obsessed world, we've both somehow managed to preserve a smile. We have lived as others dance; harmoniously, with measured steps and above all with a sense of style.

Countess And none of that pleases you any more.

Count It still seems to me to be the only way to live. It's just . . .

Countess Just what?

Count The line of my life, which stretches so elegantly and predictably from my first successful ball to my probable presidency of the Jockey Club in twenty years' time and on to my funeral in the Madeleine with all Paris in attendance – it's just struck me that although it would mean pleasant memories for my friends, and possibly even an appreciative piece in the *Figaro*, it would mean nothing to me. I didn't know why I was so cheerful all the time. Now I do – I was bored.

Countess And that girl taught you all that in the attic?

Count Yes. I love her. I had no idea what that meant. It's completely absurd. It has no sparkle, no wit, no grace. None of the things I used to think I cared for. It is merely what it is.

Countess Is this so very new, Tiger? I've seen you close to suicide on more than one occasion because some girl wouldn't give in.

Count Yes, thwarted desire is unbearable. If I was desperate for something then, yes, I'd have it straight away. This time I'm not in any kind of hurry. My greatest joy is to be with her and nothing else is any fun any more. But if for any reason you ask me to wait then I'll wait . . . quite happily . . . and I won't get tired of waiting.

Countess I won't put your patience to the test. It would be too sad if you broke your fine new resolution by pushing your luck. You know that I have never stopped you taking your pleasures.

Count My poor Eliane, we're no longer talking the same language. Which is rather worrying. It's not a question of taking.

Countess Oh, good. What is it a question of, then?

Count (*gently*) Of giving . . .

Countess Look, you've got time on your hands. And money in your pockets. So give, my dear, give. What's stopping you? Go on a trip with her. Buy her some decent clothes. You've been saying for the past ten years that you're dying to go to China. So go off to the country with my blessing, have your love-affair. I'll tell everyone you've gone to Peking.

Count Poor Eliane. I'm going to go much further than China.

Countess That's the second time you've said that! I'm not your 'poor Eliane'. Actually, I find all this terribly amusing. Do you want us to separate, Tiger? Do you want to marry her?

Count Why bother Monseigneur, your uncle, with a divorce? Why get civil servants involved with our private affairs? I can't see the point.

Countess So she hasn't suggested it yet? I give her a week. Little girls who surrender themselves at the drop of a hat in attics have a great desire for respectability, believe me.

Count This is the only estrangement I'm afraid of, Eliane – that your anger and spite might make you say something you'd regret. I've always valued and admired you, but there is still the little matter of the emerald. Let's not compound the felony.

Countess Let's just make sure I've got this right. We're going to give the party, come what may, and the next day you'll be leaving for as long as you love this girl, for as long as she loves you? Good. Fine by me. I'm not remotely worried as you can see. Have fun, Tiger, and tell me all about it when you get back.

Enter **Hortensia**, **Villebosse** *and* **Hero**, *glass in hand. The* **Countess** *rushes to* **Hortensia**. *Embraces her.*

My darling, my dear Hortensia. So good, so kind, so trusting. Men? Worthless creatures! I actually think I'm beginning to like your perfume. Hero, you're looking awfully gloomy . . . Oh, God, you're being impossible. Put down the glass. It's far too early to drink.

Hero No.

He sits away from the others.

Villebosse (*to the* **Countess**) He's appallingly drunk. He can hardly speak. I defy any of you to rehearse with him. And Damiens and the girl don't seem to be in their rooms.

Countess Tiger, it's up to you. Will you go up and get them?

Damiens *enters. In his street clothes. Strangely dark in their midst.*

Damiens You will excuse me, Madame la Comtesse, but I am obliged to give up my role and to leave the château.

Countess Now what is all this nonsense, Damiens? We open the day after tomorrow.

Damiens My god-daughter left here early this morning; alone, on foot, bound for the railway station. This sudden decision can only be a consequence of yesterday's unfortunate incident. And after that painful episode, I feel I can no longer stay here either.

Count (*suddenly pale*) How do you know she's left? She could be down in the village.

Damiens When I went to fetch her from her room just now, I found this letter, for you, sir, on her dressing-table. There was another for me.

Countess (*while the* **Count** *opens the letter*) But, Damiens, you must be dreaming! Last night we had a perfectly amicable discussion and, as far as I was concerned, the incident was closed.

Hero What does the letter say?

Count 'You are right. It was not possible. I have gone. You will never see me again.'

Hero That's all?

The **Count** *does not move.*

Countess Well, it's really quite extraordinary. Damiens, you know her . . .

Damiens Madame, you will excuse me. My train leaves shortly. I have only just enough time to get to the station. Her letter to me doesn't add a great deal – merely her determination never to see me again either. She must have been deeply hurt, more deeply than we can imagine. And now she's gone, God knows where, all alone, heart-broken. Without support, without money, without anything.

Countess Oh, that's terrible. If only we'd given her her six months' wages.

Hortensia (*to the* **Count**, *who runs out*) Tiger, where are you going?

Countess He'll take the car to search the roads. But which ones? Run and catch him, Damiens. He can drop you off at the station.

Damiens Goodbye, Madame.

He leaves.

Countess (*to* **Hortensia**) She must have caught the five o'clock bus into town. She'll have changed there and Tiger won't know where for. He doesn't have a hope of finding her again.

Hortensia She might change her mind or write to him . . .

Countess Don't you believe it. We might as well admit it, she was a girl of real quality. Her departure proves it. She was in love with him without a doubt. That is why we need not worry. After what has happened she won't ever try to see him again.

Hortensia (*as kindly as she can*) But what about poor Tiger?

Countess (*sincerely astonished*) You are so considerate, Hortensia. Sometimes I think you must have a screw loose. No. He'll be down in the dumps for a couple of months and then, gradually, he'll start having fun again. Also, I know him. His sense of social responsibility is without equal. Our first guests will be arriving this evening and for the next few days he'll only be able to think about the party. Come on, my love, let's go down and have some breakfast. All this has given me rather an appetite.

Hortensia But what about her part in the play?

Countess I anticipated her defection. Léonore, to whom Tiger originally offered the role, and who had already learnt the whole thing, has agreed to forget the dirty trick he played on her. She's flying to Le Mans and I've sent a car to meet her. She arrives in an hour. And I'll telephone Gontaut-Biron. I'm sure he's recovered from his 'flu by now.

Hortensia What? You've asked Léonore here after everything you've told me about Tiger and her.

Countess My dear Hortensia, you have many qualities and I've got a lot of time for you, but I fear, all things considered, you're not quite up to it. However you may feel, consoling Tiger must come first. And, if I know him, come the end of the week he'll only have eyes for Léonore. He can't bear to be turned down. Come and have a coffee. I think we've both earned it . . .

Villebosse (*to their exiting backs*) Eliane, I haven't had any breakfast yet either.

Hero (*calling* **Villebosse** *back*) Villebosse.

Villebosse Sir?

Hero One moment, please. I hear you're an excellent shot, sir.

Villebosse What do you mean by that, sir?

Hero I've heard you've even won several important competitions.

Villebosse That is correct.

Hero Well then. I wish to inform you that you are not as beloved as you would like to think.

Villebosse What do you mean?

Hero Of course, one is never as beloved as one would like to think. That is a general truth. But in your case, it's a particular truth. Since last night, you have been, to use a term I abhor, a 'cuckold'.

Villebosse You are drunk, sir. Take that back.

Hero I am drunk. But when I'm drunk, I know exactly what I'm saying. I stand by my word. It is the precise truth. I was not in my own room last night. I was in someone else's room. Do I make myself plain?

Villebosse Do you know what you are saying, sir?

Hero It seems clear enough to me. Do not force me to repeat that vulgar word.

Villebosse Very well, sir. At least you are frank. I have felt for some time that you were working up to this. We shall fight. I merely require time to summon two friends.

Hero Do it quickly. I want it to be tomorrow morning.

Villebosse As you wish, sir. As soon as possible.

Hero Sir!

Villebosse Sir?

Hero I want everything to be done correctly. First you must strike my face.

Villebosse No, sir. That will not be necessary.

Hero Yes, it will. If you refuse to strike me, then I will refuse to fight.

Villebosse We have already decided that the encounter should take place. The choice of weapons can be yours, sir, if that is what you're worried about.

Hero It is not mine unless you strike me. I know the rules. So, do it now. Do it at once. (*He shouts.*) At once, do you hear? Strike me for

God's sake, or I'll smash my glass in your stupid face. Go on, I'm asking you to strike me. And hard. I want to feel it. Go on, you filthy cuckold, you have to do it. You must.

Villebosse Very well, if that's what you want. You're a vulgar, pathetic fool. (*He strikes him.*) This is quite absurd.

Hero No. It's as it should be. I choose pistols.

Villebosse *exits.* **Hero** *is left alone. Slowly he drains his glass. He murmurs.*

Hero Evangéline.

And the curtain falls.

Becket

translated by Jeremy Sams

This translation of *Becket*, presented by Duncan C. Weldon, was first performed at the Theatre Royal, Haymarket, London on 7 October 1991, with the following cast:

King Henry II	Robert Lindsay
Thomas à Becket	Derek Jacobi
Archbishop of Canterbury/Baron 2/	
Monk/Earl of Arundel	Andrew Jarvis
Bishop of Oxford/Provost Marshal/	
William de Corbeil/Mariner/Priest	Alan Bennion
Gilbert Folliot (*Bishop of London*)	David Lyon
Archbishop of York/Saxon Peasant/	
Valet 1/Secretary to the new	
Archbishop	John Darrell
Scribe/Baron 3/Younger Prince/	
Monk	Ben Porter
Saxon Girl/Queen	Helen Schlesinger
Saxon Boy/French Priest/	
Valet 2/Prince Henry/Acolyte	Brenda O'Hea
Gwendoline	Phyllida Hancock
Baron 1/King Louis of France	Ken Bones
Baron 4/Priest/French Baron 2	Tom Beard
Soldier/French Baron 1	Gregor Truter
French Girl	Dariel Pertwee
Little Monk	Mark Hadfield
French Choirboy	Jane Kehoe
Queen Mother	Dilys Hamlett
Pope	Trevor Ray
Cardinal	Ronnie Stevens

Directed by Elijah Moshinsky
Designed by Michael Yeargan
Lighting by Mark Henderson
Sound by Paul Arditti
Music by Corin Buckeridge

Act One

Cathedral décor – the **King** *enters, crowned, wearing a huge cloak.*
Guards *at a distance. Shadowy figures in the background. The* **King**
hesitates, disrobes, kneels by **Becket**'s *tomb.*

King Well Thomas à Becket, *now* are you satisfied? Here I
am, naked by your tomb, and your monks are waiting in the
shadows, waiting to flog me. The end of the story, of our
story. Here we both are, you rotting away in your box, hacked
to pieces by my faithful barons – me stark naked like a half-wit
– and in this draught, waiting for your henchmen. We were
friends, I loved you – couldn't we have worked something out?

Becket *appears, dressed as an archbishop, as on the day of his death.*

Becket We could never have worked anything out.

King I said to you – 'Never forget the honour of the
kingdom'. Your turn of phrase, actually, but one I adopted.

Becket And I replied – 'Never forget the honour of God'.
We might as well have been deaf.

King God, it was freezing, last time we met, remember?
Funny that, it was always freezing cold when we were together.
When we were friends. Except at the beginning, those summer
nights. The girls ... you were in love with Gwendoline,
weren't you, Archbishop? You resented it rather didn't you,
when I took her that evening? 'Look, I'm the King', I said. Is
that why you could never forgive me?

Becket *(gently)* I don't remember.

King We were like brothers. Like two little boys. That night
I was a big kid shouting 'I'm the king of the castle'. Except I
was. I am. I was so young – not a thought in my head; you
did all my thinking for me.

Becket Stop prattling and pray.

King How do you expect me to pray? I can see them, you
know, skulking in the shadows. Big brutes your Saxons.
Terrifying. Here I am, naked, and they're going to flog me
until it hurts. And me with my delicate skin. *You'd* be terrified.
Plus I'm embarrassed by this silly charade. But I have to be
seen to repent. I need them on my side. Against my son who
wants to divide my kingdom. So I make my peace with their

saint. Don't you think that's ironic – you a saint, and me
wooing the rabble, by getting myself flogged. But I need them.
There's always a price to pay. You taught me that – when you
helped me, when you loved me. You taught me everything –
and look at us now. Those were the days – up at the crack of
dawn – well the crack of noon, dawn for us. Painting the town
red – booze, girls. You were better at all that than me. Like
most things. You'd come into my room, calm, smiling, fresh as
a daisy. You'd never know you'd been up all night.

Light changes. A curtain is drawn, we are in the **King**'s *bedchamber. A*
Page *is attending to him.* **Thomas**, *younger, enters.*

Becket   And a very good morning to your Highness.

King   Thomas – I didn't think you'd be up yet.

Becket   Oh, I've been out for a gallop – down to Richmond.
It's wonderfully cold.

King   Amazing. You actually like the cold. (*To his* **Page** *who
is rubbing him down.*) Harder, damn you, harder. That'll do –
put a log on the fire. You can dress me later.

Becket   No, my Prince, I'll dress you.

Rubs his back.

King   Oh, Thomas, you're the only one who really knows
how to do that. Where would I be without you? You were
born a gentleman, why are you happy to play the servant? If I
asked my barons, there'd be civil war!

Becket   I am your servant. I'll help you run the country, I'll
help you run your bath. All the same to me – I merely like to
help.

King   You know what they said, when I wanted to take you
on. Don't let the Saxon get too close. One day he'll stab you
in the heart.

Becket   And you believed them.

King   Um, no . . . not really. All right I was a bit nervous at
first. You know how jumpy I am. But then you seemed, well,
next to the other Saxon brutes, you seemed so well bred. How
do you manage to speak French without an English accent?

Becket   My father was able to hang onto his wealth, through a rigorous policy of, well, collaboration, with your father. So when I was young he could afford to send me away to France.

King Not to Normandy?

Becket No – not Normandy – actually he hated the Norman accent.

King Are you sure it was just the accent?

Becket Well, my father was very strict, very private. During his lifetime I'd never have delved too deeply into his innermost feelings, not while he was alive. And obviously, after his death I was none the wiser! He collaborated, he amassed a huge fortune. And since in every other way he was a man of strict principles, I presume he managed somehow to square his behaviour with his conscience. It's a neat little juggling act. When the going gets rough it's always the people of principle who seem remarkably good at it.

King And what about you?

Becket What about me?

King Yes – are you as good a juggler as your father?

Becket It's easier for me. There's less at stake. He was principled – I'm basically frivolous. So I can live with the contradictions. I love hunting – hunting is sanctioned by the Normans. I love luxury, which is very Norman. I love to live – and the Saxons are only fit to be massacred. But I also love honour.

King And honour is compatible with collaboration!

Becket (*lightly*) The first Norman nobleman who tried to touch my sister, I felt I had the right to call him out and kill him, in single combat. It's a detail, but a significant one.

King You could have slit his throat and hidden in the forest – that's what the others did.

Becket Not very practical – certainly not very comfortable. Anyway, my sister would have been raped by the next Norman in line – like all the Saxon girls. Now, she's respected.

King I don't see why you don't hate us. I would in your shoes. Admittedly you're much braver than I am.

Becket How do you know, Sir? Until the day we die, none of us really knows how brave we are.

King Anyway. You know I hate fighting. I mean in person. Even so, if France had invaded Normandy, and done a tenth of what we've done here – I wouldn't be able to pass a Frenchman in the street without instinctively reaching for my . . . what are you doing?

Becket Just getting my comb. That's because you haven't lived through a hundred years of occupation, your Majesty. It's a long time. You survive.

King Not necessarily – not if you're poor.

Becket Perhaps not – but I'm rich aren't I, *and* frivolous, and – guess what, my new gold dinner service has just arrived from Florence. Will you do me the honour of christening it with me?

King Gold? Are you mad?

Becket No, I was rather hoping it might catch on.

King I'm your monarch. And I eat off silver.

Becket Well, fair enough, you've a lot of heavy expenses. I can spend my money purely on pleasure. Only trouble is, I think it might scratch. We'll see. I've also got half a dozen forks.

King Forks?

Becket Yes. A little instrument of torture – made popular by the Devil. Now available for domestic use. For pronging bits of meat. Saves you getting your fingers greasy.

King But it gets the fork greasy.

Becket You can wash the fork.

King You can wash your fingers. I don't see the point.

Becket There is no point. It's refined, it's witty – it's not very Norman.

King Order me a dozen. I'd love to see their faces – my barons – at the next banquet. They'll think they're newfangled weapons. They'll be fighting miniature duels all round the table.

Becket Sir, it is time for the Council meeting. A dozen? They're jolly expensive.

Exit, laughing.

We are now in the Council Chamber. **King**, **Becket**, **Archbishop
of Canterbury**, **Bishop of Oxford**, **Gilbert Folliot** (*Bishop
of London*), **Archbishop of York**, **Priests**, **Monks**, **Guards**,
Attendants.

King   The Council is convened. Right. We're gathered here
to discuss one thing. The refusal of the Church to pay the
absentee tax. We have to decide who governs this kingdom –
the Church – all in good time, Archbishop – or me. I'm
anticipating a lively debate. But first, some good news. I have
decided to reinstate the position of Chancellor of all England –
Guardian of the Lion Seal – and to award it to my good and
faithful servant and subject, Thomas à Becket.

Becket (*rising, astonished*)   My Lord . . .

King   Are you going somewhere, Becket? Not off for a piss
are you? Do with one myself. God we had a skinful last night.
I'm glad I can still surprise you.

Becket (*kneeling*)   My Prince – this honour is a measure of
your trust – but one of which I fear I am hardly worthy. I am
too young. Too frivolous.

King   I'm young too. We're all . . . I'm young. But you know
more than the lot of us put together. He's studied, you know –
he can run rings round the lot of you. Even you, Archbishop.
As for his so-called frivolity – don't be fooled for a minute. He
never stops thinking. Sometimes I can feel him, next to me,
thinking. Sometimes it gets on my nerves. On your feet
Thomas. I've never lifted a finger without your advice. That
was secret, now it's public. End of story. Here's the seal.
Catch! Don't lose it. No seal, no England. We'd all have to
move back to Normandy. Right – to work!

Canterbury   With your Majesty's indulgence, may I be the
first to congratulate my young, my learned friend, the
Archdeacon. After all, I was the first, if I may allow myself the
sin of pride, to notice his promise, to pick him out, to bring
him on. And I rejoice in the presence at this Council –
bearing the mantle of such a weighty office – of our brother in
the cloth. This is a reassuring sign for the Church of this great
kingdom, the dawn of a new age of mutual understanding. A
sign that henceforward we may proceed in a new spirit of co-
operation, of trust, of . . .

King   Etcetera, etcetera. Thank you Archbishop. I knew you'd
be pleased. But don't count on Becket to do your dirty work

for you. He's my man, remember. Actually, Thomas, I had forgotten you were a deacon.

Becket So had I.

King Obviously. The girls, the booze, the bloodshed – and you a man of the cloth! But we're straying from the point. You know our customs. Every landowner must either provide one fully-armed soldier at the review of troops – or pay a tax in silver. Simple. So, where's my money?

Oxford I beg to differ.

King Beg till you're blue in the face. My mind is made up. My purse is wide open – just fill it up, would you? I'm starving Thomas, aren't you? Tell them to bring something to eat.

Becket *tells a guard to see to it.*

Canterbury Your Majesty, if a layman or a commoner shirks his duty to the state – which is to raise arms for his prince – then he must pay the tax. No one would dispute that.

King Certainly not the clergy.

Canterbury Very well. Now a clergyman's duty to the state is, by definition, different. He is to assist his prince not in war, but in prayer, in teaching and in charitable works. *Ergo* he too should be liable to a tax if he should be neglectful of these duties.

Oxford And have we refused to pray? We have not.

King Gentlemen. Come off it. Do you really think you're going to bamboozle me out of two-thirds of my tax? Rhetoric and ethics are all very well now. But not at the time of the great conquest when the pickings were richest, abbots were in there with the best of them, raping and pillaging like there was no tomorrow. Cassocks up round their waists, bums on the saddle, swords drawn. 'Help yourselves, murder the Saxon scum, it's God's will, it's God's will.' There was no stopping them.

Canterbury Those heroic days are at an end. Now we are at peace.

King Fine, then pay up. I'm not budging. What do you say, Chancellor – the weight of your new office seems to have struck you dumb?

Becket   May I be permitted to make a point, respectfully, to his Grace the Archbishop?

King   Respectfully, yes, but firmly. You are Chancellor now, remember.

Becket   England is like a ship.

King   Very good. Nicely put. I'll use that.

Becket   And on a ship there can only be one captain. Sometimes crews will mutiny – they throw their captain overboard – the result is anarchy, but inevitably a new candidate emerges, perhaps even harsher than his predecessor. But there must always be a captain and he is the only master.

Canterbury   My Lord Chancellor, my young friend. The proper wording is as follows – 'Their captain is the only master – after God.' (*He shouts.*) AFTER GOD!

King   Archbishop. Nobody here would wish to question the authority of God.

Becket   Indeed, God does guide the ship, but by inspiring the captain's orders.

Folliot   Our new Chancellor is no more than a deacon – but is, loosely speaking, still of the Church. The few years he has spent in the hurly-burly of the world will surely have taught him that it is through His Militant Church via the intermediary of his Holiness the Pope and his elected bishops that God dictates his decisions to mankind.

Becket   Every ship has a chaplain but he's not expected to organise the crew's rations or read the compass. I'm sure his Grace the Bishop of London, who I'm told is the grandson of a simple sailor, will be very familiar with this arrangement.

Folliot   (*furious*) I will not allow any personal comments of that sort to compromise the gravity of this debate. The honour of the Church of England is at stake!

King   (*pleasantly*) Keep your mitre on, Bishop. There's only one thing at stake here and that's money. I need money to fight the French. Is the Church going to cough up or not?

Canterbury   The Church of England has always acknowledged that it is its duty to give its prince every possible assistance.

King   And quite right too. Not sure about your use of the past tense, though. A little bit nostalgic.

Canterbury   I am protecting the right your illustrious forefather William awarded the Church of England.

King   May he rest in peace. Wherever he is – he doesn't need any money. I'm here on earth and unfortunately I do.

Folliot   Your Highness – it's a matter of principle.

King   I'm trying to raise an army, Bishop. I've sent for fifteen hundred German foot-soldiers, plus three thousand Swiss mercenaries. Your principles are fine and well and good. You'll find the Swiss prefer hard currency.

Becket   Your Majesty, I fear this discussion is fruitless – neither party will listen to the other. Our law and customs grant us the means to enforce our will. We will use them.

Folliot   You dare to strike out at the Mother Church – who has plucked you from nowhere?

Becket   My Lord the King has given me the royal seal. England is my mother now.

Folliot   A deacon. A wretched little deacon. A serpent in our bosom. Traitor! Sybarite! Sycophant! Saxon!

King   My dear little friend, I will ask you to pay suitable respect to my Chancellor, or I'll have to call my guards. Oh, and here they are. No, no, do excuse me – it's just my snack. I have to have a little something round about this time or I feel quite weak. And a king must never be weak, as I'm sure you'll agree. Serve it in my chapel. It'll be handy – I can pray straight afterwards. Or during. Come with me, my son.

Exits with **Becket**.

Folliot   We must appeal to Rome. We must be firm.

York   You are the primate of all England. In any matter concerning the Church your decisions are inviolable – you are the law. You have one weapon against this revolt – excommunication.

Oxford   It is a weapon which must be used with caution. Over the centuries the Church has always prevailed – but always with caution. We will be patient. A king's rage is a flashfire, terrible, but short-lived.

Folliot   That little upstart will soon be fanning the flames.

Believe me. I agree with his Reverence Bishop of York, that that fornicator must be stopped – by excommunication.

Becket *enters.*

Becket My Lords, the King has decided that the Council is adjourned. He feels that a night of meditation and prayer will help you arrive at a wiser, more equitable decision. Which you will submit to him tomorrow.

Folliot In other words it's time for the hunt.

Becket Well, to be honest your Grace, it is. Personally of course, I regret his brutal behaviour. As Chancellor of England however I will not go back on my word. We have all sworn the same oath of allegiance to our Lord and Sovereign – clergymen and laymen alike. We have all sworn to preserve his life, his health, his dignity, his honour. But I'm sure I don't need to remind you of the wording of the oath.

York You do not, my son. Any more than you need to remind us of the oath we had already sworn to God. You are young, perhaps still not quite sure what you are doing. You have taken a resolution. Its consequences may be great. Allow me, an old man, not long for this world, who in this rather sordid debate was trying to defend more than you realise – allow me to hope that you never have the bitter experience of, one day, knowing that you were wrong. I bless you my son.

Becket (*who was kneeling, springs to his feet*) No, Father, I am not worthy of your blessing. But who is worthy? And worthy of what? Who knows? Who cares?

Dances off insolently.

Folliot The insults are unforgivable. We will break him.

York I have known him for a long while. His soul is strangely unfathomable. Don't believe that he's merely the debauchee he seems to be. I have watched him, even in the riot of his pleasure. He never seems to be really there. As if he was off looking for himself.

Folliot Then break him, my Lord, before he finds himself. Or the clergy will pay dearly.

York Let us be circumspect. Our function is to look into men's hearts. I'm not convinced that his will always be against us.

Exeunt.

King (*entering*) Well, my boy. Have they gone yet? You coming hunting?

We are now in the forest. It's winter. Distant trumpets. Torrential rain. The **King** *and* **Becket** *are hunting with hawks.*

King God, it's pouring down. Do you enjoy this sport – hunting with hawks?

Becket Not really – I prefer to do my killing for myself.

King Why do you always crave danger?

Becket You have to gamble with your life to feel alive.

King You're right. The only ones who enjoy hawking are the hawks. Three hours we've been at this, I'm soaked to the skin. It seems a big price to pay for their pleasure.

Becket But my Lord, they're Norman hawks. They're from the master race. It's their birthright.

King Do you love me, Becket?

Becket I am your Lordship's humble servant.

King No, did you love me then, when I made you Chancellor? Sometimes I think you're incapable of love. Do you love Gwendoline?

Becket She's my mistress!

King Why do you have to stick labels on everything to justify your feelings?

Becket No, because without labels, the world would have no shape.

King Is it so important for the world to have a shape?

Becket Essential. Otherwise we wouldn't know what we were doing here. The weather's getting worse, your Majesty. We'd better take shelter in that hut over there.

Gallops off.

King Becket, you didn't answer my question.

Thunder – a **Peasant**'s *hovel appears.*

Becket (*to the* **Peasant**) Hey, you. We want to shelter our

horses in your barn. And rub them down. We'll stay here till
the storm dies down.

King   You, make a fire, come on, we're freezing to death
here. Come on, dog. What's he waiting for?

Becket   Wood is scarce, Sir. He probably hasn't got any.

King   In the middle of the forest?

Becket   They're only allowed two measures of dead wood. A
branch more and they're hanged.

King   Really? But they're always saying there's too much
dead wood in our forests. Anyway, that's my steward's
problem, not mine. (*To the* **Peasant**.) Go and fetch whatever
you can carry – make us a fire to shame Hell. Just this once
we won't hang you, dog.

Old man doesn't move.

Becket (*gently*)   Go on – your prince commands you. It's all
right my son.

King   Why do you call that old man your son?

Becket   Why do you call him your dog?

King   Oh, that's just habit – a figure of speech. Saxons have
always been 'dogs'. No idea why. You might as well just call
them Saxons. But your son, that smelly old sod – God what
do they eat round here, horse-shit?

Becket   No, beets.

King   What are beets?

Becket   Roots.

King   They eat roots.

Becket   That's about all they can grow in a forest.

King   Why don't they move?

Becket   If they leave the district, they're hanged.

King   Oh, I see. The slightest initiative, you're hanged for it.
That must make life much simpler in many ways – actually –
lucky them. Becket, you didn't say why you called him your
son.

Becket   He is so wretched, so naked and so poor and I am
so strong by comparison, he might as well be my son.

88   Becket

King   According to that theory, you'd have thousands of sons.

Becket   Even so – you're younger than I am and you've often called me your son.

King   That's not the same. That's because I love you.

Becket   You are our king – we are all your sons.

King   Even the Saxons?

Becket   Even the Saxons will one day be your sons. And that day England will be made.

King   You're getting on my nerves today. You're sounding like the Archbishop. And now I'm thirsty – have a look, there must be something I can drink in your son's house.

Becket *exits.*

King *finds a* **Peasant Girl***, hiding.*

King Hey, Thomas, Thomas.

Becket   You've found something to drink?

King   No, something to eat. What do you think of that – once you've cleaned it up a bit?

Becket   Pretty.

King   Stinks a bit – we can have her hosed down. Look at it, it's tiny. What do you think – fifteen? Sixteen?

Becket   It can speak, your Majesty. How old are you, my child?

Girl *is too scared to speak.*

King   You see, it can't. How old's your daughter, dog? He's dumb as well, your son. Obviously runs in the family. Or in the nation – amazing the number of dumb people I meet when I venture out of my palace. Now why would that be?

Becket   They're terrified.

King   Good. Let them stay terrified – the minute they're not, they'll terrify me. Ever seen a peasants' uprising? I did – a little one, in my father's day. Not pretty. Look at that. (*He means the* **Peasant**.) It's ugly, it's stupid, it stinks, it's vermin. The place is infested with them. (*To the* **Girl***.*) You, stay here, I want you. Now what's the point of it, d'you think?

Becket   It scratches the soil, it makes the bread.

King Pah. But look at her, a rose on a dunghill. Do you think she'll turn ugly, like the rest?

Becket Certainly.

King Do you think that if we took her back to be a whore at the palace she'd stay pretty?

Becket Possibly.

King So we'd be doing her a favour?

Becket Oh yes.

Terrified reaction from **Peasants**.

King You see, they understand perfectly.

Enter **Brother**.

Who's this?

Becket Her brother.

King How do you know?

Becket Instinct.

King I'm sorry Thomas. They're rapidly losing their rustic charm. I asked for water, dog, get it – now.

Exit **Peasant**.

Becket Theirs will be undrinkable. Let me fetch my canteen, your Majesty. You, come with me.

Exit **Becket** *with* **Brother**. *As they exit* **Becket** *attacks* **Brother**, *disarms him – an ugly knife – and cuts his own hand.* **Brother** *runs off.*

King 'My son.' Him and his sons. He always makes me *think*. It's exhausting. It can't be good for the brain. Oh, water. Good. You took your time. Drink with me. What's wrong? You're wounded!

Becket My horse, your Majesty. A bit jumpy. Doesn't like his saddle touched. I seem to have caught the side of his mouth.

King (*laughs*) I don't believe it – wonderful, wonderful. The best horseman in the land, the tamer of wild stallions, the man who makes the rest of us look ridiculous gets his hand bitten, like a stupid stable boy. You've gone pale. Why do I love you? Why do I even love seeing you hurt? Strange. Show me.

Becket It's not a pretty sight. You know you hate blood.

King Just to get me a drink. Wounded in the service of the king. Well, we'll tell the others you fought off a wild beast and saved my life. And you shall have a reward. What would you have?

Becket I'll have her. I like the look of her.

King So do I. Friendship be damned. (*Pause.*) Very well, but tit for tat, eh? You owe me a favour now. You won't forget that, will you?

Becket I will not.

King So tit for tat, you give me your word?

Becket I give my word.

King Right, you win, she's all yours. Shall we take her away or have her delivered?

Becket I'll send some guards for her.

King Wash her down, dog, delouse your daughter. Guess what, she's coming to the palace. That'll be nice, won't it. It's for this gentleman, it's all right, he's a Saxon like you are. You should be honoured. Give him a piece of gold. God, I feel good this morning.

Exits.

Becket It's all right. No one will take your daughter. Hide her better in future. Tell your son to join the others in the forest. Take this. (*His purse.*)

Girl He's beautiful that one. Am I really going to the palace?

Peasant Norman whore! (*He beats her.*)

Change to **Becket**'s *palace.*

Becket. **Gwendoline**, *strumming absent-mindedly an instrument. Distant revelling.*

Gwendoline Are they still eating, my Lord?

Becket Yes. They have an extraordinary capacity for ingestion.

Gwendoline How can my Lord spend his days and most of his nights with creatures like that?

Becket Sooner that than with learned clerks, discussing the sex of angels, my love. They're just as foolish and far less fun.

Gwendoline Sometimes, my Lord, I don't know what you're saying. All I know is that when you come to me, it's very late.

Becket But I do come to you. It is my only pleasure. Beauty is one of the few certainties, the few proofs that God exists.

Gwendoline You have won me in battle, my Lord, I'm yours completely. God granted the Norman victory over my people. Had we won the war, I would have been married to a valiant Welsh knight, at my father's castle, but it was not God's will.

Becket No, apparently not. But I *also* belong to a vanquished race – God, as usual, is moving in mysterious ways. Play some more.

Gwendoline No, I'm wrong. You are my master, with or without God. I would have followed, captive or not, and loved you. What have I said – my Lord is angry?

Becket No. It's just . . . I hate being loved. I told you that before.

King *enters.*

King Ah, there you are, my son. You left us for good. Guess what – it worked. They're fighting with the forks. And what they're particularly well designed for, it seems, is poking out each other's eyes. You'd better stop them, you don't want to ruin your nice new toys.

Becket *(exiting)* No Sir, no. Not like that. They're for the meat. Look, I'll show you again . . . *(Etc.)*

King Was that you playing just now?

Gwendoline Yes, your Majesty. *(She kneels.)*

King You can do everything. On your feet. *(He strokes her.)* Have I frightened you, my love? Don't worry, I'll make it up to you. Hey Becket, hey lads, that's enough stuffing your gobs. Come in here. A bit of music, a bit of uplift.

All enter.

Ask her to sing something sad – it's better for the digestion. You feed us far too well, Thomas. Where did you get your hands on that cook of yours?

Becket   I bought him. He's French.

King   Really? Aren't you worried he'll poison you? What's a French cook cost nowadays?

Becket   A good one, like him, almost as much as a horse, my Lord.

King   That's outrageous. God, the times we live in. No man should be worth a whole horse. But he's a good cook. Now if I were to say 'tit for tat', would that jog your memory? Remember that favour you owe me? (*Stroking* **Gwendoline**.) No – don't worry, I won't ask you for him. One can't eat that well everyday, it would be too demoralising. (*To* **Gwendoline**.) Sadder, sadder. Make her play the lament they wrote about your mother. That's my favourite.

Becket   I'd prefer not to hear that one, my Lord.

King   What? Are you ashamed of having an Arab for a mother? That's half your charm, you fool. And certainly why you're twice as civilised as the rest of us. No, I love that song and I will hear it. That's an order, Saxon.

Becket (*to* **Gwendoline**)   Sing it.

Gwendoline
Brave Sir Gilbert
Rode off to war
A soldier for Our Lord
That handsome knight
Went off to fight
The heathen, Saracen horde

Chorus:
Alas my heart is heavy
My love has gone away
Alas my heart is heavy
All the livelong day

King *sings along.*

King   And then?

Gwendoline
The thunder rolled
The sky turned black
The battlefield turned red
He was wounded there
And his fickle mare

Left him among the dead

Chorus.

A captive's fate
Is worse than death
Is harsher than the grave
In Tunis town
They chained him down
And sold him as a slave

Chorus. (**King** *sings along.*)

The daughter of an Arab prince
Was moved by what she saw
She bewailed the plight
Of the wounded knight
And loved him evermore

Chorus.

King It always makes me weepy, this story. I don't know
why. I look tough, but I'm as soft as butter. Just the way I am.
Wonder why you don't like this song? Must be wonderful to be
a love-child. God, when I think of my sour old father and my
boot-faced old mother – what a joyless coupling that must have
been! Then what happened? Let me get this right. Your
mother helped him escape and then followed him to London
town, with you in her belly. Sing the last bit. I love the last
bit.

Gwendoline
A priest baptised her
Child of God
And made her Gilbert's wife
A Christian bride
Stood by his side
He loved her all his life

Rejoice my heart is happy
For love will find a way
Rejoice my heart is happy
All the livelong day

King (*dreamily*) Did he love her all his life? That's not just
there for the rhyme?

Becket No. He did.

King It's odd. The happy ending's the saddest part. Do you believe in love?

Becket I believe in my father's love for my mother. Yes.

King (*kicking his* **Barons**) They've fallen asleep. Insensitive bastards. Is that how they appreciate music? I sometimes think we are the only two sensitive souls in England. We both eat with forks, we both have noble thoughts, we have one eye on the infinite. All I need you to do now, if you love me, is to find me a girl who will help me forget my earthly form. I'm fed up with whores. (*He goes to* **Gwendoline**.) Tit for tat. Remember.

Becket (*pale*) I am your Lordship's humble servant. Everything I have is yours. But as you have told me – I am also your friend.

King Well quite, we're friends, so share and share alike. You're fond of her, aren't you – you see, you can be fond of things. Caught you. You can't lie, can you? You'd find it, what, too unseemly, too inelegant. Your morality is simply ... aesthetics, isn't that the word? Am I right?

Becket Absolutely right, my Lord.

King This isn't such a mean trick – no, you promised me a favour – tit for tat, remember, you gave me your word.

Becket And I will stand by it ...

Silence. They look at each other.

King Right! Good. I'm going home – early night tonight. Lovely affair, Becket, you treat us royally, best food in the land. Help me wake these pigs. Come on boys, we're off. I know you love listening to good music, but enough's enough. A good evening, it was, but the best evenings always end up best in bed! Don't you agree Becket?

Becket (*stiffly*) If your Majesty will allow us a brief moment alone ...

King Of course, of course, my dear chap, I'm not a monster. I'll wait for you both downstairs. You can say goodnight to me there ...

Exits with **Barons**.

Becket You will have to go with him, Gwendoline.

Gwendoline Did you promise me to him, my Lord?

Becket I gave him my word he could have whatever he asked. I didn't realise it'd be you.

Gwendoline And if he throws me out tomorrow, will my Lord take me back?

Becket No.

Gwendoline Shall I ask the girls to pack my clothes?

Becket They'll be sent for tomorrow. You don't keep the King waiting. Say goodnight for me.

Gwendoline My Lord doesn't love anything on this earth, is that right?

Becket That is right.

Gwendoline You're like me – from a conquered race. But you've lived in luxury for so long, you've forgotten there is a part of all of us that they can never conquer.

Becket Yes, perhaps I have. There's a black hole inside me where my honour should be. Go now . . .

She exits. **Guard** *enters dragging the* **Peasant Girl**. **King** *appears, laughing.*

King My son, my son. Remember her? You're so forgetful sometimes . . . mind like a sieve. Luckily I remembered to have her picked up. It seems her father, brother and so on got a little bit killed in the process – but there you go. You see – I am your friend, you've every reason to love me. You told me you liked the look of her – and I'm happy to oblige. 'Night – have fun.

Girl Shall I undress, my Lord?

Becket Of course.

She does so. He shakes her by the shoulders.

I hope you have enough nobility of spirit to find all this pretty disgusting.

King *re-enters, running.*

King Thomas, Thomas, I didn't enjoy it Thomas. She just lay on the stairs and let me . . . like a corpse. Then she drew a little knife, God knows where from. There was blood everywhere. It was horrible. She could just as easily have killed me. Send *her* away – I'll sleep here this evening. I'm frightened.

You sleep on the other side of the bed.

Becket I'll sleep on the ground, your Majesty.

King No, I want you by my side. I don't want to feel alone.
And now you hate me. Perhaps I won't be able to trust you
any more.

Becket You have made me Guardian of the Seal. What
greater trust is there?

He blows out the candle.

King I never know what you're thinking.

Becket It'll be morning soon. You must sleep. It's off to
France tomorrow. And in a week's time we'll be facing the
French army – that'll make everything seem very simple, very
straightforward.

He lies down. **King** *groans as if in the grip of a nightmare.*

King They're after me – they're after me. They're armed.
Stop them. Stop them.

Becket My Prince, my Prince. Sleep in peace. I am here.

King Oh, is that you Thomas. They were ... they were
after me, all of them.

Becket 'My Prince.' If you really were my prince you would
be of my race. Which would make things simpler. In an
ordered world, I could love you in a simple, ordered way.
Every man beholden to another, from the highest to the
lowest. Linked by fealty and oath, loyalty and love. No blurred
edges – no contradictions. But I've wormed my way into the
ranks of the chosen – a bastard twice over. But sleep, my
Prince – as long as he can cobble together some semblance of
honour, Becket will serve you. But what if – one day it's called
into question ... and where is it, where is Becket's honour?

He shrugs. Sleeps.

Act Two

*We are now in France. Dawn. Four **Barons** are round a campfire, waiting.*

Baron 1 Becket. Who is he?

Baron 2 He's the Chancellor of England.

Baron 1 I know that – but, you know, who *is* he?

Baron 2 The Chancellor of England. The Chancellor. And that's all there is to say really.

Baron 1 No, you're not with me. Now, if I was a Chancellor, would I be the same Chancellor as Becket?

Baron 2 Are you all right?

Baron 1 Yes, why?

Baron 2 'Cos a baron who asks questions is a sick baron. For instance, take your sword – what is it?

Baron 1 It's my sword – and anyone who doubts it . . .

Baron 2 Exactly. Answered like a gentleman, and like a baron. You're up against a French soldier. Do you ask questions?

Baron 1 No.

Baron 2 Does he?

Baron 1 No!

Baron 2 You bash, don't you, you bash each other. Start asking a lot of damn fool questions – like bloody women – I mean you might as well bring a bunch of armchairs onto the battlefield. And have a debate. No if it's got this far all the questions have been asked, by bigger and better bastards than you or I.

Baron 1 All right. I'm just saying I don't like the cut of his gib.

Baron 2 Then say so. We'd've understood. No, fair enough. Nor do I. For a start, he's a Saxon.

Baron 3 He can fight though.

Baron 1 What do you mean?

Baron 3 I mean he can fight. *Really* fight. Did you see him yesterday, mowing them down to rescue the King. And how he brandished the banner, to draw the attack?

Baron 1 All right. He can fight.

Baron 3 He fights like a Norman.

Baron 1 Yes, but he's still a Saxon.

Baron 2 He'll always be a Saxon.

Pause.

Baron 1 What do you say, Reg?

Baron 4 I'm waiting.

Baron 1 What for?

Baron 4 For him to come out into the open. It's like when you're hunting a wild beast. You stalk all day. You follow the tracks, the smell. You're patient. Rush in, waving your lance, you'll never know what sort of beast you're dealing with. You have to wait.

Baron 1 What for?

Baron 4 For him to come out into the open. The beast is much more cunning, but the huntsman will always have an advantage. He knows how to wait. So I'm waiting. For Becket to . . .

Baron 1 What?

Baron 4 Come out into the open. Break cover. Only then will we know who he really is . . .

Becket *enters.*

Becket A good morning to you, gentlemen. Is the King still asleep?

Baron 1 He hasn't called for us yet.

Becket Has the Field Marshal come with the list of casualties?

Baron 1 No.

Becket Why not?

Baron 1 He's on it.

Becket Oh.

Baron 1 I saw the whole thing. A lance knocked him off his horse. The foot soldiers did the rest.

Becket Poor chap – he was so proud of his nice new armour.

Baron 2 Yes. There must have been a chink in it. They bled him to death, like veal. In the mud. French bastards.

Becket That's war.

Baron 1 That's not war. War is like every other sport. You have to play by the rules. In the old days they'd hold you for ransom. Single combat, knight against knight – now that's what I call fighting.

Becket If we learn anything from this war, it's that the old ways, the honourable ways are no longer relevant. The world is tending to butchery, so we'll have to hire cut-throats – men who play by the rules.

Baron 1 What about our honour my Lord Chancellor?

Becket The soldier's honour – let's not be hypocritical, Baron – is simply to win battles. None of us have any illusions about that. Now, we're entering the town at eight o' clock and the *Te Deum* in the cathedral is booked for nine fifteen, and we do not keep the French bishops waiting, that would be grossly impolite. We want them collaborating with good grace.

Baron 1 In my day, we'd've massacred them first, walked in after.

Becket Yes, into a ghost town. I'd prefer to give my sovereign living towns, for his greater glory and his greater wealth. Oh no, come eight o' clock this morning, I'm the Frenchman's dearest friend!

Baron 1 That's all well and good but what about English honour?

Becket English honour is simple. One way or another you always win.

Exits.

Baron 2 What sort of mentality is that?

Baron 4 You have to wait. One day he'll break cover.

Becket *enters the* **King**'s *tent. He is in bed with a* **French Girl**.

Becket My prince.

King (*yawning*) Morning, my son, sleep well?

Becket Not really. A little souvenir of France stuck in my left shoulder – kept me awake – no harm though, I got some thinking done.

King You mustn't think so much. One day it'll be the death of you. The more you think, the more problems you find, the more insoluble the problems, the more improbable the solutions, then you're in all sorts of trouble. No, better to know nothing, sleep better, live longer. What do you think of my French girl? I love France.

Becket So do I. All Englishmen love France.

King Quite right. It's warmer, the girls are prettier, the food's better. And the wine ... no, I think I'll spend a few weeks here every winter.

Becket Trouble is, it's expensive. Two thousand killed yesterday.

King Has the Field Marshal added up the losses?

Becket Yup. And he's added himself on the end.

King Wounded?

Becket *doesn't answer.*

I hate hearing about the death of people one knows. I get the feeling it gives death ideas ...

Becket Your Majesty, we must get down to business. We haven't even dealt with yesterday's despatches.

King Oh come on, yesterday we were fighting. You can't do everything.

Becket Yesterday was a holiday. Now we have to work twice as hard.

King God, you can be so boring sometimes. Being king's no fun with you around. You sound like the Archbishop. We used to be pals. When I made you Chancellor on that ludicrous salary – I thought you'd spend twice as much time and money having fun.

Becket I'm having fun, your Majesty, I'm having the time of my life.

King You like working for my subjects, do you? Do you love this nation? How can you – there are too many of them, too many to know – how can you love someone you never met? Anyhow, you don't love anything.

Becket Perhaps one thing – I love to see a good job well done.

King That's you and your aesth … aesth … can't remember the bloody word.

Becket Aesthetics. Yes my Lord.

King I'll show you aesthetics. (*Slaps the* **Girl**'s *behind.*) That's arse-thetics! Round as a peach. Some people go for cathedrals, but that is … perfection. You fancy a go?

Becket Sir, business.

King All right. Business. Spoil-sport. I'm listening. Sit down.

Becket The news is not good, my Lord.

King News never is. That's a well-known fact. Life is a tangled web of difficulties and set backs. But the knack – and there is a knack, philosophers have been researching it for generations – is to do absolutely nothing about it. Then the difficulties start swallowing each other up, then turning on the set backs. Then ten years later, when the dust has settled, you're still alive – the world's survived. No harm done. Things always work out.

Becket Yes, badly. Let me make a comparison that will hold your attention. Tennis. Aha! Now when you're on the court, do you wait for things to 'work out'? Do you stick your racquet out on the off chance that a ball will hit it?

King No, I work, I run, I sweat, I strain, I serve, I volley, I win.

Becket Well then, let me extend the metaphor to a little domestic squabble which is getting rather out of hand. And the present score is Clergy: 30, Crown: love.

King Oh, come on – we got them to pay the tax. That's something.

Becket Yes, it's a small sum of money. Just enough to mollify a monarch, as they well know. But those people are

past-masters at taking back with one hand what they give out
with the other. It's a conjuring trick they've been perfecting for
centuries.

King (*to the* **Girl**)   Little dumpling, you ought to be listening
to all this, very profound, jolly instructive.

Becket   Very well, little girl, you tell us. When you get
married – that's assuming your rather tattered virtue permits it
– but say you do – would you prefer to be mistress in your
own house, or would you prefer the priest from down the road
to come and run it for you?

King *pushes* **Girl** *under the quilt.*

King   Come on let's be serious, Becket. The priests are
plotting, I know that. They always have been – always will be.
But I can *break* them whenever I want to.

Becket   Very well, but *you* be serious, your Highness. If you
don't break them and break them now, in five years there will
be two Kings on the English throne. The Archbishop of
Canterbury and you. And in ten years there'll be only one.

King   Me?

Becket   Afraid not.

King   It will be me, Becket, it will. The House of Plantagenet
gives nothing away. Nothing. To horse, to horse, Becket – for
the greatness of our England. Let's wage war on the faithful –
that'll make a change!

The **Girl** *is still under the quilt.*

Girl   I can't breathe!

King   What are you doing there? Spying for the clergy? Get
out – get dressed and go home. For the greatness. Give her
some gold, Thomas.

Girl (*gathering her things*)   Shall I come back to the camp this
evening my Lord?

Becket   No.

King   Yes. No. Whatever, I don't know. We're discussing the
Archbishop, not you. Where was I? Yes. To horse, Thomas,
for the greatness of England! My big fist and your big brain,
we'll sort out the Archbishop between us. I'll never find
anybody that good in bed, not by this evening. Hang on. Yes,

my angel, yes my love, come back to me tonight. You have
the sweetest eyes in the whole world. You have to say that –
even if you pay them – otherwise there's no pleasure in it. You
see, it's all politics. But what will God say if we ... I mean
they are His bishops.

Becket   We're not little boys any more. We both know that
we can always come to some arrangement with God – at least
in this life. Quick, get dressed – we're due in town at eight
and nine fifteen, *Te Deum* in the cathedral – they'll appreciate
our punctuality.

King   You're such a cynic. And I do love you – at least
when you're not being boring.

Becket   Come on, we'll be late.

King   All right, all right. Do you think I ought to trim my
beard?

Becket   Two days in battle – it might be wise.

King   All for a bunch of defeated Frenchmen. Sometimes I
think you're getting a bit too fussy.

Exit.

Enter **Soldiers** *with* **Little Monk**.

Becket   Who's this?

Soldier   We've just arrested him my Lord. He was prowling
round the camp. He had a knife under his robe – we were
taking him to the Provost.

Becket   You French?

Little Monk   No, English.

Becket   Where from?

Little Monk   Hastings.

Becket   Oh. Leave him with me – I'll interrogate him myself.

Soldier   He's a vicious bugger, saving your Grace. Took four
of us to get the knife off him. He wounded the sergeant. Just
so you know.

Becket   Thank you. Stay close by. (*Plays with the knife.*) Now
why do you need a knife in a monastery?

Little Monk To slice my bread with.

Becket Oh yes, and who else? It's not up to much – good for one murder at most. So it wouldn't just be a Norman soldier.

Little Monk I'm prepared to die.

Becket Yes of course – but afterwards, before would be a bit dumb, don't you agree? Look, they'll put you to the torture. Do you know what that means? I've had to be present a couple of times, in a professional capacity. One thinks one's strong-willed. But they're really ingenious – I mean their particular knowledge of anatomy and pain – they'd put most doctors to shame. And believe me, you always talk – every single time. You don't die, you talk. So if I tell them that you talked to me first – then it'll be swifter, less painful, which is worth taking into account. Plus there's an amusing little coincidence. When he made me Chancellor, the King entrusted to my particular care the abbey of Hastings. The rather cruel irony of which did not, I am sure, escape him. I pretended not to notice.

Little Monk You are Becket?

Becket Yes. This is a real Saxon's knife. Stinks of onions. You didn't say who it was meant for? For me? Well I have it in my hand – so thank you. For the King? Trouble is he's got three sons and royalty breed like rabbits. Did you expect to liberate the Saxon race in a single blow?

Little Monk No, I wanted to liberate myself.

Becket From what?

Little Monk My shame.

Becket How old are you?

Little Monk Sixteen.

Becket The Normans have occupied our island for a hundred years. Your father and your grandfather have drunk their fair share of shame. The cup's probably empty now.

Little Monk It is not.

Becket So, one fine morning, you woke up, sixteen years old – woke up in your cell – first bell, first light, and the bells told you to bear the burden, personally, of all that shame . . .

Little Monk How did you know that?

Becket You know I'm a Saxon like yourself?

Little Monk Yes.

Becket (*smiling*) Spit at me then, I know you want to.

Little Monk *spits at him.*

Becket Now that's better isn't it? Obviously whether you live or die is neither here nor there, but I'd like to keep you alive for a while, it is rare for fate to bring us face to face with the ghost of one's youth. Soldier.

Soldier *enters.*

Becket Bring the Provost. Lovely morning isn't it? I love this hot sunshine shrouded in cold mist. Gorgeous. But I'm like you. I prefer England. Round Hastings. Good solid fog – you know where you are. Sunshine is a luxury. And luxury – well, our race rather mistrusts it ... it's not in our blood.

Provost *arrives.*

Becket Ah, Provost. Your men arrested this monk – he was found skulking around the camp. He's from the abbey of Hastings and therefore falls under my direct jurisdiction. You will arrange for him to be taken back to England, to Hastings, where his abbot will keep an eye on him until my return. There will be no specific charge against him, not for the moment. I want him closely guarded, but without brutality, is that clear? I will hold you personally responsible for his well-being.

Provost Very good my Lord, come on lad.

Exit with **Little Monk** *and* **Soldiers**.

Becket (*looks at knife*) Touching that. Still stinks of onions though.

Enters the **King**'s *tent shouting.*

Are you ready, Prince? Have you got your gladrags on? Mustn't keep the Bishop waiting, must we?

The street. Bells – guard of honour, trumpets. **King** *and* **Becket** *ride in triumph.*

King They love us, they absolutely love us.

Becket They jolly well ought to – they're being paid enough.
The common folk that is. The bourgeoisie is at home, skulking.

King Patriots?

Becket Not at all, I just couldn't afford them. There are also
various members of your Highness's guard, in disguise. Just in
case enthusiasm starts to flag.

King Why must you always shatter my illusions? I was sure
they loved me for myself. You are thoroughly amoral, Becket,
or is it immoral?

Becket That depends. The only thing which is completely
immoral is to not do that which has to be done. When it has
to be done.

King So, morality isn't a medicine you believe in?

Becket Yes, but for external use only.

King *She's* nice. Up there on the balcony. Shall we stop a
moment?

Becket The timetable is actually quite strict.

King Be more fun than seeing a bishop! Make a note of the
house – we'll pop in later on.

Becket You remember what you have to say?

King Yes, yes, but what the hell's it matter what I say to a
French bishop whose city I have just conquered?

Becket It matters a great deal. For future policy.

King Look, I'm the victor aren't I? I'm stronger.

Becket Today you are. Which is why you have to be
particularly polite. Then you'll seem a thousand times stronger.

King Polite? To a defeated bishop? My grandfather would
have massacred the lot of them. We've grown soft over the
years.

Becket Never drive your enemy to despair. That makes him
strong. Gentleness is the best policy. It emasculates them. To
occupy effectively, do not crush, merely corrupt.

King What's this, a Saxon giving us lessons in occupation?

Becket Yes and quite right too. We've had a hundred years
to think about it.

King   What about my pleasure? I don't want to hear their *Te Deum* – I want to get at them, now. I'm the conqueror, after all, it's my right.

Becket   It would be a mistake sir. Worse. A weakness. One may indulge one's whims, of course, but never one's weaknesses.

King   Yes daddy, no daddy. You're a pompous ass today, you really are. God, look at that redhead over there.

Becket   The timetable.

Antechamber of the cathedral. **King**, **Barons**, **Priest**, **Choirboy**; **King** *pacing*.

King   Where the hell is Becket? What are we waiting for?

Baron 1   He said to wait Sir. He said there was something wasn't quite right.

King   All this carry-on for a French bishop. Look at me, pacing about like a teenage bridegroom.

Baron 4   I don't see why we don't just go in. After all it's your bloody cathedral if you don't mind me saying so. Shall we just burst in – swords drawn. Shall we do it Sir?

King (*silence*)   Nah. It'd upset Becket. He knows what to do and what not to do. Better than we do. If he's making us wait, and he is, there's bound to be a reason.

Enter **Becket**.

Becket, there you are. We're freezing to death here. What's going on? Why are we locked in this damn sacristy?

Becket   I gave the order Sir. A security measure. My spies informed me that the French were planning an attack during the ceremony.

Baron 2 (*draws his sword – others do the same*)   Bastards!

Becket   Put up your swords. The King is safe here. There are guards at every door.

Baron 2   Won't you let us go and deal with it Sir? I promise it won't take us long.

Baron 4   Let me at them.

Becket I forbid it. There's only a handful of us. I've alerted
our troops – they will evacuate the cathedral. Until then, the
King's person is under your protection. But sheathe your
swords – and no provocation. I have only fifty men stationed
in the town.

King Becket – what about the priest? He's French.

Becket Yes my Lord, but he belongs to the Bishop – and
the Bishop belongs to us.

King We can't even trust English bishops, let alone French
ones … he's got a shifty look about him.

Becket Who, the Bishop?

King No, this priest.

Becket I should think he has my Lord – he's got a squint.
Apart from that, you needn't upset yourself about him. Even if
he had a dagger – he'd have to get past four barons and one
chainmail coat. Excuse me – I must help evacuate the church.

Makes to go.

King Becket, what about the choirboy?

Becket (*laughing*) He's only so high!

King He could be a dwarf. You never know with the
French. Look Becket, we were talking a bit … carelessly this
morning. What if this is God, taking his revenge?

Becket (*smiling*) I think not, Sir. Merely my police being
overzealous, they see murderers round every corner – it justifies
their salary. But come on, who cares. We'll hear the *Te Deum*
in an empty church, that's all.

King (*bitter*) And just now I thought that people loved me.
Perhaps you didn't pay them enough.

Becket One cannot buy those who are not for sale, my
Lord. And they, by definition, are not dangerous. As for the
others, well, we're as cunning as they are. I'll be back to
reassure you soon.

Exits.

King Barons.

Barons (*thunderously*) Your Majesty!

King (*calming down*) Please. Keep this man under surveillance

... If he so much as twitches, then jump on him.

Knock at door.

Enter.

A **Soldier** *enters.*

Soldier   A messenger from London, your Majesty. He's come from the camp – they sent him here. It's extremely urgent.

King   Sounds fishy to me. Go and see, Baron.

Baron 4 *goes, returns, reassured.*

Baron 4   It's William de Corbeil, your Highness. With most urgent letters.

King   Are you sure it's him? It's not a Frenchman made up to look like him? It's the oldest trick in the book.

Baron 4   It's him.

Enter **Corbeil**. *Presents letters.*

King   Thank you. Well, William de Corbeil, you have a fine beard. Let's see if it stays on.

Corbeil   Ow! Thank you your Majesty. (*Exits.*)

King *reads letters.*

King   Good news, gentlemen. We have one enemy less.

Becket *returns.*

King   Becket!

Becket   Everything's fine my Lord. The troops are on their way. So we only have to wait.

King   Everything *is* fine, Becket. Couldn't in fact be better. God, it seems, is not angry with us – he's done us a favour. The Archbishop of Canterbury is dead.

Becket (*seriously*)   That little old man ... so much strength in that feeble body.

King   Now, now, don't squander all your sorrow. Not on him. I think that is excellent news.

Becket   He was the first Norman to take an interest in me. He was a true father to me – I hope he is with God.

King   He certainly ought to be – he's been fighting His cause

for long enough. No. He'll be in Heaven – and infinitely more
use to God than he's been to us. So – that's all worked out for
the best. Becket, don't you see, the ball's in our court – and
we can score an easy point. You see, I've had an extraordinary
idea. A masterstroke. I think I've woken up *brilliant* this
morning. Perhaps it was having that French girl all night –
some native wit has rubbed off. I feel subtle. I feel
unfathomable. Makes me feel giddy. Are you sure deep thought
doesn't have adverse side-effects? Thomas, Thomas – are you
listening.

Becket   Yes, my Lord.

King   You're not listening. Now *listen*. You always said that
the best ideas are the stupidest ideas – but you have to think
of them first. Listen. Thomas. Now. Custom forbids me to
tamper with the privilege of the primacy. With me so far?

Becket   Yes, my Lord.

King   But what if the Primate is my man? What if the
Archbishop of Canterbury is on the side of the King? Then his
power is my power and it can't hurt me.

Becket   It's ingenious my Lord, but the Primate is chosen by
free election, don't forget.

King   No. Don't *you* forget. What about the Royal veto? If
the elected candidate doesn't suit the King, he can send his
representative to the synod and veto their choice. And for once
it works in my favour. Not for a hundred years have they
voted against the Royal decision . . .

Becket   That's true your Majesty, but we know what your
bishops are like. Which of them can you trust?

King   Who can I trust? You know who I can trust –
someone whose head is screwed on properly – someone who
isn't easily scared – not even by God. Thomas – now I'm
being serious. There's work for you to do, my son. You'll have
to give up all this for the time being – French girls, battles –
you'll have to go to England.

Becket   At your command.

King   Have you guessed why?

Becket (*a sick horror growing in his face*)   No, my Lord.

King   Very well. This is your mission. You will take personal letters from me to every bishop in the land. Containing – guess what, I think you have – an expression of the Royal desire to see you elected as Primate of all England.

Becket (*tries to laugh*)   You're joking – of course you are. Look at me. A shining example of devotion and self-denial. These simple vestments. (*He shows off his expensive costume; the* **King** *is laughing too by now.*) You are joking – I know you are.

King (*stops laughing*)   I am deadly serious. I'll draft the letters this morning. You will assist me.

Becket   But for God's sake, I'm not even a priest!

King   You are a deacon. That's a start. You'll pronounce your vows tomorrow – you'll be ordained in a month.

Becket   Have you even considered what the Pope will say?

King   He'll say what I pay him to say.

Becket   I don't think you're joking any more. Don't do this to me.

King   Why ever not?

Becket   It scares me.

King (*harder than ever*)   Becket – it's an order.

Becket   If I become Archbishop I can no longer be your friend.

Organ music breaks out clamorously.

An **Officer** *appears.*

Officer   Your Majesty, the church has been cleared. The Bishop and his clergy await your Highness's pleasure.

King   You hear that, Becket? Pull yourself together. This is no way to receive good news. Snap to it – we can proceed now.

The cortège forms – **Becket** *by the* **King**.

Becket (*softly*)   This is absolute madness, my Lord. Don't do it. I cannot serve God and you.

King   You have been loyal to me, Thomas. I'm certain you will continue to be so. I trust you – it is my wish – you will leave this evening. Now come on.

Becket's *room, two* **Valets** *packing rich garments.*

Valet 2   Even the sable jacket?

Valet 1   Everything, he said.

Valet 2   That sable, for beggars? They won't make a penny dressed like that – they'll starve.

Valet 1   No, they'll eat the fur. No – idiot – they'll sell it and get money that way.

Valet 2   But what about him? He'll have nothing to wear.

Becket *enters, simply dressed.*

Becket   I want everything packed and out of here by this evening. I want nothing here but bare boards. Stan, get rid of that fur bedspread.

Valet 1   But you'll freeze.

Becket   Do what I say.

He does so.

Has the steward organised the evening meal? Dinner for forty in the Great Hall.

Valet 1   The gold service won't stretch my Lord – shall we add on the silver?

Becket   Wooden bowls, earthenware spoons, the service has been sold.

Valet 1   Very good your Lordship. The steward was a bit worried about the guest list. We've only got three footmen and time's rather against us.

Becket   There is no guest list. Open the great gate and go into the streets. The poor will be my guests tonight.

Valet 1   Very good my Lord.

Becket   I want everything to be impeccable. Serve them with the ceremony due to princes. All right. Off you go.

They exit.

He looks into the packing cases.

It was lovely stuff. I am being rather vulgar, rather theatrical about the whole thing. A truly saintly man would never have done all this on one day. No one would take him seriously. (*To a crucifix.*) My Father, I hope you're not filling my head with these saintly notions just to make me look ridiculous. It's all so new, I'm still not very good at it. Mind you, you can talk – pretty rich yourself, gleaming rubies set into your bleeding body. I'd better give you away too.

Looks around.

Off on my holidays! Pray forgive me, God in Heaven – but I haven't had so much fun in years and years. Was that part of your Grand Design? That I should enjoy this? I believe in God the Father, the God of joy, the God of laughter.

Goes behind curtain. We hear him whistling – reappears – sackcloth, sandals.

So there we are! Farewell Becket. I just wish it'd felt like more of a sacrifice. My Father – are you sure you're not just tempting me? It all seems far too easy . . .

He kneels and prays.

Curtain.

Act Three

A room in the palace. The **Queen** *and the* **Queen Mother** *working on their tapestries. The* **King's Sons** *playing in a corner.*

King Forty beggars! He invited forty beggars to dinner.

Queen Mother You see – he's as extravagant as ever. I always told you, my son, that your trust had been misplaced.

King Excuse me, Madam, but I am very strict about where I place my trust. I have only dared to give it once in my life – and I remain convinced that I did the right thing. And anyway how can we posssibly know the whole story? Thomas is a thousand times cleverer than the whole lot of us put together.

Queen Mother Excuse me, but you are talking about the Royal family, my son.

King Yes. But I'm talking about intelligence. It's not like wealth or birth. It's shared out on a rather different basis. No, the forty beggars must be symbolic, they must correspond to something in his soul. Their poverty, his riches ... I can't work it out. But he'll tell us himself. I've ordered him here this morning.

Queen I hear his gold plate, his jewel boxes and all those gorgeous clothes have been *sold*. To a Jew! He now wears a simple monk's habit.

Queen Mother To me that smacks of ostentation. Men do become saints, it's true, but not overnight.

King It's all a joke. He's pulling our leg. Has to be. If you knew him – he was always playing jokes, dressing up. Once he dressed up as a dockside whore and paraded round town on my arm all night.

Queen *(after a pause)* I've never liked that man. And as for you, you were mad to allow him so much power.

King *(shouts)* He's my friend.

Queen Mother *(bitterly)* More's the pity.

Queen He's not your friend – the man who has driven you from the bosom of your family – away from your duties and to taverns and to whores.

King Nonsense Madam. I didn't need anyone to drive me

away from you, my family, or my duties. There are other
bosoms more alluring, believe me. I sired three children by you
– diligently – God knows, I've done my bit.

Queen   When this fornicator's wicked influence over you has
waned, then, only then, will you appreciate the true joys of
family life. Let us hope he disobeys your orders.

King   The joys of family life are rather limited. To be frank,
you all bore me witless. Your endless bitching and bickering –
forever picking away at your tapestries. It's not even as if you
were any good at it. Look at that – really mediocre!

Queen   We only have the gifts we are born with . . .

King   And yours, Madam, are negligible.

He checks the time. Looks to the window.

I've been here a month – nobody to talk to – and I'm bored.
Of course, so soon after his nomination – I didn't want to rush
things. Then he had to undertake his pastoral tour of duty.
Fair enough. Now he's coming back, on my orders – and he's
late. Aha – there's someone at the sentry post. No. Some
monk.

Looks at his children, playing.

Look at them. Charming. Him. A grown man in miniature.
Already dark, sly, moody. Funny. You're not quite old enough
to hate or to mistrust. Which of you is the eldest?

Prince Henry   Me, sir.

King   And what was your name again?

Prince Henry   Henry the Third.

King   Not yet it isn't. Number two is still alive and kicking. Is
this what you're teaching them Madam? You already think of
yourself as Queen Regent. Are you surprised I keep away from
your bedchamber. Who wants to make love to his widow?

Officer *enters.*

Officer   I bring a message from my Lord Archbishop, your
Majesty.

King (*furious*)   A message! A message! I ordered the
Archbishop to appear in person. (*Suddenly concerned.*) Perhaps he's
ill. That would explain everything.

Queen (*bitterly*) And be too much to hope for.

King You both want him dead, don't you. Just because he's my friend. But that must be it. He's not here – he's dying. Oh, Thomas.

Officer *leads in a* **Monk**.

King Is Becket unwell?

Monk No, your Majesty. My master is very well. He has ordered me to deliver – with his profound regrets – this letter – and this, to your Highness.

King (*looks at what he has been given*) The seal! Why has he returned the seal? (*Reads in silence, visibly chilled.*) Very well. Your mission is completed. Go now.

Monk Has your Highness a reply which I may communicate to his Grace, the Archbishop?

King (*hard*) No.

Monk *exits.*

A silence. The women glance at each other conspiratorially.

Queen Mother Well my son, what has your nice friend to say for himself?

King Get out! Get out of here, both of you. And take the Royal brats – vermin! Leave me alone here.

General exit, leaving the **King**, *who is racked by a great sob.*

Thomas! (*He pulls himself together, teeth set, fists clenched.*) You send me back the seal – like a little boy who doesn't want to play any more. You think you must protect the 'Honour of God'. To protect you, I would have all England at war, I would have sacrificed the honour of this whole Kingdom, like that, and laughed about it. For you. But I loved you and you never loved me. That's the difference. Thank you, though, for this parting gift. This going-away present. I'll have to learn to be alone from now on.

Exit.

Fade. Lights up on an empty church. **Gilbert Folliot**, *Bishop of London, has just said Mass. He enters with his clergy. A man, half-disguised, is waiting for him in the shadows. It is the* **King**.

King My Lord Bishop. Psst.

Folliot (*rudely*) Who are you – what d'you want?

King My Lord Bishop.

Folliot Your Majesty.

King Bishop, will you hear my confession?

Folliot I am Bishop only of London – the King has his own confessor. An important court position which has its own prerogatives.

King Even a king has a free choice of confessor, Bishop.

Folliot *indicates that the clergy should leave.*

King Don't worry, my confession will be brief – and I have not come to ask for absolution. At least not precisely. I have committed something more serious than a mere sin. I have committed an error. A stupid error. I forced Thomas à Becket on you at the Council of Clarendon. And now I repent it.

Folliot We bowed before the Royal Will.

King Reluctantly, I know; it took me thirteen weeks of patient authority to convince the small stubborn minority that their position was ill-considered – and you led that minority. On the day of the Council you looked a very funny colour. They told me you became seriously ill afterwards.

Folliot God has cured me.

King Good of him – but then he always seems to look after his own. I am still sick – but I can cure myself without divine intervention. My sickness is the shape of an archbishop who is stuck in my craw. A sizeable blockage, as you can imagine. I need to vomit him up. So. What do the Norman clergy think of him?

Folliot (*guardedly*) His Grace seems to have a firm grip on the reins of the Church in England. There are even some close to him who talk of sainthood.

King God, that's a bit sudden – but nothing would surprise me. It's the nature of the beast, he's capable of anything – good or bad. Now Bishop, you'll have to be frank. Is the Church particularly interested in saintliness.

Folliot The Church, in her wisdom, is well aware the temptation of saintliness is one of the Devil's most subtle traps.

To administer the kingdom of souls, with all its concomitant difficulties one requires, as in all administrations, efficient and effective administrators. The Roman Catholic Church has its saints – it begs for their generous intercession – it prays to them. But it has no need to make more. That would be superfluous and dangerous.

King   It is becoming clear to me, Bishop, that you are a man I can do business with. I misjudged you. My friendship blinded me.

Folliot (*still guarded*)   Friendship is a precious thing.

King   It's like a favourite pet – a warm, living thing. You only see its two big, soulful eyes, staring at you, warming you. You don't notice its teeth. But it is an animal with a peculiar property – it can only really hurt you when it's dead.

Folliot   Do I take it that the King's friendship for Thomas à Becket has died, your Highness?

King   Yes. Very suddenly. Heart failure, you might say.

Folliot   A curious phenomenon, your Highness, but not uncommon.

King (*taking his arm*)   I hate him. I hate Becket. I'll have to turn this hatred loose on him, but I am the King – and what seems to be my greatness is a slight obstacle. So I need somebody to help me.

Folliot   I will serve only the Church.

King   Look, let's talk like grown-ups. You and I, Church and Crown, have conquered England arm-in-arm, together we ransacked and we pillaged. We have had our disagreements – mostly over money of course, but Heaven and Earth have many interests in common. For instance, guess what I've just received from the Pope in Rome? His blessing for us to go and disembowel Ireland and the Irish – all in the name of the Faith. Yes, a holy war – a new crusade if you like, to impose Norman clergy, Norman barons, Norman values. So you'll be busy blessing the flags and swords – Constantinople all over again. Only one condition: a little piece of silver per household per year, for St Peter's pence, which the Irish clergy seem unwilling to cough up. I've agreed to soften their reluctance. It's a tiny sum, but year by year it all adds up. God's bankers in Rome know how to do their sums.

Folliot (*shocked*) Your Highness, there are certain things which are better unsaid. Indeed it is better not to know too much if one is not directly responsible.

King (*smiles*) We are alone, Bishop. The church is empty.

Folliot The church is never empty. An eternal flame is burning on the altar.

King (*impatient*) Look, Bishop, I enjoy games – but don't insult my intelligence. I'm not one of your stupid flock. Whoever that flame honours knows all about us – He has read our hearts long, long ago. He sees your cupidity – my hatred.

Silence.

Folliot (*venomously*) If I disregard, as I must, my personal feelings on the subject – then I am forced to say that the new Archbishop has yet to do anything which directly impugns the interests of the Mother Church.

King Well, my little friend, I think I can see what you are up to – I see that you're not going to come cheap. But thanks to Becket – the clergy are now paying their absentee tax – so I think I can probably afford you. And I also think it perfectly right – morally right – that some of the Church's gold should return, *via* you, to the Church. And since we're talking about morality, your Holiness, you yourself will agree that the greatness of Church and State are inextricably linked, and you will be wishing to safeguard and strengthen the Catholic faith when, as I feel you will, you work for me.

Folliot I had always mistaken your Highness for an overgrown adolescent lout, concerned only with his own sensual pleasure.

King It is often easy to misjudge people, Bishop. I misjudge myself. (*Suddenly he cries out.*) Thomas, Thomas.

Folliot You love him, Highness. You *still* love him. You love that bastard Saxon, that pig in a mitre, that imposter, that guttersnipe.

King (*jumps on him*) Yes I love him. But listen, vicar, that's none of your business. All I'll confess to you is my hate – I'll pay you to get rid of him, but if you say a word against him in my hearing, you'll have me to deal with. Man to man.

Folliot You're choking me, your Majesty.

King (*suddenly letting him go – a different, matter-of-fact tone*) We'll meet tomorrow, my Lord Bishop, to discuss our detailed plan of action. You will be ordered to my palace on some pretext – let's say my charitable work in your diocese – I am, after all, its most important resident! But we won't be talking about the poor. Oh no, the poor can wait – their kingdom, if anywhere, is in the hereafter.

Exit **King**. *Then exit* **Folliot**, *rejoined by his clergy. He replaces his mitre, knocked off in the struggle.*

Crossfade. The Archbishop's palace. A **Priest**, **Two Monks** *and the* **Little Monk** *we met earlier.*

Priest His Grace will receive you here.

The **Monks** *are impressed – they jostle the* **Little Monk**.

Monk 1 Come on, stand up straight. Kiss his Lordship's ring – speak when you're spoken to and be polite or I'll skin you alive.

Monk 2 Perhaps you thought he'd forgotten all about you. Great men never forget. And behave yourself – don't act all high and mighty.

Becket *enters in a simple monk's habit.*

Becket Well, well brothers. Good weather in Hastings?

Monk 1 Fog, my Lord.

Becket Well, that's very good, for Hastings. We were thinking fondly of our abbey there the other day, and it is our firm intention to visit it soon. How has this young man been behaving?

Monk 2 Stubborn as a mule, your Grace, and that's the truth. Our Father Abbot tried to cure him with kindness as you suggested, but after a while we had recourse to the dry bread, the dungeon and the scourge. Still no good. He's as pig-headed and foul-mouthed as ever. He's fallen into evil ways my Lord, the sin of pride. Nothing can help him.

Monk 1 A good boot up the arse would help him, saving your Lordship's presence. Stand up straight, will you.

Becket Yes, stand up straight – do as he says. Strange, normally the sin of pride has the opposite effect. Look me in the eye. Good. We will take you to the kitchens, my brothers – a little refreshment before you leave. I've told them to treat you well. Don't be offended – we'll permit you to abstain from abstinence – just for today.

Monk 2 What about the boy?

Becket We'll keep him here.

Monk 2 Don't trust him, my Lord. He's a bad one.

Becket We are not afraid.

Exit **Monks**.

Becket Why do you stand so badly?

Little Monk I'm not going to look anyone in the face. Not any more.

Becket I'll teach you the way. And that'll be our first lesson. Look at me. No better than that.

Little Monk *does so.*

Becket You're still bearing the weight, the shame of England, on your shoulders, aren't you? Is that what's bending your back?

Little Monk Yes.

Becket If I take half, will that help? (*Aside.*) It is time for my council with the serried ranks of England's bishops. (*To the* **Priest**.) Show their Lordships in. (*To the* **Little Monk**.) You'll see that being alone is not a privilege reserved exclusively for you.

Little Monk Look, how can I serve you? I can't read, I can't write. I only had my head shaved to escape being a serf.

Becket I need you. Is that not reason enough? I need you to look me in the face, the way you are looking at me now. I've got a hair shirt. I wear it all the time. Trouble is, I've got used to it – I think if I took it off, I'd catch a cold. I need something else to scratch me, to prick my conscience – to remind me what I am and who I am. There has to be the odd thorn on the road to righteousness – otherwise I'd be enjoying myself too much.

As the **Bishops** *enter,* **Folliot**, **York**, **Oxford** *and others, with attendant clergy,* **Becket** *guides the* **Little Monk** *into a corner.*

Becket   You sit there and shut up. One thing. Don't leap at their throats – it'd only complicate matters.

Folliot   This meeting may well be pointless. You have dared – against our advice – to attack the King directly. You have asked us to sanction three excommunications, but before they were even made public, the King has struck back. His Attorney General has a legal summons for you to appear tomorrow before his Court of Justice and to answer the charges against you.

Becket   What are these charges?

Folliot   Embezzlement, principally. His Privy Council have examined the accounts and it seems there is still a sizeable sum outstanding from your tenure at the Treasury.

Becket   When I resigned as Chancellor I left all my registers with the Attorney General, who declared me free of any debt or obligation. What does the King say I owe?

Oxford   Forty thousand marks in gold.

Becket   I don't think there was that much in the Treasury all the time I was there. But you never know, a clever clerk, some creative accounting ... The King has begun to tighten his fist – and I'm just a little fly, caught inside it ... well, there we are. Try not to look so smug.

York   We did warn you against open opposition.

Becket   William of Aynesford was excommunicated because he struck and killed the priest I appointed to his parish. He had the King's complete support, because the King disapproved of my choice. What do they expect me to do, stand aside and watch my priests be attacked?

Folliot   It is not for you to appoint a priest to a fiefdom created by William the First. No Norman cleric or layman would ever allow it. It is contrary to the whole legal system of the Conquest. England is the land of law, and of the most scrupulous respect for the law.

Becket   Bishop, must I remind you that we are all men of God and as such we have his honour to defend.

Oxford   To excommunicate William of Aynesford was, we felt, insensitive, not to mention provocative. He is a friend of the King.

Becket   I know him well – very pleasant fellow. We used to get drunk together.

York   And his wife is my second cousin!

Becket   Well I'm sorry about that, my Lord Bishop, but he struck one of my priests. If I do not protect my clergy, who will? To my next case, Gilbert de Clare, who has dared to arraign a clerk, who comes under my direct jurisdiction.

York   Oh my heart bleeds for your clerk. He was accused of rape and murder and is certainly guilty of that and worse and deserved the gallows a hundred times over. Let him hang and be done with it.

Becket   It is a matter of supreme indifference to me what this man is accused of. If I let my priests be tried in a secular court, or let the likes of Robert de Vere, who is my third excommunicant, continue to abduct tonsured monks, as he has been doing, from my monasteries on the pretext that they are merely there to escape serfdom – well I don't hold out much hope for our liberty, even for our existence five years from now. William of Aynesford, Gilbert de Clare, Robert de Vere are excommunicated. The Kingdom of God must defend itself – like any other kingdom. It's not enough to have a just moral cause. You must have and use the power to protect it.

York   These are empty words. The King is the law.

Becket   He is the written law – there is another law, not written – but which topples even the greatest of kings. I was a libertine, a profligate, or let's say a man of the world. I loved life. I loved pleasure. I laughed at all this sort of stuff. But now I bear the burden you have passed on to me – nothing will persuade me to set it down.

Folliot   It's all very well to observe ecclesiastical law to the letter – but by doing so you are sanctioning the theft – yes, the theft of Saxons from their Norman masters. Thanks to this law, any peasant's son can take refuge and then it's snip, snip, half a benedictus and they're in! For life. And the master can't touch him. Is this justice, I ask myself, or sleight of hand?

Becket   I am touched to see your concern for Norman landowners, my Lord. I do freely admit that most of the serfs who seek sanctuary do so to escape slavery. But I would sacrifice everything, the whole security, the life of the Church, if I thought that hidden among a thousand impostors there was

one single Saxon, sincere in his faith, whom we prevented from
coming to God.

Silence.

Folliot (*smiling*)   The parable of the lost sheep. Very touching.
Never fails. Politics, however is a different matter, as you
yourself have shown us.

Becket   Only when I was a politician. I am no longer a
politician. You wish to bring me into line – for me to be a
good boy. Well I won't be good – not according to your sense
of the word ... I thank your Lordships, the council is
adjourned. My mind is made up. The excommunications stand.
And I will appear at the Court of Justice.

Exit **Bishops**.

The shame weigh less heavy now?

Little Monk   Yes.

Becket   Then stand up straight.

The Court of Justice. The **King** *is trying to spy on the proceedings,
possibly through a curtain. Enter* **Folliot**.

King   What's happening now? I can't see anything.

Folliot   Justice is taking its course, your Majesty. He has been
summoned for the third time. He has not appeared. In a
moment he will be condemned in absentia. The Bishop of
Chichester will go to him and read him the Charter –
repudiating him, absolving us of our vows of obedience,
etcetera. Then it's me. As Bishop of London. I'll accuse him
publicly, referring to him simply as Becket, former Archbishop,
of celebrating a sacrilegious mass at the instigation of the Devil.

King   Isn't that a little heavy-handed?

Folliot   Yes, of course. Nobody's fooled – but it always does
the trick. Then the Assembly will vote and return a verdict of
guilty. It's already drawn up.

King   Is it unanimous?

Folliot   Naturally, we are all Normans. As for the rest – it's
in your Highness's hands. It will merely be a matter of
carrying out whatever sentence you see fit.

King Oh, Thomas.

Folliot Your Majesty, the machine can still be stopped if you wish.

King (*hesitates, then –*) No. Go now.

Enter **Queen** *and* **Queen Mother**.

Queen Is he broken?

King (*heavily*) Yes.

Queen Thank God.

King (*loud*) I forbid you to be happy about it.

Queen Not happy to see your enemy crumble?

King (*bursting out*) Yes, Becket is my enemy, but soul for soul, Madam, before God, that bastard, naked as his mother bore him, is worth a thousand of you, even with your crown, your jewels and your bloody father thrown into the bloody bargain. Yes, Becket attacks me. Yes, Becket betrays me. And yes, I'm having to fight him, and to break him, but at least he gave me something; freely, unasked, he gave me the tiny particle of good which is in me. All you have given me is your picky mediocrity – your endless fussing about your bloodless body, your rights! That's why I forbid you – when he dies – I forbid you to smile.

Queen (*cut to the quick*) I have given you my youth. I have given you children.

King I do not like my children. As for your youth – it was fine at twelve – but now it's a faded flower, pressed between the pages of your prayerbook, a sad souvenir, white and brittle, no sap, no blood. Throw it away, chuck it on the fire. Get older – perhaps bigotry and bitterness will give you a bit of character. Your belly was a barren ditch which duty made me sluice from time to time. But you have never been my wife. And Becket was my friend, my active, living friend. Every sinew coursing with life and generosity and strength. Oh Thomas.

Queen Mother And what of me, my son – have I also given you nothing?

King (*nicer now*) Yes, my life. So thank you, Madam, for that. But afterwards I only caught the odd fleeting glimpse of you, in the corridor, off to a ball, or in crown and ermine ten

minutes before some ceremony, which I was obliged to be by
your side. My principal memory is of always being alone. No
one on this earth has ever *loved* me. No one but Becket.

Queen Mother   Very well then, re-call him, pardon him, if
you love him so much – give him back all his power. Do
something!

King   I am. I'm learning to be alone again. It seems a trick
you never forget.

Enter a **Page**, *breathless.*

Very well, where are we up to now?

Page   My Lord. Thomas à Becket – just as he was no longer
expected – suddenly appeared. Looking haggard and ill, in full
Archbishop's dress with the heavy cross of silver which he
carried himself. He slowly crossed the hall and no one dared to
stop him. As Robert of Leicester, who was to pronounce his
sentence, began the sacred proclamation, Becket stopped him
with a wave of his hand, forbidding him in the name of God,
to pass judgement on his own Spiritual Father – and saying he
would be answerable only to the Holy See. Then he walked
back through the speechless crowd, which parted for him as he
went . . .

King (*overjoyed*)   Well played Thomas! One point to you. (*Stern.*)
What about my barons?

Page   They reached for their swords, crying 'Traitor, perjurer,
arrest him. Wretch, hear your sentence'. But no one dared to
move or touch the sacred ornaments.

King   Fools, I'm surrounded by fools. And the only clever
man in the kingdom is my enemy.

Page   At the threshold, he calmly turned and looked at them
all with a long, cold stare. They were furious, baying for his
blood, but impotent.

King (*jubilant*)   So he said that not so long ago he could have
fought them man to man, but that was no longer in his power
– but not to forget that fact. He could beat them all, thrash
the lot of them. With the mace, the lance, the sword, any way
he wanted.

Page   And his gaze was so icy, so ironic that, although he
had no weapon save his simple curate's staff, one by one, they
fell silent. Then, and only then, did he slowly turn and leave.

They say that at his lodgings he has invited all the poor of the town to join him for dinner.

King (*now darker*)   What of my man whom I sent to pulverise him? What of Gilbert Folliot, Bishop of London?

Page   He cursed and raged and swore in apoplexy, seeking to incite the Assembly to riot. In the end he fainted. He's being seen to.

King *laughs.*

King   That is the funniest thing I've heard ... that is so funny.

Queen Mother   Come tomorrow, the laughter will freeze on your lips, my son. If you do not stop him, Becket will reach the coast by tonight, and seek asylum with the King of France. Then he will jeer at you with impunity from across the water.

Exeunt.

Fade to French court. **King Louis** *with his* **Barons**.

King Louis   Look I'm sorry, but this is France, and as the old song goes, to hell with the King of England.

French Baron 1   Your Majesty may not refuse to see these ambassadors extraordinary.

King Louis   Extraordinary, ordinary or downright boring, I'm at home to all of them. I have to see ambassadors, alas, it goes with the job.

French Baron 1   They have been waiting in your Majesty's antechamber for half an hour now.

King Louis   Let them wait – that's *their* job. I know what they're after anyway.

French Baron 2   Extradition of criminal subjects is a courtesy for all crowned heads.

King Louis   That may be. But my courtesy doesn't extend beyond the interests of France. And it is in the interests of France to make life as difficult as possible for England. God knows they do the same for us. The Archbishop is a thorn in Henry's side, so long live the Archbishop. Plus, I actually like the fellow.

French Baron 1   Allow me, you Majesty, to introduce two ambassadors extraordinary sent by his Majesty Henry of England. His Grace the Bishop of London and the Earl of Arundel.

King Louis   My Lord, my friend, I salute you. I still remember your skill at the tournament at Calais. Are you still such a wizard with the lance?

Earl of Arundel   I trust so, Sire.

King Louis   Let us hope that now the difficulties between our two kingdoms have been, how shall I put it, ironed out, such gentlemanly peace-like pursuits may be resumed, in the spirit of friendship. And that we may again have the pleasure of seeing your prowess . . .

Folliot *is slowly unrolling a parchment.*

King Louis   My Lord Bishop, I see you have a little something from your master. Read it, we will listen . . .

Folliot (*bows, reads*)   To my Lord and friend, Louis, King of the French: Henry King of England, Duke of Aquitaine, Count of Anjou, wishes to inform your Majesty that Thomas, former Archbishop of Canterbury, after a public trial, before a full Assembly of the barons of my realm has been convicted of fraud, of perjury, and of treason against my Royal person. And that as a result he has fled my kingdom, traitorously and with avowed malicious intent. It is therefore my fervent desire and prayer that you should not permit this convicted criminal, nor any of his adherents to sojourn on the soil of your kingdom, nor that any of your subjects should lend my greatest enemy their counsel, succour or support. For I protest that none of your enemies receive such support from myself or my people. I expect you to assist me in this case, to help me to avenge my honour and to chastise my sworn enemy: just as you would wish me to assist you, should the need arise.

Folliot *bows, gives scroll carelessly to* **Louis** *who crumples it carelessly and passes it to a* **Baron**.

King Louis   Sirs, we have listened attentively to our noble cousin's entreaty – our Chancellery will draw up a suitable reply which will be in your hands tomorrow. In the meantime we must confess a mild surprise at your request. We have heard no news – have we? – no, it seems we have not – of the presence of the Archbishop of Canterbury on our soil.

Folliot (*sharply*) Sir, the *former* Archbishop has taken refuge at the abbey at Saint Omer.

King Louis Bishop, we flatter ourselves that there's some vestige of order in this land. If he were here, we would most certainly be informed of the fact.

He indicates that they may leave.

Bring in Thomas à Becket and leave us.

Enter **Thomas** *in a monk's robe. Kneels.*

Please, arise Thomas à Becket. And greet us as befits the Primate of all England. So, a bow I think is sufficient – I *think* this is right, which I return with an almost imperceptible lowering of the head. (*Does so.*) You missed it. Now if the visit were official I would also kiss your ring. But somehow I get the feeling that it is not.

Becket No sir. I am but an exile.

King Louis In France that is also a title worthy of respect.

Becket I fear it is the only one I have to my name. My goods have been seized and divided amongst my enemies. Letters have been sent all over France enjoining various noblemen to seize me. The Bishop of Poitiers, on the mere suspicion of harbouring my person, has been poisoned.

King Louis (*smiling*) All in all, you are a very dangerous individual?

Becket (*also smiling*) So it would seem.

King Louis Good. We rather enjoy danger, Becket. And if France were perpetually cringing before England, the balance of Europe would be upset. No – we will extend our Royal protection as long as you are on our soil.

Becket I thank your Majesty, in all humility. However, I feel I could never buy this protection with any act of disloyalty to my country.

King Louis No, no, you do us wrong. That is, of course, completely understood. After so many years in office, learning on the job, as it were, we know instinctively whom to recruit as our spies or our traiters. So we would not wish to impose. But ... which is a big word in politics, as you well know; but – my only concern is my country and its interests. Those of Heaven I have, alas, to leave to others. So it's entirely possible that in a month, who knows, or a year, I could summon you here and tell you that the balance of power had subtly shifted and that I would, with infinite regret, be obliged to banish you – or simply wrap you up and send you back. Archbishop – I believe you are no stranger to intrigue, to dirty tricks ...

Becket   No Sir, I have done my share. And not so very long ago.

King Louis   You know, I really like you Becket. Mind you, if you had been a French bishop I would have had you clapped in irons and serve you right. However, circumstances being as they are, you have the right to my protection. Do you appreciate frankness, Becket?

Becket   I do indeed, Sir.

King Louis   In that case I'm sure we'll get on. Are you going to visit the Holy Father?

Becket   If your Highness will guarantee me safe conduct.

King Louis   I can and I will – but a word of advice. Between friends. Don't trust him. He'll sell you for thirty pieces of silver. God knows, he needs the money.

We are now in Rome. The **Pope**, *thin. The* **Cardinal**, *swarthy. The whole scene is a bit grubby, considering the sumptuous surroundings.*

Pope   I don't agree at all, Zambelli. Not at all. The plan is flawed. We're not going to sacrifice our honour, not for a measly three thousand silver pieces.

Cardinal   Your holiness – it's not a question of sacrificing our honour, but merely of accepting the sum offered by the King of England and thus buying time. To refuse the money, and to turn him down flat would not benefit the Holy See, nor Thomas à Becket, nor indeed the greater good of the Church. But if we were to accept the money – a tiny sum I agree, but surely meant merely to whet our appetite – it would be seen as a gesture of appeasement on our part, made in the interests of peace in Europe. And this, after all, is our duty is it not?

Pope   It's become embarrassing. Becket has been hanging around in Rome for a month now, waiting for an audience. If we receive him we can hardly also receive this money. It's one or the other.

Cardinal Or, of course, both, your Holiness. The one could be seen to sanction the other. To take the money would exonerate us from any suspicion of complicity or subversion in granting the Archbishop an audience – and seeing the Archbishop would mollify our humiliation at having to accept the money in the first place.

Pope I'd rather not receive him if I can help it. It seems he's rather earnest – you know, sincere. And sincere people depress me on the whole.

Cardinal Sincerity is a ploy like any other, your Holiness. Recognise it for what it is – then it is defused. When circumstances have demanded it, I've even used it myself. It always unsettles one's opponents. Trouble is they sometimes do it back at you – that is when matters get really complicated.

Pope Do you know what Becket has come to ask me?

Cardinal I've no idea, Holy Father.

Pope Zambelli – don't play your little games with me. You're the one who told me in the first place.

Cardinal (*found out*) Oh, sorry, I forgot. Or rather, even as your Holiness was asking the question, I felt that he himself might have forgotten the answer, so I took the chance that . . .

Pope Zambelli, come on. If we run these endless rings round each other, we'll never get anywhere.

Cardinal Sorry, your Holiness. It's a reflex – I do it without thinking.

Pope He has asked me to strip him of the rank and functions of Archbishop. But do you know why he wants this . . . ?

Cardinal (*frank, for once*) Ah . . . yes, your Holiness.

Pope No, you don't! Rappallo told me and Rappallo is your sworn enemy.

Cardinal That's true, but I have a spy in Rappallo's palace.

Pope (*winks*) Ah yes, you mean Culograti.

Cardinal No. Culograti's function is that Rappallo should think he's a spy. But I have someone else spying on Culograti. So the real spy is spying on the spy, but the spy's spy is . . .

Pope Enough! Becket claims that his nomination and election

were rigged. And thus that the honour of God of which he
seems to be the self-appointed guardian – does not allow him
to bear this title which was criminally acquired. He wishes
merely to be a simple priest.

Cardinal Is there no end to his ambition?

Pope Nevertheless, he is no fool – he realises his position
and his functions are his only safeguard against the King's
wrath. Were he not Archbishop, I would not put much value
on his life.

Cardinal (*thoughtfully*) He is playing a very clever game. But
we have a great advantage, Holiness. We haven't the faintest
idea what to do. No, hear me out. Total uncertainty of
intention often gives one astonishing freedom for manoeuvre.
(*Thinks.*) Ah, I have it, Holiness, a plan, a *combinazione*. Your
Holiness believes him – pretends to believe him – receives him,
agrees with him, agrees that he would be relieved of his post.
You perform the ceremony. But then, as recompense for his
zeal in defending the Church in England, or some such, you
re-appoint him Archbishop, only this time it's perfectly legal
and above board. Thus the threat is dissipated – you score a
point against Becket – you also score one against the King.

Pope It's a dangerous game. The King has a long arm.

Cardinal Not as long as that of Becket's protector, the King
of France – at least for the moment. So our policy should
consist of measuring those two arms at regular intervals. Plus
we can cover ourselves. It's simple. We can send secret letters
to the English court explaining that the new nomination is
merely a formality and that we have in truth repealed the
excommunications pronounced by Becket, but at the same time
we can warn Becket of the existence of these secret letters,
swearing him to secrecy, making it clear to him that they are
without weight and meaningless.

Pope (*who is getting interested*) Then there's no point in making
them secret in the first place?

Cardinal Oh, but there is – because then we may proceed
to manoeuvre as if neither party knew the contents of the
letters – whereas, in reality, we will have made sure that both
parties do. The important thing for us is to know that they
don't know that we know that they know. A child of ten would
understand that.

Pope   That's all very well, but whether he's Archbishop or not, what are we to do with Becket?

Cardinal   Oh, that's easy. Put him in a monastery somewhere. A French one, we mustn't forget Louis' protection. With the Cistercians in Pontigny, say. Yes, that's perfect – they have a very strict regime. That'll do the old reprobate good. Let him experience poverty at first hand.

Pope   This is good advice, Zambelli. Bread and water and prayers are the surest cure for too much sincerity. I have one last question.

Cardinal   Holiness?

Pope   Why is it in your interest to give me such good advice . . . ?

Cardinal *is slightly embarrassed.*

Fade.

We are now in **Becket***'s cell. Empty, save a wooden cross –* **Becket** *is praying. The* **Little Monk** *is in the corner, toying with a knife.*

Becket   Yes, that would be simple enough. Too simple perhaps. Saintliness is also a temptation. Father in Heaven – it's so hard to get an answer from you. Praying to you is something new to me. But I cannot believe that those more worthy than I, who have been on speaking terms with you for years and years, find it any easier to comprehend your Grand Design. It's all so new to me – I'm a beginner – a first-year student. When I studied Latin at school – I made such ridiculous mistakes, my teacher, the old priest, would howl with laughter. And thus I learned. But I don't think I can learn your language in quite the same way – there isn't a grammar, a lexicon, a book of idioms. I'm sure the hardened sinner, who suddenly one day falls to his knees and splutters your name in his astonishment – I'm sure he hears your voice straight away – clear and simple. And I'm sure he understands. I have served you like a dilettante. I still take delight in you. And for a long time, my delight, my pleasure has embarrassed me. This life once seemed the proper road to you – but now I understand their hair-shirts, their fasting, being summoned by bells at all hours of day and night, summoned to meet you on a slab of ice-cold marble, brutalised in your service. All this seems to me to be merely a safety-net to catch the weak of purpose. I now know that in power, in luxury, even in the pleasures of the flesh, I will never cease to speak to you. You are also the God of the rich man, of the happy man and that, Father, seems to show the true depth of your justice. You do not spurn the man who was born with everything. You have not forsaken him, abandoned him to the snare of affluence. And who knows, perhaps he is the true lost sheep ... the poor, the misshapen have all the advantages from birth. They overflow with your essence. You are their insurance policy – and their poverty is their premium. But sometimes, I think, come the Day of Judgement, their proud heads will be bowed as low, lower even than the high and mighty.

For your order, which we mistake for justice, is not *just*, it's more unknowable, deeper than that – will punish them equally – you are the impartial schoolmaster, strict, but fair, who beats the fat rumps of kings and the wizened flesh of the poor with equal vigour. For the differences between them, which dazzle us and blind us, what are they to you? Beneath the crown, beneath the grime, you perceive the same pride, the same vanity, the same petty smugness. My Lord, my Father, now I see that you wished to tempt me – to tempt me with the mortification of the flesh – the hair-shirt, the perpetual prayer, the winter's cold we gladly bear – quite absurd – the empty cell, the solitude. A life of service, of self-denial – of nothingness. It would be so simple to buy you at so cheap a price. I will leave this sanctuary – where you are so closely guarded and cosseted. And I will find you in the world. I will take up my mitre, my golden vestments, my silver cross and I will return to the battlefield to fight with the weapon with which you have seen fit to arm me. It was your will that I should be Primate of all England – a simple pawn who dares to stand up against the King. I will return to my place, to my rank and resume the game. Let the world accuse me of pride – I will return to perform what I believe to be my life's work. My purpose on this earth. As for the rest – may your will be done.

He makes the sign of the cross. The **Little Monk** *is still playing with his knife. Suddenly, he takes it – throws it down – it sticks, quivering in the floor.* **Becket** *turns away.*

Curtain.

Act Four

Same cell. **Becket**, **Father Superior** *and two* **Monks**.

Father Superior   You took your refuge here – you honoured us with your choice. So God forbid you should think that we should influence you in any way. However . . .

Becket (*smiles*)   However . . .

Father Superior   This is merely by way of a friendly warning – to better inspire your judgement, so you may proceed with the proper caution.

Becket   One can be too cautious. We are on French soil – I have the King's protection.

Father Superior   The Cistercian order is based here, my son. But it is an international concern – we have considerable possessions abroad, as I am sure you know, in England, Normandy, in Anjou, in Aquitaine.

Becket   Ah yes, my Lord Abbot – and how hard it is to protect God's honour when one has such considerable possessions. Let me list mine – a clean shirt, and a change of linen. I've been packed for a while – do not worry, I am leaving here today.

Father Superior   And it is quite a relief my son, that this difficult decision is one you have taken for yourself.

Becket (*rather arrogantly*)   Do not call me your son, Father. His Holiness has re-appointed me Archbishop, Primate of the English Church – I was happy to accept that honour. As I embark on this uncertain journey, it is I who should bless you.

He holds out his ring to be kissed, **Father Superior** *does so with a grimace.*

(*To* **Little Monk**.)   Come on, little chap. Don't forget your knife. We may need it.

The court of **King Louis**.

King Louis   Well I told you intrigue was a messy business. And now, guess what? England and France seem to be the best of friends. Or to put it more precisely, it is now considerably to our advantage to settle our differences with the

Holy Emperor. So, not wishing to expose my rear, as it were, or fight on two fronts at once, I require a truce with Henry of England, before marching to the east. There is of course a price to pay – the King has sent me the bill – and you, not unnaturally, are on it. Indeed, you have pride of place – his other demands are negligible. Strange man. His best policy would be to profit from the Emperor's aggression and seal the trap – but he has sacrificed this opportunity – quite deliberately – for the pleasure of seeing you banished. Does he really hate you that much?

Becket   Your Majesty, I believe that he can never forgive me for having preferred God's love to his.

King Louis   Your King is not doing his job, Archbishop. Passion is clouding his judgement. But there we have it. He's chosen to score a point off you and let me off the hook. I will do as he wishes – though not without a certain sense of shame. Where will you go?

Becket   I am a shepherd who has neglected his flock. His Holiness has honoured me by re-appointing me Archbishop. I will return to England. My mind was already made up.

King Louis   So martyrdom is to your taste? You disappoint me; I had always credited you with much more sense.

Becket   Where's the sense in going begging on the highways and byways of Europe, looking for a place where my carcass could be safe? The honour of God and commonsense – which for once seem to coincide – dictate my course of action. Rather than be struck down by the roadside by an unseen hand, I will go to my death – if that is to be my fate – amongst my flock, in my cathedral. There is no place more fitting.

King Louis   And I'm sure you're right. Dammit, it's such a bore being King, when one meets a man as astonishing as you . . . you were born on the wrong side of the Channel. No, then you'd have been a thorn in my side, Becket. The Honour of God is a heavy burden to bear. No – I'm fond of you – probably too fond of you. So let me indulge myself, allow me a moment of humanity. Let me try something even at the risk of your master doubling his demands. After all, banishing you costs me nothing, an ounce or two of honour, nothing more. I'm meeting Henry's son, to discuss our treaty. I will try to convince him that the two of you should settle your differences.

Would you agree to talk to him?

Becket My Lord, ever since our separation, I have never *stopped* talking to him.

Darkness. Trumpets. Two **Guards** *watch a distant plain.*

Guard 1 Open your eyes – have a good long look. You'll never see the like again. This is history in the making.

Guard 2 Will it be long in the making? It's freezing.

Guard 1 At least we're sheltered – out there on the plain – *they're* freezing.

Guard 2 Archbishop's not bad on a horse. Look at him – not bad at all.

Guard 1 Before he was Archbishop he was a champion – won all the tournaments.

Guard 2 (*watching*) There they go. They're both there – alone. What'll they say, d'you think?

Guard 1 They're not like us. They're not going to exchange family news – they're not going to talk about their chilblains. The fate of the world hangs in the balance out there. What they'll say, we wouldn't understand it. Probably not even the words they use . . .

Empty plain. Cold winter wind blows throughout this scene. **King** *and* **Becket** *face each other in silence.*

King You're older, Thomas.

Becket So are you, your Highness. Aren't you cold?

King Yes, I'm freezing to death. All right for you though isn't it? You're in your element. Barefoot as well, I can't help noticing.

Becket (*smiling*) Yes. My latest affectation.

King Even with these fur boots I've got terrible chilblains. Haven't you?

Becket Yes, of course.

King And I suppose you're offering yours to God?

Becket I have better things to offer.

King Look, if we carry on like this we'll end up arguing. Let's talk about something else. Something less important. You know my son's fourteen now? He's of age.

Becket Is he any nicer?

King He's a little idiot – as sly and sulky as his mother. Never get married, Becket.

Becket The matter is rather out of my hands now. Your Majesty saw to that. He had me ordained.

King Don't start all that. Not yet. Let's talk about something else.

Becket Has your Highness been out hunting a lot?

King Every day. And it's no fun any more!

Becket With new hawks?

King Best that money can buy. They don't fly straight.

Becket And your horses?

King The Sultan sent me four superb stallions, magnificent beasts, on the tenth anniversary of my accession. No one can ride them – they throw everybody off.

Becket I'd like to see that one day.

King They'd throw you off as well. Then we'd see your bum under your cassock. At least I hope so. Then we might at least get a laugh out of you.

Becket You know what I miss most of all, your Highness? The horses.

King Not the women?

Becket I don't think so.

King Hypocrite. You became a priest, you became a hypocrite. Did you love her – did you love Gwendoline?

Becket I don't remember.

King You did! You loved her! That's the only way I can explain it all.

Becket No, no my Prince, in all conscience, I did not love her.

King Well then, you've never loved anything. And that's even worse. Why did you call me your Prince, like you used to?

Becket Because you will always be my Prince.

King Then why are you hurting me so much?

Becket Let's talk about something else.

King Well, what about? I'm cold.

Becket I've always told you that you fight fire with fire, and cold with cold. So strip naked every morning and wash with cold water.

King I used to, when you were there to help. Nowadays I don't wash at all. I stink like a pig.

Becket I heard.

King (*shouts suddenly*) Becket – I'm so bored!

Becket My Prince. I'd love so much to be able to help you.

King What are you waiting for? I'm going mad.

Becket I'm waiting for the honour of God and the honour of the King to become one and the same.

King You'll wait a long time.

Becket Yes. I feel I will.

Silence. Wind.

King If there's nothing else to say, I'm going to go and get warm.

Becket There's everything to say. We will not get this chance again.

King Well make it quick. Otherwise we'll freeze to death, two frozen statues, stuck here for all eternity. I am your King, you owe me the first move – I can forget many things, but not that I am King – you taught me that.

Becket And never forget it. Not even face to face with God. He has given you your work. Steer the ship.

King And what's yours?

Becket To resist with all my might, when I see you steering against the wind.

King   One is always steering against the wind. God and the King, working together? It never happens, except in fairy stories. No, nine times out of ten there's a head-on wind to deal with. So you need someone to keep watch.

Becket   And someone else to cope with the irrational whims of the wind – and of God. Two jobs – to be shared. Unfortunately, the sharing fell on us, and we were friends.

King   The King of France – and I still don't see what's in it for him . . . lectured me for three whole days – drove me mad, trying to talk me into seeing you. What good was it your trying to provoke me?

Becket   None.

King   You know that I am King, and must act like a King. What were you hoping to see, my weakness?

Becket   No. That would devastate me.

King   To conquer me then, to overpower me?

Becket   The power is entirely in your hands.

King   What then, talk me round?

Becket   Nor that. I cannot talk you round. All I can do is say 'no'.

King   Oh come on. Let's at least be logical.

Becket   No. Logic is irrelevant. We can only do the tasks we have been given – however absurd the consequences.

King   Ten years! Ten years I've known you. To say 'absurd' – that isn't like you.

Becket   Perhaps I'm not like myself any more.

King (*mocking*)   Oh, you're touched by grace now are you?

Becket   Not in the way you mean. I am not worthy of that.

King   So you feel you're a born-again Saxon do you? Your father's hearty collaboration notwithstanding?

Becket   Not even that.

King   What then?

Becket   That day in that empty cathedral somewhere in France, I felt I'd been given a purpose – for the first time – and in a very simple way. It was a burden that you ordered me to bear. I had no honour, none at all. And then, suddenly, I had. And not the honour I'd ever dreamt of possessing. But something fragile and unfathomable; the honour of God.

King Look – if we're going to talk about it, can we at least be precise. Or use words that I can understand. Otherwise we'll be here all night. They're waiting for us.

Becket I am being precise.

King Then answer my questions precisely. Will you rescind the excommunication of William of Aynesford and the others you have pronounced against my men?

Becket No. It is the only weapon I have to protect what I must protect.

King Very well, will you accept the twelve propositions agreed to by bishops in your absence, particularly concerning criminal protection of fugitive Saxons?

Becket No, your Majesty. I am obliged to look after my flock, and they are of my flock. Nor will I allow others to elect my clergy, nor will I accept that a cleric is answerable to any jurisdiction other than that of the Church. Those are my pastoral duties – I may not give them up. But I will readily accept the other nine articles, in the spirit of appeasement and in respect of the fact that you are, after all, the King. In everything save in the honour of God.

King Very well. So be it. I will help you to protect your God, since it seems to be your new vocation, in memory of the good friend you have been to me. In everything – save in the honour of my kingdom. You may come back to England Thomas.

Becket Thank you my Lord. It was always my intention to come home, and to give myself up. For on English soil, on my native earth, you are my King. And in everything which is on that earth and of this earth, I owe you my obedience.

King Very well, let's go back. We have finished. And now I'm cold.

Becket And so am I.

Silence. Wind.

King (*suddenly*) You never loved me, did you?

Becket Yes. Inasmuch as I was capable of love, yes, I did.

King But then you started to love God? (*Shouts.*) You're still a stubborn bastard aren't you? Answer the question.

Becket I started to love God's honour.

King Go back to England. I give you my word you will go in peace. I hope you don't find you're wrong. I won't come begging to you again. I shouldn't have seen you. It hurt me too much. (*He is racked by a sob.*)

Becket My Prince.

King No – no pity. It disgusts me. Get away. Go to England. Back to England! It's too cold here.

Becket Farewell, my Lord. Will you give me the kiss of peace?

King No. I'm not coming near you. I don't want to see you. No. Later, later. When it doesn't hurt so much.

Becket I will set sail tomorrow. Farewell, my Lord. I know that we will never meet again.

King How dare you say that. After I've given you my Royal word? You call me a traitor?

Becket *looks at him pityingly – then exits. Wind.*

King Thomas!

But **Becket** *does not hear.* **King** *exits.*

Elsewhere on the plain – the **King of France** *and his entourage, watching.*

King Louis It's all over, they have parted.

French Baron 1 He didn't give the kiss of peace.

King Louis Yes, I noticed that. I fear our intercession was fruitless. Fire and water – irreconcilable. He's here.

Enter **Becket**.

Well, Becket.

Becket Thank you, I have made my peace.

King Louis What peace? – with your King or with your soul?

Becket With the King, your Majesty. The peace of my soul depends on another King.

King Louis Don't go back Becket – your King did not give you the kiss of peace. You cannot trust him.

Becket I leave tomorrow – I'm expected.

King Louis Yes, but by whom? (*Trumpets.*) Henry's troops are leaving. This interview is at an end.

Thunder, tempest. Boat tossed hither and thither. **Little Monk** *vomiting* – **Mariner** *trying to steer.*

Becket Go on my boy, cough it all up. That's the way – everything we've been given – we've got to spew it all out.

Mariner Hold tight, Father. It's bad but I've seen worse. But God will hardly drown me with a holy man on board.

Becket You can never be sure. I could be in disguise. So pray, my son, pray.

Mariner No, you pray – I've got a rudder to see to.

Becket You're right. We'll each stick to our jobs. You steer, I'll pray.

Big wave.

Mariner That's the stuff, Father, keep at it. (*Another wave.*) A couple more Hail Marys and we'll be home and dry.

Becket God is at his exercise. Batting us about for fun. He and I both know that this is not how I am meant to die!

The boat plunges down in an enormous wave and disappears. Empty beach. Cold grey dawn.

I think I know where we are. We can get back to Canterbury by the back roads.

Little Monk They'll be expecting us.

Becket No. God has sent the storm to help us. No one will think we set sail in this weather. The assassins will be tucked up in bed.

Little Monk Will we have to die?

Becket Without a doubt. But when and where? It's in God's hands. I hope we can get home, to my church. I feel it may well be there. Are you afraid?

Little Monk Oh, no. As long as we can fight. As long as I
can get one of them before they get me. So if I can kill a
Norman first – just one, I don't ask for much, that would seem
fair to me. I mean, it's good, it's better to die for a reason,
isn't it. So you can say, all right, I'm just a grain of sand, but
one day, eventually, all that sand will clog up the machine and
it'll grind to a halt.

Becket And then?

Little Monk Then we'll build a new machine, bright and
shiny and well-oiled – except it'll be the Normans that get
crushed inside. That's justice isn't it.

Becket Yes. I suppose it is. Right, off we go – we must be
there by morning. Come on, whistle something cheerful – or is
that sinful, considering where we are going? God in his wisdom
sends us His trials, and we must submit to them of course. But
I'm sure he never said anything about not whistling. Come on.

They exit, whistling.

Throne room. **King**, **Prince Henry**, *both* **Queens** *and* **Barons**.
Torches. Shadows.

King Today, for once, I will not be the first to sit down.
(*Bows ironically to his son.*) You Sir, are the King. Go on, sit
down. Take the place of honour – come on, come on.

Queen Mother My son . . .

King I know what I'm doing Madam. Yes you, go on, sit
down. You may be King – but you're still thick as pigshit.

Prince Henry, *startled, sits.*

King Barons of England, behold your second King. For the
good of our dominions I require as it were, a Royal colleague.
Reviving the ancient custom, we have appointed a successor in
our lifetime. We share our responsibilities with him and ask
that you pay him due homage and honour, as you would to
ourself. Take your places gentlemen, I will serve you.

Food arrives. **King** *serves his son.*

Queen (*to* **Prince Henry**) Sit up straight. And now you're
in the place of honour, watch your table manners.

King Sorry about him, he's the best I could do.

Queen Mother My son, that will suffice. This foolish game
is unworthy of you and of us. You insisted on tomorrow's
coronation – against my express wishes – now at least you
must carry it through with honour.

King I'll play my games however I wish. This is of course a
vulgar charade – and quite meaningless if your new King
deigns to step out of line, let me know and I'll give him a
Royal boot up the train – but it has a point and an
appreciable one. It clearly demonstrates to our new Archbishop
Primate that we can quite happily do without him. For if there
is one privilege the Primacy clings to with an iron grip, it's
their right to anoint the Kings of this land. So tomorrow, that
old toad the Archbishop of York – yes, with the authorisation
of the Pope – and yes, I paid for it, of course I paid for it –
will anoint my son in our cathedral. And that'll show him. It's
a ridiculous farce – but it'll show him. God, I'd love to see his
face when he hears about it! Right, that's enough, thick head.
Go back to the end of the table – you're not official till
tomorrow.

Prince Henry *returns scowling to his place.*

King Did you see his face? What a way to look at your
father. You want this to be for real don't you? You can see
yourself already, number three, and daddy stiff in his tomb.
Well, you'll have to wait. Daddy's fine. Daddy is in the best of
health. And don't you forget it!

Queen Mother My son, God knows I have castigated you
enough for your attempts at reconciliation with this filthy
wretch – who has caused us so much pain – and God knows I
sympathise with your undisguised hatred for him. But beware.
Do not be seduced into a reckless gesture, the consequences of
which may be greater than you can tell, merely for the
pleasure of wounding his pride. Henry is still a child, it's true.
But remember you yourself were not much older when you
seized the crown, in direct opposition to my wishes. And
ambitious men, self-seekers and parasites – and find a prince
and you'll find enough of them – may advise him, turn him
against you, and exploit this rash coronation as an excuse to
split your fragile kingdom down the middle. Reflect on what I
say – it is not yet too late.

King We are still here, Madam, and fully in command. I
can't wait to see his face when he sees his most fundamental
privilege whisked away from under his very nose. I conceded a

few points the other day, he is three articles to the good. But I
have the trump card.

Queen Mother You are answerable to history and to a
great nation, not to your whims. You must think of England,
my son. And forget your hatred – or rather your thwarted love
for that man.

King Madam, who gave you the right to meddle in my
affairs? Who I love or hate, what is that to you?

Queen Mother This rancour is neither healthy nor manly.
Your father the King would never have born such a grudge –
he was a man of action. He would have his enemies done to
death and never mention them again. If Thomas à Becket had
been a woman who had deceived you, a woman you still
loved, in what way would your behaviour have been different?
For God's sake, man. Rip him out of your heart, once and for
all. Heavens, if I were a man . . .

King (*humorously*) Well let us all thank God that he gave you
your dugs, Madam. Not that I had anything to do with them.
I was suckled by a peasant girl.

Queen Mother That's probably why you are so oafish, my
son.

Queen Am I not allowed to speak? I have put up with your
mistresses Monsieur, and your whores but must I now put up
with this? I have had enough of this man. He has polluted our
lives. It was almost better when you loved him. I am a
woman. I am your wife, I am your queen. I will not be treated
like this. I will appeal to my father, I will appeal to my uncle,
to all the Kings of Europe. I will appeal to God.

King Why not start with God? I hope you appeal to him
more than you appeal to me. Go on, go to your chapel. Get
out. Get out, both of you. Go to your secret advisers, sit in
your webs of intrigue. Horrible hairy spiders – I hate you – I
stamp on you – you sicken me. And, oh yes, Henry the Third
– here's my boot up your Royal bum. Go to God, go to the
Devil, the whole pack of you. Get out, get out.

General exit, in disorder.

Turns to his **Barons**.

Now gentlemen. Let's get drunk. That's about all you're good
for. Let's get drunk like men. Till we roll off the table and

vomit ourselves into oblivion. My four fools. My fetid stable mates. Warm, comforting, half-witted. (*Taps their skulls.*) Hello? Anyone home? Before he came, I was like you. What did you do to me, Becket? Has he landed? I hear the sea's been too rough to cross the Channel.

Baron 1 He has landed sir. In spite of the sea.

King So God chose not to drown him.

Baron 1 No.

King Was no one there to intercept him? He must have some enemies in England.

Baron 1 We had men waiting. But Englishmen from all the coastal towns formed an armed escort to bring him home to Canterbury.

Baron 3 And the Dean of Oxford told the barons that it would be treason to shed his blood, since you, your Majesty, had promised him safe conduct. Is it true?

King It's true, I did.

Baron 1 All along the road to Canterbury, peasants, workmen, shopkeepers, came out to meet him, cheering him, escorting him from village to village.

Baron 2 Not a single rich man, not a single Norman dared to show his face.

King Only the Saxons?

Baron 1 Vermin; armed with ploughshares, pitchforks. A huge crowd, God knows where they came from, camped around Canterbury to protect him.

Baron 2 I'd no idea there were so many people in England.

King And I brought him up from nothing. Nothing! I loved him. I loved him. Oh God. Enough. Enough.

Baron 1 (*timidly*) Your Majesty . . .

King I can do nothing. I am powerless. Limp, like a girl, as long as he is alive. He amazes me. I stand in wonder – and I am the King. Will no one rid me of him?! A priest, a measly priest – who goads me, torments me. Am I the only coward here? Surely not. Are there no men left in England? Oh my poor heart, it will burst, it will kill me. I cannot bear it.

The **Barons** *rise.*

Oh Thomas!

We are now in Canterbury Cathedral.

The **Little Monk** *is helping* **Becket** *to dress.*

Becket   Come on, hurry up. I want to look my best.

Little Monk   All these laces. You need a girl's hands.

Becket   Men's hands are what we need today. Leave it open. Quick, my cope, my stole.

Little Monk   No. If it's worth doing, it's worth doing well.

Becket   You're right. If it's worth doing, it's worth doing well. Tie up all the laces, every one. God will give us time.

Little Monk *works assiduously, his tongue out.*

Becket   Don't stick your tongue out like that, it's rude.

Little Monk   Will it be today?

Becket   I thinks so. Are you so very set on killing one?

Little Monk   One would be nice. There we are, all done.

Becket   Now my mitre.

Little Monk *goes to find it.*

Becket   Father, you forbade Peter to strike the Roman centurion. I won't be so strict. He has had little enough pleasure on this earth.

Little Monk *returns with mitre.*

Becket   Give me the silver cross. I want to carry it.

Little Monk   God, it's heavy. A well-aimed blow with that and they'd feel it. Let me carry it.

Becket (*stroking his hair*)   You're lucky. It all makes so much sense to you, doesn't it? So Father, I am dressed. Dressed for your feast. Please God, while I am waiting, please don't let me feel any doubt, that . . .

Hefty knocks at door. A **Priest** *enters, terrified.*

Priest   My Lord, my Lord. There are four armed men at the door. They say they must see you, in the King's name. I barricaded the door, but they're breaking it down. They've got battleaxes. Quickly! You must hide in the back of the church – I will have the choir gates closed. They're strong. They'll hold.

Becket But William, it's time for vespers, we don't shut off the choir during vespers, do we? That wouldn't be right, would it?

Priest No, of course, but . . .

Becket Everything must be as it should be. We will not close the choir. Come on my boy, let us go to the altar. We'll be happier there. The ultimate folly, it is time.

We hear the **Barons** *shouting:*

Barons Where is the traitor? Where is the Archbishop? Where is Becket?

A great noise. The door gives way. The four **Barons** *enter, armed to the teeth.* **Becket** *turns calmly to them. Silence.*

Becket I am here and no traitor to the King. Why do you come armed into the House of God? What do you want?

Baron 1 Your death.

Baron 2 You have shamed the King. Fly the country or you are dead.

Becket It is time for the service.

He turns to the altar. The four men advance like automata. The **Little Monk** *brandishing the cross, trying to protect* **Becket**, *is felled by a single blow.*

Becket Not even one. Shame. He would have enjoyed that so much. (*Cries out.*) Oh God, you make everything so hard – your honour is such a burden to bear. (*Softer.*) And poor Henry.

The four men jump on him. He falls. They hack him like butchers. The **Priest** *flees, screaming. Blackout.*

When light returns, the **King**, *naked, is being flogged by four* **Monks**, *as at the opening of the play.*

King Now are you satisfied, Becket? Are we even now? Tit for tat? Is God's honour satisfied?

The four **Monks** *stop, then kneel, heads bowed. Plainly it is a ritual.*

King Thank you, thank you. No, no. It was permitted. I pardon you. Thank you again.

A **Page** *covers the* **King** *in a cloak. Helps him to dress. His* **Barons** *help too. He scowls and growls.*

King Pigs. The Norman bishops just went through the motions. All very symbolic. But those Saxon swine. They really got their money's worth.

Baron 1 (*who has been looking outside*) Sir, it has worked. The Saxon mob outside is screaming. Screaming for you, and for Becket in the same breath. If the Saxons are for us then Prince Henry's followers are done for.

King It seems the honour of God is worth having on your side. Thomas à Becket – our friend Becket – always said so. And he was right. So England's victory over chaos and disorder was thanks to him – and he will, quite properly, henceforth be venerated as a saint. Come gentlemen. The Council will decide how we may best honour his memory, and punish his murderers.

Baron 1 Your Majesty, no one knows who they are.

King Our justice will find them out, Baron, and I will place you in charge of this inquiry. No one must be in any doubt as to our Royal desire to protect the honour of God. And the memory of our dear departed friend.

Organ music. Cheers.

Curtain.

Eurydice

translated by Peter Meyer

Translator's Note

The play was written in 1941, but the absence of food
rationing and the freedom of movement show that it is meant
to take place in the 1930s. The only mention of 'the war' in
the text clearly refers to 1914–18.

This translation was commissioned by BBC Radio to celebrate
the author's seventy-fifth birthday and was first broadcast on 14
July 1985. An earlier translation by Kitty Black was staged in
England as *Point of Departure* and in the USA as *Legend of Lovers*.

This translation of *Eurydice* was first produced on stage at the Chichester Festival Theatre on 6 June 1990 with the following cast:

Orpheus, *a street musician*	William Oxborrow
His Father, *a street musician*	Peter Halliday
Monsieur Henri, *a young man*	Simon McBurney
Waiter	Sidney Malin
Cashier	Suki Turner

Members of a theatrical touring company:

Eurydice	Shirley Henderson
Her Mother	Patricia Brake
Vincent	Ben Aris
Michel	Richard Bates
A Girl	Jane Picking
Second Girl	Trilby James
Stage Manager	Jasper Britton
Dulac	Davyd Harries
Hotel Waiter	Milton Johns
Police Secretary	Richard Bates
Bus Driver	Terry John

Directed by Michael Rudman
Set Designer Penny Brown
Costume Designer Binnie Bowerman
Lighting by Nigel Hollowell-Howard
Sound by William Glancy

Act One	A provincial station buffet. A hot summer afternoon in the 1930s
Act Two	A cheap hotel bedroom in Marseilles, the following evening
Act Three	Same as Act One. Late that night
Act Four	Same as Act Two. The following evening

Act One

A provincial station buffet. Pompous, shabby, dirty. Marble tables, mirrors, threadbare red velvet banquettes. Above her large till, like a Buddha on an altar, the **Cashier**, *with enormous breasts and her hair in a large bun. An old, bald, dignified* **Waiter**. *Stinking dishcloths in shiny metal bowls.*

Before the curtain rises, a violin has been heard. It is **Orpheus**, *playing quietly in a corner next to his* **Father**, *who is absorbed in his sordid accounts in front of two empty glasses. Upstage a solitary customer, a young man in a raincoat, his hat pulled down over his eyes, absorbed in his thoughts. It is* **Monsieur Henri**. *Music for a moment.*

Father (*stops counting and looks at* **Orpheus**) My boy?

Orpheus (*goes on playing*) Father?

Father You don't mean to make your father start begging in a station buffet?

Orpheus I'm playing for myself.

Father (*continuing*) A station buffet with only one customer anyway and he's pretending not to listen. An old trick that. They pretend not to listen, then they pretend not to see the plate when you hold it out in front of them. Well I pretend not to see they're pretending.

Pause, during which **Orpheus** *goes on playing.*

You enjoy playing the violin that much? I wonder you can still like music when you're a musician. When I've scraped away for hours to fools playing cards in a café, all I want to do . . .

Orpheus (*goes on playing*) Is go and play cards in another café.

Father (*surprised*) As it happens, yes. Who told you that?

Orpheus I've suspected it for the last twenty years.

Father Twenty years. You're exaggerating. Twenty years ago I still had talent. How time flies . . . Twenty years ago, in the symphony orchestra days, who'd have told your father he'd finish up twanging a harp round the cafés. Who'd have told him he'd be reduced to begging with a saucer?

Orpheus Every time you got the sack, mother . . .

Father Your mother never loved me. You don't either. All you think about is humiliating me. But don't you believe I'll go on drifting like this for ever. You know I've been offered a job with the harp in the casino at Palavas?

Orpheus Yes, father.

Father And I turned it down because there was no vacancy for you and your violin?

Orpheus Yes, father. At least, no, father.

Father No, father? Why, no, father?

Orpheus You turned it down because you know you play so badly you'd be sacked the next day.

Father (*turning his back, deeply hurt*) I won't even answer that.

Orpheus *has picked up his violin again.*

Father You're going on playing?

Orpheus Yes. Does it bother you?

Father It confuses me. Eight times seven?

Orpheus Fifty-six.

Father You're sure?

Orpheus Yes.

Father Funny. I was hoping it would be sixty-three. Yet eight times nine are seventy-two right away ... You know we've not much money left?

Orpheus Yes.

Father Is that all you can say?

Orpheus Yes, father.

Father You're thinking about my white hair?

Orpheus No, father.

Father Good. I'm used to it. (*Diving back into his addition.*) Eight times seven?

Orpheus Fifty-six.

Father (*bitterly*) Fifty-six ... You shouldn't have to tell me twice! (*He closes his notebook and gives up his accounts.*) We didn't eat badly tonight for twelve francs seventy-five.

Orpheus No, father.

Father You were wrong to take the separate vegetables. If you can, you take a main dish with vegetables included and they'll let you change your separate vegetables for a second dessert. In set price menus it's always better to take two desserts. The Neapolitan slice was a marvel . . . In one sense, you know, we ate better tonight for twelve francs seventy-five than for thirteen fifty à la carte yesterday in Montpellier . . . You'll say they had real napkins instead of paper ones. The place had class, but it was no better in the end. And did you see they charged three francs for the cheese? At least if they'd brought the platter like the really good restaurants . . . Not on your life! Once I was taken to Poccardi's, you know, Boulevard des Italiens. They brought me the platter . . .

Orpheus Yes, father, you've told me a dozen times.

Father (*deeply hurt*) All right, all right. I won't go on.

Orpheus has started playing again. *After a moment his* **Father** *gets bored and decides to stop sulking.*

Father You know, my boy, that tune of yours is very sad.

Orpheus My thoughts are sad too.

Father What are you thinking about?

Orpheus You.

Father Me? Well, well! What are you up to now?

Orpheus (*having stopped playing*) About you and me.

Father Our position's not very bright, I know, but we do what we can, my boy.

Orpheus I'm thinking that since mother died, I follow you around cafés with my violin, I watch you struggle with your sums each night, I listen to you talking about the set price menus, then I go to bed and next morning I get up.

Father When you reach my age, you'll realise that's what life is!

Orpheus And I'm thinking you'd never be able to survive with the harp on your own.

Father (*suddenly worried*) You want to leave me?

Orpheus No. I don't expect I'll ever be able to leave you. I've more talent than you, I'm young and I'm certain life's got something else in store for me. But I couldn't go on living if I knew you were starving somewhere.

Father   It's right, my boy, to think about your father.

Orpheus   It's right, yes, but it's a burden too. Sometimes I dream about what might part us ...

Father   Come now, we get on so well ...

Orpheus   A wonderful job where I'd earn enough to pay you an allowance. But that's a dream. A musician can never earn enough on his own to pay for two rooms, four meals a day.

Father   Oh, I don't need much, you know. A twelve franc seventy-five meal like tonight, coffee, brandy and a three sous cigar and I'd be the happiest man alive. (*A pause. He adds.*) If necessary, I could do without the brandy.

Orpheus (*goes on dreaming*)   Then there's the level-crossing where a train knocks one of us down ...

Father   Steady on, my boy! Which one of us!

Orpheus (*quietly*)   Oh, I don't mind ...

Father (*surprised*)   You're a strange lad. Not me! I don't want to die! Your thoughts are very grim tonight, dear boy. (*He dismisses them with an elegant gesture.*) That rabbit was good. Dammit, you make me laugh. At your age I thought life was wonderful. (*He suddenly eyes the* **Cashier**.) And love? Have you ever thought that love exists?

Orpheus   Love? What do you believe love is? The girls I might meet with you?

Father   Oh, dear boy, no one ever knows where they'll meet love. (*He draws nearer.*) Tell me, I don't look too bald? That cashier's charming. A little buxom maybe. More my taste than yours. How old do you think she is, forty, forty-five?

Orpheus (*smiles sadly and taps him on the shoulder*)   I'm going out on the platform for a moment ... We've an hour before the train goes.

Orpheus *goes out.*

His **Father** *gets up and walks round the* **Cashier**, *who crushes this wretched customer with a look. He suddenly feels ugly, poor and bald; he passes his hand across his bald patch and sadly goes back to collect his instruments before going out.*

Eurydice *enters hurriedly.*

Eurydice Excuse me, was someone playing the violin here?

Father Yes. That was my son. My son, Orpheus.

Eurydice That was a pretty tune he was playing!

The **Father** *bows, flattered, and goes out with his instruments.*
Eurydice's **Mother** *makes a triumphal entry. Boa, feathered hat. She has not stopped growing younger since 1920.*

Mother Eurydice, there you are! … It's so hot … I loathe waiting in railway stations. This tour's so badly organised, as always. That stage manager ought to arrange things so the leads at least don't have to spend their lives waiting for a connection. When you've been in a fury all day in a waiting room, how can you be expected to give your best in the evening?

Eurydice There's only one train, mother, for the leads and everyone else, and it's an hour late because of the storm yesterday. There's nothing the stage manager can do about it.

Mother Oh, you always stand up for idiots!

Waiter *(who has approached them)* Can I get you anything?

Mother Do you think we might?

Eurydice Now you've sat down here in triumph, perhaps we'd better.

Mother Have you a really good peppermint? A peppermint then. In Argentina or Brazil when the heat was overwhelming, I always relied on a peppermint before I went on stage. Sarah – *(Throwing it away.)* Bernhardt – gave me the tip. A peppermint.

Waiter *(to* **Eurydice***)* And … ?

Eurydice A coffee.

Mother Sit up straight. Why aren't you with Michel? He's wandering about like a soul in torment.

Eurydice Don't worry about him.

Mother You shouldn't infuriate the boy like this. He adores you. You should never have had him as a lover in the first place, I told you so at the time. What's done is done. Anyway we all start and finish with actors, all of us. At your age I was prettier than you, I could have been kept by anyone, but I wasted my time with your father ... You see what that's led to ... Sit up straight.

Waiter (*having brought the drinks*) A little ice?

Mother Never, my dear fellow, because of the voice. This peppermint's appalling. I hate the provinces, I hate tours. But all Paris raves about now are little idiots with no breasts who can't speak two lines without drying ... What's that boy been up to, you didn't get in the same compartment when we left Montélimar? My dear Eurydice, a mother's a friend you can confide in, especially when she's your own age, I mean when she's a very young mother. So tell me, what's he been up to ... ?

Eurydice Nothing, mother.

Mother Nothing, mother, that's meaningless. One thing's certain, he adores you. Maybe that's why you don't love him. We're all of us the same. We'll never change. Is that coffee good?

Eurydice You have it, I don't want it.

Mother Thank you. I like it very sweet. Waiter! Another lump of sugar for the young lady. You don't love him any more?

Eurydice Who?

Mother Michel.

Eurydice You're wasting your time, mother.

The **Waiter** *sulkily brings the sugar.*

Mother Thank you my dear fellow. It's covered in fly droppings, that's charming! I've been all round the world in the grandest hotels and I descend to this. Ah well. It'll melt ... (*She drinks.*) I suppose you're right. You must follow your instincts. I've always followed mine like the real theatre animal I am. It's a fact, there's not much of the artist in you. Sit up straight. Ah, there's Vincent, the dear man. He looks exhausted. Be nice to him please. You know I'm very fond of him.

Vincent *enters, silver hair, handsome and soft beneath an energetic manner. Wide gestures, a bitter smile, empty eyes. Hand-kissing.*

Vincent My dear, I've been looking for you everywhere.

Mother I was here with Eurydice.

Vincent That wretched stage manager's completely impossible. Apparently we've over an hour's wait here. We'll have to perform without dinner again. It's becoming a habit. It's infuriating, my dear, one may have the patience of an angel, but it's infuriating.

Eurydice It's not the stage manager's fault there was a storm last night.

Mother I'd like to know why you always stand up for that little fool.

Vincent A minus quantity, the man's a minus quantity ... I can't understand why Dulac keeps anyone so useless in that job. The latest news is he's lost the trunk with all the wigs and beards in it. With a matinée of *Lear* tomorrow! Can you imagine *Lear* without a single beard or wig!

Eurydice He'll find the trunk. It was probably left in Montélimar.

Vincent In that case he may get it back tomorrow, but tonight, *Genevieve's Disgrace* ... Hopeless! He says it doesn't matter because it's a modern play ... But I've warned Dulac, I will not play the Doctor without a goatee.

Waiter (*approaching*) What will you have, sir?

Vincent (*superb*) Nothing, my dear fellow. A glass of water.

The **Waiter** *withdraws, defeated.*

Acts One and Two will get by, but you'll understand, my dear, with the best will in the world, I can't play my big reconciliation scene in Act Three without my goatee. What would I look like?

Eurydice *moves away angrily.*

Mother Where are you going, darling?

Eurydice Outside for a moment, mother.

Eurydice *goes out quickly.* **Vincent** *watches her go, Olympian.*

Vincent (*after she's gone*) You know, my dear, I don't usually get on my high horse, but that girl's attitude to me is, frankly speaking, scandalous.

Mother (*simpering, trying to take his hand*) Pussycat ...

Vincent   Our situation may be delicate, I grant her that – though after all you are free, you're separated from her father – but really she seems to delight in making it worse.

Mother   She's a silly girl. You know she protects that man the way she protects every poor creature, old cats, stray dogs, drunks. God knows why? The thought that you might persuade Dulac to sack him upsets her, that's all.

Vincent   She may be upset, but there are such things as manners.

Mother   That's exactly what she lacks ... the child's good at heart, but she's a little animal.

Michel *enters hurriedly. He's unshaven, gloomy, tense.*

Mother   Oh, hullo, Michel.

Michel   Where's Eurydice?

Mother   She's just gone out.

Michel *goes out.*

Mother (*watching him go*)   Poor boy. He's mad about her. She was very nice to him till recently, but I don't know what's got into her the last few days. It's as though she's looking for something, or waiting ... What for? I don't know ...

Orpheus' *violin can be heard in the distance.*

Mother   What's that idiot up to, scraping away at his violin the whole time? It gets on your nerves.

Vincent   He's waiting for the train.

Mother   That's no reason. Him and the flies ... It's so hot!

The violin draws nearer. They listen. During the following scene **Eurydice** *passes across upstage, as though looking for it.*

Mother (*suddenly, in a different voice*)   You remember the Grand Casino at Ostend ...

Vincent   It was the year they launched the Mexican tango ...

Mother   How handsome you were!

Vincent   At that time I still had side-whiskers ...

Mother   You had such a way with you ... You remember the first day: (*Adopting his voice.*) 'Will you do me the honour of this tango?'

Vincent (*adopting her voice*) 'I can't dance the Mexican tango.'

Mother 'There's nothing easier. I hold you and all you have to do is relax.' The way you said that! ... You took me in your arms, then everything became confused, the look from the old fool who was keeping me, he stayed in his chair, furious, the look from the barman who was pursuing me, he was Corsican, he'd said he'd kill me, the waxed moustaches of the gypsy orchestra, the great mauve irises and pale green hellebores decorating the walls ... Oh, it was delicious! We all wore broderie anglaise that year ... My dress was completely white.

Vincent I'd a yellow carnation in my buttonhole and trousers with a little green and brown check.

Mother When we danced, you held me so tight, the embroidery on my dress was printed red on my skin ... The old idiot noticed, he made a scene, I slapped his face and there I was in the street without a penny. But you'd hired a carriage, it had pink tassels, and we drove beside the sea, the two of us, till evening ...

Vincent Oh, the uncertain, the disturbing first day! We seek each other, explore, conjecture. We don't yet know each other, but we do know it will last a lifetime ...

Mother (*suddenly, in a different tone*) Why did we part after a fortnight?

Vincent I don't know. I can't remember now.

Orpheus *and* **Eurydice** *have entered. He has stopped playing. She is facing him. They look at each other.*

Eurydice That was you playing just now?

Orpheus Yes. That was me.

Eurydice You play so well!

Orpheus Do you think so?

Eurydice What's it called, the tune you were playing?

Orpheus I don't know, I was making it up.

Eurydice (*in spite of herself*) What a pity ...

Orpheus (*smiling*) Why?

Eurydice   I don't know. I'd have liked it to have a name.

*A **Girl** passes along the platform.*

Girl (*sees **Eurydice** and calls*)   Eurydice! There you are!

Eurydice (*continuing to look at **Orpheus***)   Yes.

Girl   I've just seen Michel. He's looking for you.

Girl *goes out.*

Eurydice   Yes. (*Looking at **Orpheus**.*) Your eyes are pale blue.

Orpheus   Yes. I don't know what colour yours are.

Eurydice   They say it depends what I'm thinking.

Orpheus   At this moment they're dark green like deep water by a harbour wall.

Eurydice   They say that's when I'm very happy.

Orpheus   Who's they?

Eurydice   People.

*The **Girl** passes along the platform again.*

Girl (*calling*)   Eurydice!

Eurydice (*without turning round*)   Yes.

Girl   Don't forget Michel!

Eurydice   Yes. (*Asking suddenly.*) Do you think you'll make me very unhappy?

Orpheus (*smiling quietly*)   No, I don't.

Eurydice   It's not that I'm afraid of being unhappy as I am now. No, that hurts, but on the whole it's good. What I'm afraid of is being unhappy and alone when you leave me.

Orpheus   I'll never leave you.

Eurydice   Do you swear that?

Orpheus   Yes.

Eurydice   On my head?

Orpheus (*smiling*)   Yes.

They look at each other.

Eurydice (*suddenly, quietly*) I like it when you smile.

Orpheus You don't smile?

Eurydice Never when I'm happy.

Orpheus I thought you were unhappy.

Eurydice So you don't understand anything? You're a real man? What a business! Oh, we are in trouble, the pair of us, standing here face to face, with everything that's going to happen to us already prepared behind us.

Orpheus You think a lot of things are going to happen to us?

Eurydice (*serious*) Everything. Every single thing that can happen to a man and a woman on earth, one after the other . . .

Orpheus Things that are amusing, nice, terrible.

Eurydice (*quietly*) Shameful, beastly too . . . We're going to be very unhappy.

Orpheus (*taking her in his arms*) What happiness!

Vincent *and the* **Mother**, *who have been dreaming, their heads touching, start to talk quietly.*

Vincent Oh, love, love! You see, my dearest, here on this earth where we are forever shattered, forever deceived, forever hurt, it's a wonderful consolation to know we still have love . . .

Mother My pussycat . . .

Vincent . . . All men are liars, false, gossips, hypocrites; proud or cowardly, despicable or sensual. All women are faithless, artful, vain, inquisitive or depraved. The world is just a bottomless sewer where shapeless beasts writhe and crawl on mountains of mire. But in this world there is one thing holy and sublime; that is the union of two of these imperfect frightful creatures.

Mother Yes, pussycat. I've always loved that play – *One ne badine pas avec l'amour.*

Vincent (*stopping surprised*) Is it? I've played it so often.

Mother Do you remember? You played it that first evening at the Grand Casino in Ostend. I was playing *The Mad Virgin* at the Kursaal, but I was only on in the first act. I came and waited in your dressing room. You arrived, still throbbing with those beautiful words of love you'd just spoken on stage and you loved me there immediately in your Louis Quinze costume . . .

Vincent   Oh, Lucienne, our nights of love! The union of two hearts, two bodies! The moment, the unique moment, when we no longer know if it's our flesh or our soul that's a-quiver . . .

Mother   You know, you've been a marvellous lover, my big bow-wow!

Vincent   And you the most adorable of mistresses!

Mother   I'm crazy, you weren't a lover. You were *the* lover. The inconstant and the faithful, the strong and the tender, the mad. You were love. How you made me suffer . . .

Vincent   Ah, we are often deceived in love, often hurt, often unhappy, Lucienne. But we love. And when we are on the edge of the grave, we turn round to look back and say: 'I have often suffered, sometimes made mistakes, but I have loved. It is I who have lived, not some artificial being created by my pride and my despair.'

Mother (*applauding*)   Bravo, pussycat, bravo!

Vincent   It's the same play again?

Mother   Yes, pussy.

Orpheus *and* **Eurydice** *have been listening, tight against each other, as if terrified.*

Eurydice (*whispering*)   Make them shut up, please, make them shut up.

Orpheus *goes towards them.* **Eurydice** *hides.*

Orpheus   Excuse me, you're certainly not going to understand this. You'll think it strange. Very strange. Well, you must leave.

Vincent   Leave?

Orpheus   Yes.

Vincent   You're closing?

Orpheus   Yes. We're closing for you.

Vincent (*getting up*)   Well, really . . .

Mother (*having also risen*)   He doesn't work here. I recognise him, he's the man who was playing the violin . . .

Orpheus   You must vanish right away. I assure you I'd explain if I could, but I can't. You wouldn't understand. At this moment something very important is happening here.

Mother   The boy's mad!

Vincent   Dammit all, this is insane! This place is open to everyone.

Orpheus   Not any more.

Mother   Oh, this is too much! (*Calling.*) Cashier! Waiter!

Orpheus (*pushing them towards the door*)   No, don't, please. Just go. I'll pay your bill.

Mother   We're not going to be treated like this!

Orpheus   I'm a very peaceful man, very kind, very shy in fact. I assure you I'm shy. Before now I'd never have dared to do this.

Mother   I've never heard of such a thing!

Orpheus   No, no one has. At least I haven't.

Mother (*to* **Vincent**)   You stand there saying nothing?

Vincent   Come along, you can see he's not in a normal condition.

Mother (*disappears, shouting*)   I'll complain to the station master!

The **Mother** *goes out, followed by* **Vincent**.

Eurydice (*emerges from her hiding place*)   Oh, they were so ugly, weren't they? So ugly, so stupid!

Orpheus (*returns towards her, smiling*)   Sh! Don't let's talk about them any more. How everything falls into place, now we're alone! How luminous and simple everything is! I think I'm seeing things for the first time, chandeliers, plants, metal bowls, chairs . . . How charming a chair is! Like an insect, listening to the noise of our footsteps and about to flee with one bound of its four thin legs. Careful! Don't move. Or else, run!

He leaps forward, dragging **Eurydice** *with him.*

. . . Got it! How useful a chair is! We can sit down . . .

He makes her sit down with a ceremoniously comic gesture, then looks at her very sadly.

What I don't understand is why they produced the other one.

Eurydice (*pulls him down and gives him a tiny corner of her chair*) That's for people who don't know each other.

Orpheus (*takes her in his arms and shouts*) I know you! Just now I was playing the violin and you passed by on that platform and I didn't know you ... Now everything's changed! I know you. It's extraordinary. Everything around us has suddenly become extraordinary. Look ... How beautiful the cashier is, with her two huge breasts delicately placed on the marble counter! And the waiter! Those long flat feet in those button boots, that distinguished bald head! And that noble air! So noble ... It really is an extraordinary evening. We were fated to meet. And to meet the noblest waiter in France. A waiter who could have been a mayor, a colonel, a member of the Comédie Française! (*Calling.*) Waiter ...

Waiter (*approaching*) Sir?

Orpheus You are charming.

Waiter But, sir ...

Orpheus Yes, you are. Don't protest. I mean it, and I'm not used to paying compliments. You are charming. This lady and I will always remember you and the cashier. You'll tell her, won't you?

Waiter Yes, sir.

Orpheus Oh, it's so amusing to be alive! I didn't know it was exciting to breathe, to have blood flowing through your veins, muscles that move ...

Eurydice Am I heavy?

Orpheus Oh, no! You're just the right weight to keep me down on earth. A moment ago I was too light, I was floating, bumping into furniture, people. My arms were stretching so far, my fingers dropped things ... It's funny. All the mathematicians were so ignorant when they calculated gravity! I now realise I needed exactly the addition of your weight to be part of this atmosphere ...

Eurydice Oh, darling, you frighten me! At least you're really part of it now? You'll never fly away again?

Orpheus Never.

Eurydice If you left me, what would I do, all alone here on earth, like an idiot. Swear you won't leave me.

Orpheus I swear.

Eurydice Yes, but it's easy to swear like that! I hope you don't intend to leave me! If you want me to be really happy, swear you'll never want to leave me, even in the future, even for one minute, even if the prettiest girl in the world looks at you.

Orpheus I swear that too.

Eurydice (*having suddenly got up*) See how false you are! You swear you won't want to leave me, even if the prettiest girl in the world looks at you. But to know she's looking at you, you must have been looking at her. Oh, I'm so miserable! You've scarcely begun to love me and you're thinking about other women already. Swear you won't even see that silly girl . . .

Orpheus I'll be blind.

Eurydice Even if you don't see her, people are so wicked, they'll rush and tell you, to hurt me. Swear you won't listen to them.

Orpheus I'll be deaf.

Eurydice No, there's something much simpler. Swear now, sincerely, of your own free will, not to please me, swear from now on you'll never think any other woman's pretty . . . Even so-called beauties . . . which doesn't mean anything anyway.

Orpheus I swear.

Eurydice (*distrustful*) Even if she looks like me?

Orpheus Even then. I wouldn't trust her immediately.

Eurydice You're swearing of your own free will?

Orpheus My own free will.

Eurydice Good. Of course it's on my head?

Orpheus On your head.

Eurydice You do know, when you swear on someone's head, that means the other person dies if you don't keep your oath?

Orpheus I do know.

Eurydice (*after thinking for a moment*)   Good. Even so, it's not because, I mean with that angelic air about you, I think you're capable of anything, it's not because you're really thinking: 'I can easily swear on her head. What do I risk? If she dies at the moment I want to leave her, it would really be much better. Death makes parting easy. No scenes, no tears . . .' Oh, I know you!

Orpheus (*smiling*)   Very ingenious, but I didn't think that.

Eurydice   Really? You know, it would be better to tell me right away.

Orpheus   Really.

Eurydice   Swear it.

Orpheus (*raising his hand*)   There!

Eurydice (*approaching*)   Good. Then I'll tell you. I only wanted to test you. We haven't made real oaths. To make a real oath, it's not enough to make a tiny gesture with your hand, a tiny equivocal gesture you can interpret any way you like. You must stretch out your arm, like this, spit on the ground . . . Don't laugh, you know what we're going to do now is serious. Some people say, if you break your word, the other person doesn't just die immediately, he suffers terribly as he dies.

Orpheus (*seriously*)   I'm making a careful note of it.

Eurydice   Good. Now you really know what could happen to me if you tell a lie, even a tiny one. So please, darling, you're going to stretch out your hand and spit on the ground and swear that all you've sworn was true.

Orpheus   I spit, I stretch out my hand, I swear.

Eurydice (*after an immense sigh*)   Good. I believe you. Anyway it's easy to deceive me, I'm very trusting. You're smiling. You're laughing at me?

Orpheus   I'm looking at you. I'm realising I haven't had time to yet.

Eurydice   Am I ugly? Sometimes when I've been crying or I laugh too much, I get a little red mark at the corner of my nose. I'd rather tell you now, so you don't have a nasty surprise later.

Orpheus   I'll make the best of it.

Eurydice And I'm thin. Not as thin as I seem to be, no. Actually I think I've a fairly good figure when I wash. But, well, I'm not the sort of woman you could lean on comfortably.

Orpheus I wasn't expecting to be very comfortable.

Eurydice I can only give you what I have, can't I? So you mustn't imagine things ... I'm stupid too, I can't say anything, so you mustn't rely on me much for conversation.

Orpheus (*smiling*) You're talking all the time.

Eurydice I talk all the time, but I can't reply. Actually that's why I talk all the time, to stop people asking questions. It's my way of being silent. I do what I can. Of course you hate that. It's my luck. You're going to find you don't like anything about me.

Orpheus You're wrong. I like you talking too much. It makes a little noise that's restful.

Eurydice I don't believe it. I'm sure you like mysterious women. The Greta Garbo type. Women six feet tall, with big eyes, big mouths, big hands, who wander around in the woods and smoke all day. I'm not that sort at all. You'll have to say goodbye to all that right away.

Orpheus It's done.

Eurydice Yes, you say that, but I can see your eyes ... (*Throwing herself into his arms.*) Oh, darling, darling, it's too sad not being the sort of girl you like! What do you want me to do? Grow taller? I'll try. I'll do gymnastics. Or acquire a gaunt look? I'll open my eyes wide, I'll use more make-up. I'll try to be melancholy, I'll smoke ...

Orpheus No, don't!

Eurydice Yes, yes, I'll try to be mysterious. Oh, being mysterious isn't very complicated. All you have to do is think of nothing, any woman can do that.

Orpheus You're mad!

Eurydice I shall be, you can rely on that! And sensible too and extravagant and economical; and docile too, like a little odalisque you turn over in bed, or terribly unfair on days you want to be rather unhappy because of me. Oh, but those days, simply don't worry. I'll make it up to you the days when I'm maternal, so maternal I'll be infuriating, days when you've toothache or a boil. And I can be a housewife, a prude, vulgar, ambitious, exciting, dull, for days when there's nothing else to do.

Orpheus You think you'll be able to play all these parts?

Eurydice I'll have to, darling, to keep you, because you'll be desiring every other woman . . .

Orpheus When will you be you? You make me worried.

Eurydice In between. When I've five minutes, I'll manage.

Orpheus It's going to be a dog's life!

Eurydice That's what love is! . . . With dogs, the female has the easy part. She just has to let herself be sniffed at a little and then trot dreamily on for a few yards, pretending not to notice anything. Men are much more complicated.

Orpheus (*pulls her to him, laughing*) I'm going to make you very unhappy!

Eurydice (*snuggling up against him*) Oh, yes! I'll make myself tiny and so easy to please. All you have to do is to let me sleep on your shoulder at night and hold my hand all day . . .

Orpheus I like sleeping on my back across the bed. I like long walks on my own.

Eurydice We'll try to lie across the bed side by side. And on your walks I'll follow just behind you, if you like. Not far. Almost next to you actually! I'll love you so strongly too! And I'll always be so faithful, so faithful . . . Only you'll have to talk to me the whole time, so I shan't have a moment to think of nonsense . . .

Orpheus (*after dreaming for a moment in silence with her in his arms, whispers*) Who are you? I seem to have known you for a long time.

Eurydice Oh, why ask who I am? Who I am, means so little . . .

Orpheus Who are you? It's too late, I know that, I can't leave you now . . . You suddenly loomed up in this station. I stopped playing my violin and now I'm holding you, here in my arms. Who are you?

Eurydice I don't know who you are either. But I don't want to ask. I'm happy. That's enough.

Orpheus   I don't know why I'm suddenly afraid things may go wrong.

The **Girl** *passes along the platform.*

Girl   Oh! You're still there? Michel's waiting for you in the third-class waiting room. If you don't want another row, my dear, you'd really better run along . . .

Girl *goes out.*

Orpheus (*having released* **Eurydice**)   Who is this Michel?

Eurydice (*quickly*)   Nobody, darling.

Orpheus   That's the third time they've come to say he's looking for you.

Eurydice   He's a boy in the company. Nobody. He's looking for me. All right, he's looking for me. He's probably got something to tell me.

Orpheus   Who is this Michel?

Eurydice (*shouting*)   I don't love him, darling, I've never loved him.

Orpheus   He is your lover?

Eurydice   Oh, you know, it's so easy to say something. The same word can mean so many things. But I'd rather tell you the truth now, of my own free will. Everything must be open between us. Yes, he is my lover.

Orpheus *falls back a little.*

Eurydice   Oh, don't draw away. I do so wish I could say: 'I'm a young girl, I've been waiting for you. Your hand will be the first to touch me.' I do wish I could say that. I know it's silly, but it seems that's how it really is . . .

Orpheus   Has he been your lover for long?

Eurydice   I don't know. Six months maybe. I've never loved him.

Orpheus   Then why?

Eurydice   Why? Oh, don't ask questions. When we still don't know each other very well, still don't know all about each other, questions, more than words, are terrible weapons . . .

Orpheus Why? I want to know.

Eurydice Why? Well, he was unhappy, I was tired. I was lonely. He loved me.

Orpheus And before?

Eurydice Before, darling?

Orpheus Before him.

Eurydice Before him?

Orpheus You haven't had another lover?

Eurydice (*after an imperceptible hesitation*) No. Never.

Orpheus Then *he* taught you how to make love. Tell me. Why do you stand there saying nothing? You said you wanted only the truth between us.

Eurydice (*shouting desperately*) Yes, darling, but I'm trying to think what would hurt you least! ... If it's him and you may meet him, or someone else a long time ago you'll never meet ...

Orpheus It's not a question of knowing what will hurt me least! It's a question of knowing the truth!

Eurydice All right, when I was still very young, a man, a stranger, took me almost by force ... It lasted a few weeks, then he went away.

Orpheus You loved him?

Eurydice I suffered, I was frightened, I was ashamed.

Orpheus (*after a pause*) That's all?

Eurydice Yes, darling. You see, it was very silly, very pitiful, but quite simple.

Orpheus (*dully*) I'll try never to think of them.

Eurydice Yes, darling.

Orpheus I'll try never to imagine their face next to yours, their eyes on you, their hands on you.

Eurydice Yes, darling.

Orpheus I'll try not to think they've ever held you in their arms. (*He has taken her in his arms again.*) There, everything's starting all over again. *I'm* holding you.

Eurydice (*very quietly*) It's nice in your arms. Like a little house, tightly shuttered in the middle of the world; a little house, which no one can ever enter now.

Orpheus *bends over her.*

Eurydice Here?

Orpheus Here. I'm ashamed the whole time when people look at me, but now I want this place to be crowded ... It will be a wonderful wedding! Our witnesses will be the cashier, the noblest waiter in France, and a modest little man in a raincoat, who's pretending not to see us, but I'm sure he does ... (*He kisses her.*)

M. Henri *who has remained silent upstage since the beginning of the play, looks at them, rises quietly and comes and leans against a pillar near them. They don't see him.*

Eurydice (*suddenly releasing herself*) Now you must leave me. There's something I have to do. No, don't ask questions. Go outside for a moment, I'll call you ... (*She accompanies* **Orpheus** *upstage.*)

Orpheus *goes out.* **Eurydice** *goes quickly to the door which is wide open onto the platform. She stops and remains for a moment in the doorway, not moving. We can feel she's looking at someone invisible who is also looking at her.*

Eurydice (*suddenly, sharply*) Come in.

Michel *comes in slowly, never taking his eyes off her. He stops in the doorway.*

Eurydice You saw? I kissed him. I love him. What do you want?

Michel Who is he?

Eurydice I don't know.

Michel You're mad.

Eurydice Yes, I'm mad.

Michel For the last week you've been running away from me.

Eurydice For the last week I've been running away from you, yes; but not because of him, I've known him for an hour.

Michel *looks at her and her look terrifies him.*

Michel (*drawing back*)   What are you going to tell me?

Eurydice   You know.

Michel   You know I can't live without you.

Eurydice   Yes. I love him.

Michel   You know I'd rather die straight away, than go on with this life alone, now I've had you with me. I'm not asking for anything, just not to be completely alone ...

Eurydice   I love him.

Michel   Can't you think of anything else to say?

Eurydice (*quietly, pitilessly*)   I love him.

Michel (*going out suddenly*)   All right, you asked for it.

Michel *goes out.*

Eurydice (*running after him*)   Listen, try to understand. I like you, but I love him ...

Eurydice *and* **Michel** *have gone out.* **M. Henri** *watches them go, then slowly goes out after them. The stage remains empty for a moment. A bell rings, then a train whistles in the distance.* **Orpheus** *has come in slowly and watches* **Michel** *and* **Eurydice** *go out. His* **Father** *bursts in behind him with his harp, while the train whistles and the bell asserts itself.*

Father   The train's been announced! Platform two ... Come on. (*He takes a step, then looks thoughtful.*) Hm, have you paid? I think you ordered the drinks.

Orpheus (*quietly, not looking him in the face*)   I'm not coming, father.

Father   Why do you always wait till the last moment? The train will be here in two minutes and we have to use the tunnel. With the harp we've only just enough time.

Orpheus   I'm not taking this train.

Father   Not taking this train? Well, why not, if you please? If we want to be in Palavas this evening, it's the only one.

Orpheus   Then take it. I'm not going.

Father   That's a new idea, dammit! What's got into you?

Orpheus   Look, father. I'm fond of you. I know you need me and this is going to be terrible, but it had to happen one day. I'm leaving you . . .

Father (*acting as though he's thunderstruck*)   What did you say?

Orpheus (*shouting suddenly*)   You understood! Don't make me say it again to give you a chance of a pseudo-pathetic little scene! Don't hold your breath to look pale; don't start pretending to tremble and tear your hair out! I know every one of your little tricks. They were okay when I was a kid, but they don't work any more. (*Repeating in a whisper.*) I'm leaving you, father.

Father (*changes tactics and suddenly drapes himself in an exaggerated dignity*)   I refuse to listen to you, my boy. You've taken leave of your senses. Come along.

Orpheus   Dignity's no use either. I tell you I know all your tricks.

Father (*deeply hurt*)   Forget my white hair, forget my white hair! I'm used to this . . . I tell you again I refuse to listen to you. That's clear, isn't it?

Orpheus   You've got to listen, because you've only two minutes to understand. That's your train whistling.

His **Father** *laughs nobly.*

No noble laughs, please. Listen! You've got to take this train on your own. It's your only chance to get to Palavas in time to take that harpist's job you've been offered.

Father (*shrilly*)   I refused the job! I refused for your sake!

Orpheus   You can say you've thought it over, you're leaving me and you accept. Tortoni may not have found another harpist. He's a friend of yours. He'll give you preference.

Father (*bitterly*)   Ah, friends, children, all one holds sacred! One fine day they vanish with the wind. I've discovered that to my cost. Tortoni's friendship! Ha! (*He laughs bitterly.*)

Orpheus   You think he won't give you the job?

Father   I'm sure he won't!

Orpheus   He offered it to you . . .

Father   He offered it to me, but I refused it. He drank the shame to the dregs. Don't forget he's Italian. They never forget.

Orpheus   All the same do take this train. As soon as you've gone, I'll ring the casino, I promise I'll persuade him to forget you refused.

Father (*shouting in a voice one would never suspect in this feeble body*)   Never!

Orpheus   Don't shout! He's a decent fellow, I'm sure he'll listen.

Father   Never, do you hear! Your father will never stoop so low!

Orpheus   I'm doing the stooping! I'll say it's my fault.

Father   No, no!

The train whistles, much nearer.

(*Frantically seizing his parcels.*) The train, the train! Orpheus, don't continue this painful scene. I can't understand one word of it. Come with me, you can explain on the journey.

Orpheus   I can't go, father. I may join you later.

Father   Why join me, for God's sake? We've two tickets.

The train whistles.

Orpheus   I'll phone right away. (*Going to the* **Cashier**.) Can I phone from here?

Father (*catching him*)   Listen, my boy, don't ring him. I'd rather tell you right away, that harpist's job . . .

Orpheus   Yes.

Father   Well, he never offered it me.

Orpheus   What?

Father   I said that to make you think better of me. I got wind of the job. I begged him to take me. He refused.

Orpheus (*after a short pause*)   Oh, all right . . . (*Quietly.*) I thought you could get that job. It tied things up neatly.

A pause.

Father (*quietly*)   I'm an old man . . .

The train whistles again.

Orpheus (*suddenly, urgently*)   Take this train all the same, please, father. Go to Palavas, there are cafés there, it's the season, you'll earn a living, I promise you.

Father With just a harp ... you're joking!

Orpheus What impressed people was the harp. You hardly ever see one. Every beggar plays the violin in cafés. The harp, you often said so yourself, that's what made us seem like artists.

Father Yes, but you played the violin so well and women thought you young and nice, so they nudged their men to make them put twenty sous in the plate. For me on my own they'd never nudge anyone.

Orpheus (*trying to laugh*) Yes, father, yes, more mature women! You know you're an old Don Juan.

Father (*after a look at the* **Cashier** *who humiliated him a moment ago, caressing his bald head*) Oh, between ourselves an old Don Juan for maids in cheap lodging houses ... ugly ones at that.

Orpheus You're exaggerating, father, you still have a lot of success!

Father I tell you these stories, but it doesn't always happen exactly how I say ... Besides, I've never told you, my boy, I brought you up, I had my pride as a father, but I don't know if you've ever noticed, I ... I play the harp very badly.

A terrible silence.

Orpheus (*lowers his head, unable to help smiling a little*) One can't help noticing, father.

Father You see, you say so yourself.

Another silence. The train whistles, very near.

Orpheus (*suddenly shaking him gently*) Father, there's nothing more I can do for you. If I were rich, I'd give you money. I haven't any. Go and take this train, keep all we have, and good luck. There's nothing else I can say.

Father A moment ago you said you could never leave me!

Orpheus A moment ago yes. Now I can.

The train is heard entering the station.

There's your train. Hurry up, take the harp.

Father (*still resisting*) You've met someone, that's it?

Orpheus   Yes, father.

Father   The girl who came and asked me who was playing the violin just now, that's it?

Orpheus (*on his knees in front of the suitcases*) Yes, father. (*He takes things from one case and puts them in the other.*)

Father   I've talked to these people. She's an actress: a third-rate company, playing in fourth-rate theatres. She'll take every penny you've got.

Orpheus   Yes, father. Hurry up . . .

Father (*also on his knees, searching in the cases*)   I might have found you a wonderful girl, like a statue, first prize at the Marseilles Conservatoire, a Greek profile. A pianist! We'd have been a trio! I'd have learnt the cello . . . I would never have believed you could do such a thing!

Orpheus   Nor would I, father, hurry up.

Father   Let my curses be upon your head! You'll pay for this!

Orpheus   Yes, father.

Father (*rising*)   Laugh, go on, laugh! I've my ticket, I can earn a living. You'll have nothing!

Orpheus (*laughs in spite of himself and takes his* **Father** *by the shoulders*)   Father, my old father, my terrible father. I'm fond of you, you know, but there's nothing more I can do for you.

Loudspeaker (*outside*)   The train at platform two is now leaving for Beziers, Montpellier, Sète and Palavas. Close the doors, please.

Orpheus   Quick, you'll miss it. You've the harp, the big suitcase? I've two hundred francs on me, keep all the rest.

Father   Oh, no need to be generous, there's not all that much.

Loudspeaker   The train at platform two is now leaving for Beziers, Montpellier, Sète and Palavas. Close the doors, please.

Father (*suddenly*)   Do you think I can cash your ticket?

Orpheus (*embracing him*)   I'm happy, father. I love her. I'll write to you. You should be a little glad I'm happy. I do so want to live!

Father (*loading up*) I'll never be able to carry all this myself.

Orpheus I'll help you, you can get a porter.

Father (*in the doorway, shouting like a ridiculous curse, which makes him drop some of his parcels*) You're leaving your father for a girl! She may not even love you!

Orpheus (*also shouting as he follows him*) I'm happy, father!

Voices (*off*) Close the doors! Close the doors! Close the doors!

Father (*before going out*) I shall die!

Orpheus (*pushing him*) Quick, father, quick!

Orpheus and his **Father** *go out. Whistles, noise of carriage doors, smoke. Immediately the train can be heard starting.*

Eurydice *enters with a small suitcase. She goes and sits in a corner, very small.* **Orpheus** *enters. He goes to her. She looks at him.*

Orpheus There, it's done.

Eurydice (*oddly*) Me too, it's done.

Orpheus (*lowering his head*) I apologise. He's rather ridiculous. It was my father.

Eurydice You mustn't apologise to me. That woman gurgling about love just now was my mother. I didn't dare tell you.

They are facing each other. They smile quietly.

Orpheus I'm glad you're ashamed too. It's almost as if we were little brothers.

Eurydice (*smiling*) I can see you as a tiny boy, trailing your violin along behind you ...

Orpheus He had a job in an orchestra, but even then he made me play in cafés between performances. One day a policeman arrested us. Father told him he'd catch it, *he* was the minister's cousin. The policeman laughed. I was ten, I cried, I was ashamed. I thought I'd end up in prison ...

Eurydice (*shouting, tears in her eyes*) Oh, darling, and I wasn't there! I'd have taken your hand, I'd have gone with you when they arrested you. I'd have told you it was nothing serious. At ten, I knew everything already.

Orpheus   He played the trombone in those days. He's tried to play everything, poor fellow, without success. I said at the door of the cinema: 'I'm the trombone player's son', and they let me in ... *Mysteries of New York*. It was wonderful!

Eurydice   And *The Mask With White Teeth*! It was such agony we couldn't stand any more by the fourth episode ... Oh, I wish I'd been next to you on those hard little seats ... I wish I'd eaten oranges with you in the interval and asked you if Pearl White's cousin was really a traitor and what the Chinaman could be thinking ... Oh, I wish I'd been a child with you! It's such a pity ...

Orpheus   Now it's all vanished. There's nothing we can do about it. The oranges have been peeled and the cinemas repainted and the heroine must be an old lady.

Eurydice (*quietly*)   It's not fair ...

A bell. The whistle of an approaching train.

Loudspeaker   The train for Toulouse, Beziers and Carcassone is now arriving at platform seven.

Another Loudspeaker (*further off, repeating*)   The train for Toulouse, Beziers and Carcassonne is now arriving at platform seven.

The members of the troupe pass by with their suitcases, beyond the door which is wide open onto the platform.

Girl (*to the* **Second Girl**)   Hurry up! We're going to have to stand the whole way again. The leads of course travel second. Who pays the extra, I wonder, who pays the extra?

Second Girl (*continuing her story*)   So, do you know what she said? She said: 'I don't care, I have to protect my position ...'

They pass on. The **Mother** *and* **Vincent** *follow, weighed down with hatboxes, suitcases.*

Mother   Pussycat, the green hatbox and the big case?

Vincent   I've got them. Go on.

Mother   Be careful, the strap's broken. That reminds me of Buenos Aires. Sarah's hatbox flew open in the middle of the station. There were ostrich feathers everywhere, all over the lines ...

They pass on. A fat man, **Dulac,** *follows.*

Dulac (*puffs, calling behind him*) Hurry up, for God's sake, hurry up! And check the loading of the luggage van, you fool. Get in the last carriage. We're all at the front.

Eurydice There go all the characters in my life . . .

Running, yet unable to, comic, pitiful, the little **Stage Manager** *finally passes, carrying too many suitcases, too many parcels, falling everywhere. All this among distant shouts, the approaching whistles of the train.*

Eurydice (*quietly to* **Orpheus**) Shut the door.

Orpheus *goes and shuts the door. Silence suddenly envelopes them.*

Eurydice There! Now we're alone in the world.

Loudspeaker (*further away*) The train for Toulouse, Beziers and Carcassonne is now arriving at platform seven.

Orpheus *has quietly come back towards her. Clamour of the train entering the station, and a shout, a shout that is transformed into an uproar which swells and suddenly gives place to a terrible silence. The* **Cashier** *has stood up and is trying to see. The* **Waiter** *runs across the stage.*

Waiter (*flinging it to them as he passes*) Someone's jumped under the express, a young man!

People run past on the platform, **Orpheus** *and* **Eurydice** *are face to face, not daring to look at each other. They say nothing.* **M. Henri** *appears on the platform. He enters, closes the door behind him and looks at them.*

Eurydice (*quietly*) There was nothing I could do. I loved you and I didn't love him.

There is silence. They look straight in front of them. **M. Henri** *has approached them.*

M. Henri (*in a neutral voice, looking at them all the time*) He jumped under the engine. He must have died instantly.

Eurydice How horrible!

M. Henri No. He chose rather a good way. Poison is slow and very painful. You're sick and you writhe, it's dirty. Like barbiturates – some people think they're going to fall asleep. Nonsense! A death with hiccups and nasty smells . . . (*He has approached quietly, smiling.*) Believe me, when you're very tired, when the idea's been with you for a long time, the easiest way is to slip gently into water, like a bed . . . You choke for a second, with a great wealth of images ... Then you go to sleep ... At last!

Eurydice   You think he didn't suffer when he died?

M. Henri (*quietly*)   No one ever suffers when they die. Death never hurts. Death is gentle ... What makes you suffer with certain poisons, certain clumsy wounds, is life. What's left of life. You must trust death completely, like a friend, a friend with a hand that's delicate and strong.

Orpheus and **Eurydice** *are huddled together.*

Eurydice (*quietly, like an explanation*)   There was nothing else we could do. We're in love.

M. Henri   Yes, I know. I was listening to you just now. A beautiful girl and a handsome young man! Ready to play the game without cheating, through to the end. Without those little concessions to comfort or the easy way, that are made by aging, well-to-do lovers. Two brave little animals, with supple limbs and long teeth, ready to fight till dawn, as is proper, and then fall, wounded, together.

Eurydice (*whispering*)   We don't know you ...

M. Henri   I know you. I'm delighted we've met. You're going away together? There's only one more train this evening. For Marseilles. You're going to take it perhaps?

Orpheus   I suppose so, yes.

M. Henri   I'm going there myself. I may have the pleasure of seeing you.

M. Henri *bows and goes out.* **Orpheus** *and* **Eurydice** *turn round to face each other. They are standing, very small, in the middle of this big, deserted room.*

Orpheus (*quietly*)   My love.

Eurydice   My dear love.

Orpheus   Our story's beginning ...

Eurydice   I'm rather frightened ... Are you good? Are you bad? What's your name?

Orpheus   Orpheus. And yours?

Eurydice   Eurydice.

The curtain falls.

Act Two

A bedroom in a provincial hotel, big, gloomy, dirty. The ceiling is too high and lost in shadow. Dusty curtains, a great iron bed, a screen, a miserly light. **Orpheus** *and* **Eurydice** *are lying on the bed, fully dressed.*

Orpheus Just think, it might never have happened! ... You might have passed by on the right and me on the left. Not even that, the flight of a bird, the shout of a child might have made you turn your head for a second. I'd now be scraping my violin with father in a café in Perpignan.

Eurydice I'd be playing *Orphans in the Storm* in the municipal theatre in Avignon. The orphans are mother and me.

Orpheus I've been thinking about all the luck we had to have. Thinking about that unknown little boy and girl who set out years ago towards that provincial station ... Just think, we might not have recognised each other; picked the wrong day or the wrong station.

Eurydice Or met too soon, with parents who'd have taken our hand and dragged us away by force.

Orpheus Luckily we didn't pick the wrong day, the wrong minute. No one stopped us in the whole of that long journey. Oh, we're very strong.

Eurydice Yes, darling.

Orpheus (*strong, but meek*) We're tremendously stronger than anyone else in the world, the two of us!

Eurydice (*looking at him, with a little smile*) My Hercules! But you were very timid yesterday when we came into this room.

Orpheus Yesterday we weren't stronger than anyone else. I didn't want our love to be at the mercy of this last little possible chance.

Eurydice (*quietly*) There are things in life we don't want, but they're there, so quiet, so huge, like the sea.

Orpheus Just think, we could have been nothing when we leave this room: not even a brother and sister like now; just two enemies, smiling, distant, polite, talking about other things. Oh. I hate love ...

Eurydice Sh! You mustn't say that ...

Orpheus Now at least we know each other. We know the weight of our sleeping heads, the noise of our laughter. Now we've memories to defend ourselves with.

Eurydice A whole evening, a whole night, a whole day! How rich we are!

Orpheus Yesterday we had nothing, we knew nothing. We came into this room by chance, under the terrible eye of that waiter with the moustache who suspected we were going to make love. We began to undress quickly, standing, facing each other . . .

Eurydice You hurled your clothes into every corner of the room like a madman . . .

Orpheus You were trembling. You couldn't undo the little buttons on your dress and I watched you tearing them off, without moving a finger. Then, when you'd nothing on, you were suddenly ashamed.

Eurydice (*lowering her head*) I thought I had to be beautiful too and I wasn't sure . . .

Orpheus We stood for a long moment facing each other, not daring to say a word, not daring to move . . . Oh, we were too poor, too naked; it was too unfair, having to risk everything at the same time like that; until a sudden pang of love brought a lump to my throat because you'd a little red spot on your shoulder.

Eurydice Then afterwards everything became so easy . . .

Orpheus You rested your head against me and went to sleep. The weight of your head suddenly made me feel strong. It seemed as though we were lying naked on a beach and my love was an incoming tide that slowly covered our outstretched bodies . . . As if our struggle and nakedness on this rumpled bed were necessary for us to become really two little brothers.

Eurydice Oh, darling, you thought all that and let me go on sleeping . . .

Orpheus You told me lots of other things in your dreams that I couldn't answer.

Eurydice I spoke? I always do when I'm asleep. You didn't listen, I hope?

Orpheus (*smiling*) Yes.

Eurydice   Oh, you traitor! Instead of sleeping honestly, like I was, you spied on me. How do you expect me to know what I say when I'm asleep?

Orpheus   I only understood three words. You breathed a terrible sigh. Your mouth hardened a little and you said: 'It is difficult.'

Eurydice *(repeating)*   It is difficult . . .

Orpheus   Well, what was so difficult?

Eurydice *(remains for a moment without answering, then shakes her head and says quickly in a tiny voice)*   I don't know, darling. I was dreaming.

*A knock at the door. It's the **Waiter**, who enters immediately. He has a huge grey moustache, a strange manner.*

Waiter   You rang, sir?

Orpheus   No.

Waiter   Oh, I thought you did, sir. *(He hesitates for a moment, then:)* I'm sorry, sir.

Waiter *goes out.*

Eurydice *(as soon as he's gone)*   Do you think it's real?

Orpheus   What?

Eurydice   His moustache.

Orpheus   Definitely. It looks false. Only false ones look real. It's a well-known fact.

Eurydice   He doesn't look as noble as our waiter in the station last night.

Orpheus   The one from the Comédie Française? He was noble, but conventional. And at heart under that imposing manner he was wet. This one's definitely more mysterious.

Eurydice   Yes. Too mysterious. I don't like people who are too mysterious. He frightens me rather. Not you?

Orpheus   Rather. I didn't dare tell you.

Eurydice *(snuggling up against him)*   Oh, darling, let's hold each other tight. How lucky there are two of us!

Orpheus   We've characters in our story already . . . Two waiters, one who's noble and wet, one who's bizarre with a moustache, the beautiful cashier with her enormous breasts . . .

Eurydice   What a pity the beautiful cashier never spoke to us!

Orpheus   There are silent characters in all stories. She never spoke to us, but she watched us the whole time and if she weren't silent for ever now you'd see everything she'd tell us about ourselves . . .

Eurydice   And that railway official.

Orpheus   The one with the stutter?

Eurydice   Yes, that charming little man with the stutter. So small and so nice! I'd have liked to hold his hand and take him with his big watch chain and lovely peaked hat to a teashop and fill him up with cakes.

Orpheus   You remember how he recited the names of all the stations where we mustn't change, to make us understand without any possible mistake the one where we really had to!

Eurydice   Oh, that dear little man with the stutter! He definitely brought us luck. But the other, that dreadful brute, the inspector . . .

Orpheus   Oh, that idiot! The one who refused to understand that with one third-class ticket for Avignon and another third-class ticket for Perpignan, we wanted to pay extra for two second-class tickets for Marseilles?

Eurydice   Yes, him. He was so ugly and stupid. And squalid and smug, with his dirty, big cheeks, full of heaven knows what, over-shaved and much too red, resting on his celluloid collar.

Orpheus   He's our first unpleasant character. Our first villain. There'll be others, you'll see . . . A happy story's full of villains.

Eurydice   Oh, I won't have that one! I wipe him out. You can tell him I wipe him out. I don't want a fool like that in the memories I share with you.

Orpheus   It's too late, darling, we're not entitled to wipe anyone out.

Eurydice   Then for the whole of our life that big dirty self-satisfied man will be part of our first day?

Orpheus   The whole of our life.

Eurydice   And the dreadful old lady in black I stuck my tongue out at when she lost her temper with her thin little maid. She'll always be there too?

Orpheus   Always. With the little girl who never took her eyes off you in the train and the big dog who insisted on following you and all our charming characters.

Eurydice   You think we couldn't remember a first day with just the big dog, the little girl, the gypsies who danced on stilts in the square at night – and the nice little man with the stutter? You're sure we can't weed out the bad characters and only keep the good ones.

Orpheus   That would be too wonderful.

Eurydice   Don't you think we might try to imagine them a little less ugly, just for this first day ... Make the inspector a little less self-satisfied, the nasty woman in black a little less sour, a little less of a hypocrite ... or her tiny maid a bit fatter and her luggage not quite so heavy?

Orpheus   Impossible. They've gone now, the good and the bad. They've taken their few steps in your life, said their few words ... They're a part of you, like that, for ever.

A pause.

Eurydice (*suddenly asking*)   Then supposing we've seen a lot of ugly things in life, they all remain part of us?

Orpheus   Yes.

Eurydice   Carefully stored away one by one, all the nasty thoughts, all the people, even those we've hated, even those we've run away from? All the sad things we've heard, you think we keep them all deep down inside? And all the gestures we've made, our hand still remembers them, you believe that?

Orpheus   Yes.

Eurydice   You're sure that even the words we've said unintentionally and never been able to take back, they're still in our mouth when we talk?

Orpheus (*trying to kiss her*)   Yes, you crazy little ...

Eurydice (*breaking away*)   Wait, don't kiss me. Explain all this first. What you've said is a fact or only *you* think that? Other people have told you?

Orpheus   Of course.

Eurydice   Sensible people? I mean people who ought to know, people you can trust?

Orpheus   Yes.

Eurydice   Then with all that around us we're never alone. We're never sincere, even when we long to be ... If all the words are there, all the nasty laughter, if all the hands that have touched us are still stuck to our skin, then we can never become someone different?

Orpheus   What are you saying?

Eurydice   (*after a pause*)   You think we'd be the same, if we'd known as a child that one day it would be essential to be completely spotless? And when we say things? When we say I made this gesture, I said or heard this word, I let someone ... (*She stops.*) When we say these things to someone else ... someone we love for instance ... do your sensible people think that destroys them?

Orpheus   Yes. It's called making a confession. Afterwards apparently you're washed bright and clean.

Eurydice   Oh! They're sure of that?

Orpheus   So they say.

Eurydice   (*after thinking for a moment*)   Yes, yes, but if they're wrong, or if they said that to discover things about you; if those things went on living, twice as strong, twice as vivid for having been said a second time; if the person you told them to began remembering, always ... tell these friends of yours I don't trust them, I think it's better to say nothing ...

Orpheus   *looks at her. She sees this and adds quickly, snuggling up against him.*

Or else, darling, when it's quite simple, like with us yesterday, say everything of course, like me.

The **Waiter** *knocks and enters.*

Waiter   You rang, sir?

Orpheus   No.

Waiter   Oh, I'm sorry. (*He takes a step, then adds from the* *doorway.*) I was going to say, the bell doesn't work, so if you want to ring, it's best to shout.

Orpheus Right.

The **Waiter** *seems to be about to go out, but he changes his mind, crosses the room and checks the curtains, closing them, then opening them again.*

Waiter The curtains work.

Orpheus So we see.

Waiter In some of my rooms it's the other way round. The bell works, but the curtains don't. (*He is about to go out, then says again.*) Anyway if you try them in a moment and they don't work, you only have to ring ... (*He stops.*) I mean shout, because, as I said, the bell ... (*He makes a gesture.*)

The **Waiter** *goes out.*

Orpheus There's our first odd character. We'll have others. He's probably a decent country fellow with no harm in him.

Eurydice Oh no, he stares at me the whole time. Didn't you notice he stared at me the whole time?

Orpheus You're dreaming.

Eurydice Oh, I preferred the other one, I much preferred the one from the Comédie Française ... You felt that even in tragedy he'd never be really dangerous.

The **Waiter** *knocks and enters. We have the clear impression that he was waiting outside.*

Waiter I'm sorry, I forgot to tell you, sir, the manageress is asking for you downstairs to complete your form. There's something missing. It has to be sent in this evening.

Orpheus She wants me to go down right away?

Waiter Yes, sir, if you can, sir.

Orpheus All right, I'll be with you in a moment. (*To* **Eurydice**.) Get dressed while I'm gone and we'll go and have dinner.

The **Waiter** *opens the door to let* **Orpheus** *go out and follows him. He enters again almost at once and goes towards* **Eurydice**, *who has stood up.*

Waiter (*holding out an envelope*) Here's a letter for you. I was told to give it to you when you're alone. The manageress isn't downstairs. I was lying. It's only one floor, you've half a minute to read it.

He remains standing in front of her.

Eurydice, *trembling a little, has taken the letter. She opens it, reads it, tears it into small pieces without any expression on her face and is about to throw them away.*

Waiter Not in the basket!

He goes to the basket, kneels and starts picking up the bits of paper which he puts in his apron pocket.

Have you known each other long?

Eurydice One day.

Waiter That's usually still a good time.

Eurydice (*quietly*) Usually, yes.

Waiter I've seen lots of people use this room, lying on the bed, like you just now. Not just handsome couples either. The bloated, the scrawny. Monsters! All wasting their saliva talking about 'our love'. Sometimes when evening arrives like now, I think I see them all, together. The place is swarming with them. Oh, there's nothing beautiful about love.

Eurydice (*imperceptibly*) No.

Orpheus *enters.*

Orpheus (*as he comes in*) You're still here?

Waiter No, sir. I'm going.

Orpheus The manageress wasn't there.

Waiter I must have taken too long coming to tell you. She probably got fed up waiting. It doesn't matter, sir, this evening will do.

Waiter *looks at them both and goes out.*

Orpheus What was he doing here?

Eurydice Nothing. He was telling me about all the couples he'd seen in this room.

Orpheus How exciting!

Eurydice He says he sometimes sees them all together. The whole room's swarming with them.

Orpheus   You listened to nonsense like that?

Eurydice   Perhaps it isn't nonsense. You know so much, you said all the people we've ever known live on in our memory. Perhaps the room remembers too ... Everyone who's been here is around us, embracing, the bloated, the scrawny, monsters.

Orpheus   Darling, you're crazy!

Eurydice   The bed's full of them; actions are ugly things.

Orpheus (*wanting to take her away*)   Let's go and have dinner. The street is pink with the first lights coming on. We'll eat in a little bistro that smells of garlic. You'll drink from a glass where a thousand lips have drunk already and the thousand bottoms that have hollowed out the moleskin banquette will make a little space for you, where you'll manage to be comfortable. Come along.

Eurydice (*resisting*)   You laugh, you always laugh. You're so strong.

Orpheus   Since last night! A Hercules ... you said so yourself.

Eurydice   Yes, yes, a Hercules, but you hear nothing, feel nothing, you're sure of yourself and go straight ahead. Oh, you can be frivolous, you men, yes, as soon as you've made me serious ... You say things, you recreate, at the moment I least expect it, all the beastly couples who've ever done anything between these four walls, you snare me in a mass of horrid words, then you don't give it another thought. Off you go to dinner, saying 'It's nice, the lights are lit, it smells of garlic.'

Orpheus   You'll say the same in a moment. Come on, let's get out of this room.

Eurydice   I don't think it's nice now. It doesn't smell nice. How short it's been ...

Orpheus   What's the matter? You're trembling.

Eurydice   Yes. I'm trembling.

Orpheus   You're so pale.

Eurydice   Yes.

Orpheus   And those eyes! I've never seen your eyes like this.

He tries to pull her towards him.

Eurydice (*turning away*) Don't look at me. When you look at me, I feel the touch of your look. It's as though you've put your hands on my thighs and entered me like a flame. Don't look at me.

Orpheus I've been looking at you since yesterday.

He pulls her to him, she lets him do so.

Eurydice (*conquered, whispering, against him*) You're strong you know ... You look like a thin little boy, but you're the strongest person in the world. When you play your violin, like yesterday in the station, or when you talk, I become a tiny snake. All I can do is creep gently towards you ...

Orpheus (*wrapping her in his arms and warming her*) Are you all right, little snake?

Eurydice Sometimes you say nothing and I think I'm free, as I was before. With all my strength I pull on my thread for a whole minute. But you start talking again, the thread winds back on its reel and I return to my basket, only too happy ...

Orpheus You're a little snake that thinks too much. Little snakes should bask in the sun, drink their milk and purr very gently.

Eurydice (*quietly*) It's cats that purr.

Orpheus (*stroking her hair*) Never mind, purr, you're in my arms.

Eurydice You're a traitor. You scratch my head gently and I go to sleep in the warmth of your sun.

Orpheus But you say, 'It's difficult.'

Eurydice (*breaking away with a sudden shout*) Darling!

Orpheus Yes.

Eurydice I'm afraid it may be too difficult.

Orpheus What is?

Eurydice The first day everything seems so easy. The first day we only have to invent. Are you sure we haven't invented everything?

Orpheus (*taking her head in his hands*) I'm sure I love you and you love me. Sure as stone and wood and iron.

Eurydice Yes, but perhaps you thought I was someone else.

Then when you look into my face and see me as I really
am . . .

Orpheus I've been looking into your face since yesterday.
I've been listening to you talk when you're asleep.

Eurydice Yes, but I didn't say much. Suppose I go to sleep
again tonight and say everything?

Orpheus Everything? What everything?

Eurydice Old messy words, old stories. Or if somebody, one
of the characters in them, came and told you . . .

Orpheus What do you expect anyone to come and tell me
about you? I know you better than they do now.

Eurydice You think so? (*She raises her head and looks at him.*)

Orpheus (*continuing with a happy strength*) My little soldier! I've
had you under my command for a whole day; I know you.
Because I have been rather horrid since yesterday, haven't I,
always playing the captain. 'Quick, here's the train. Get in the
last carriage. Keep the seats, I'll go and hire pillows. Wake up,
it's Marseilles. Get out. Be brave, the hotel's some way from
the station, but we've no money for a taxi . . .' And the little
soldier, bewildered eyes still crumpled with sleep, grasps the
suitcases with a willing smile. And left, right, left, right, follows
the captain in the dark . . . Just think, I might have brought
along a lady with feathered hats and high clacking heels! I'd
have died of fright when I asked for the room. And in the
carriage with all those men staring at you and pretending to be
asleep so they could undress you in their minds . . . who
knows? She might have smiled, pulled up her skirt with a little
flick of her hand, let her head fall to one side, rather glad that
the whole compartment desires her when they're pretending to
be asleep . . . Oh, I'd have died of shame . . . But my silent
little brother next to me immediately turned into a statue. Legs
vanished, skirt mysteriously long, hands buried, stiff as a
ramrod. A little Egyptian mummy, with no eyes, so the
disappointed so-called sleepers began to forget her, as one after
the other they started to snore . . . I haven't thanked you.

Eurydice (*quietly, her head lowered*) You mustn't.

Orpheus I haven't thanked you either for your courage . . .

Eurydice (*stammering*) Courage?

Orpheus For the days which are not far off, when you let the dinner hour slip by as we smoke the last cigarette, one puff for each of us. For the dresses you pretend not to see in shop windows; the sneering shopkeepers, the hostile hotel-owners, the concierges ... I haven't thanked you for making the beds, sweeping the rooms, doing the washing-up, your red hands and the glove with the hole in it, the smell of cooking in your hair. Everything you gave me, when you agreed to come away with me.

Eurydice's *head is lowered. He looks at her in silence.*

Orpheus   I didn't think I'd ever meet the comrade who'd come away with me, tough and vital, carrying her own bag, not wanting to smile the whole time, any more than me. The little silent friend who'd toil all day and at night is warm and lovely in my arms. For me alone, a woman, more secret, more tender than the sort men have to have drag along behind them the whole time in glamorous dresses. My timid bird, my wild beast, my little stranger ... I woke up last night and wondered if I wasn't as dull as other men, with their stupid pride and clumsy hands, wondered if I deserve you.

Eurydice *has raised her head and stares at him in the darkness which now fills the room.*

Eurydice (*very quietly*)   You really think all that about me?

Orpheus   Yes, my love.

Eurydice (*after thinking again for a moment*)   It's true. That's a very charming Eurydice.

Orpheus   It's you.

Eurydice   Yes. You're right, that's just the wife for you. (*A pause, then quietly, in an odd little voice, stroking his hair.*) Eurydice, your wife ...

Orpheus (*having got up, happy*)   I salute you! Now will you finally agree to come and eat? The snake charmer can't blow his flute a moment longer. He's starving.

Eurydice (*in a different voice*)   Turn the light on now.

Orpheus   A sensible word at last! Every light in the place! Floods of light! Exit ghosts!

He turns the light switch. A harsh light floods the room and makes it hideous.

Eurydice (*having got up*)   Darling, I don't want to go to a restaurant and see people. If you like, I'll go down and buy something and we'll eat it here.

Orpheus   In this room, swarming with people?

Eurydice   Yes, it doesn't matter any more now.

Orpheus (*moving*)   It'll be fun. I'll come with you.

Eurydice (*quickly*)   No, let me go alone.

He stops.

I want to go shopping for you, like a wife.

Orpheus   Then buy lots of things.

Eurydice   Yes.

Orpheus   We must have a banquet.

Eurydice   Yes, darling.

Orpheus   Exactly as if we had money. It's a miracle rich people will never understand ... Buy a pineapple, a real one, one of God's pineapples, not a sad American one in a tin. We haven't a knife. We'll never manage to eat it. But it's only fair for the pineapple to defend itself.

Eurydice (*a little laugh, with her eyes full of tears*)   Yes, darling.

Orpheus   Buy flowers for dinner too, lots of flowers ...

Eurydice (*stammering, with her poor little smile*)   We can't eat them.

Orpheus   True enough. we'll put them on the table. (*He looks around him.*) We haven't a table. Never mind, buy lots of flowers. And fruit. Peaches, enormous peaches, apricots, greengages. A little bread, to show the serious side of our character, and a bottle of white wine. We'll drink it in the toothglass. Hurry up, I'm starving!

Eurydice *goes and takes her little hat and puts it on in front of the mirror.*

Orpheus   You're putting your hat on?

Eurydice   Yes. (*Turning round suddenly, in a strange harsh voice.*) Goodbye, darling.

Orpheus (*shouting to her with a laugh*)   You're saying goodbye like they do in Marseilles?

Eurydice (*in the doorway*) Yes.

She looks at him for another second, smiling, pitiful, and goes out quickly. **Orpheus** *remains for a moment motionless, smiling at the departed* **Eurydice**. *Suddenly his smile disappears, his face hardens and he is seized by a vague anxiety.*

Orpheus (*runs to the door, calling*) Eurydice!

He opens the door and falls back, amazed. **M. Henri**, *the young man who spoke to them in the station, is in the doorway, smiling.*

M. Henri She's just gone downstairs.

Orpheus *is not sure if he recognises him.*

M. Henri You don't remember me? We met yesterday in that station buffet, when the accident happened . . . you know, the young man jumped under the train. I took the liberty of coming in to say hullo. I liked you so much. I'm in the room next door. Number eleven.

He takes a step into the room and holds out a packet of cigarettes.

Do you smoke?

Orpheus *automatically takes a cigarette.*

M. Henri I don't. (*Takes out a box of matches and lights* **Orpheus**'s *cigarette.*) A light?

Orpheus Thank you. (*He closes the door and asks automatically.*) Who have I the honour of . . . ?

M. Henri When one meets people on one's travels, I think it's rather charming not knowing exactly who they are. My surname would mean nothing to you. Let's just say Monsieur Henri.

He has come into the room. He looks at **Orpheus** *with a smile;* **Orpheus** *looks back, as if fascinated.*

A lovely town, Marseilles. This swarming humanity, the rabble, the filth. People aren't killed around the old port as much as they're said to be. Still it's a lovely town. Do you expect to stay here long?

Orpheus I don't know.

M. Henri It was rather rude of me to speak to you yesterday. But you were so touching, the pair of you, snuggling up against each other in the middle of that great deserted room ... Rather beautiful, didn't you think? Red, and gloomy, with night falling and those station noises in the background ... (*He looks at him for a long moment, then smiles.*) Orpheus and Eurydice ... One doesn't have a windfall like that every day ... I needn't have spoken to you ... I don't usually speak to anyone. What's the point? You, I don't know why, I couldn't resist the urge to get to know you better. You're a musician?

Orpheus Yes.

M. Henri I like music. I like everything that's gentle and happy. In fact I like happiness. But let's talk about you. Talking about me's not interesting. First of all have a drink. That makes conversation so much easier.

He gets up and rings the bell. He looks at **Orpheus** *with a smile during the short wait.*

I'd very much like to have a chat with you for a moment.

The **Waiter** *has entered.*

M. Henri What will you have? A brandy?

Orpheus If you like.

M. Henri A brandy, please.

Waiter Just one?

M. Henri Yes. (*To* **Orpheus**.) Forgive me, I don't drink.

The **Waiter** *has gone out.*

M. Henri (*looks at* **Orpheus** *again, smiling*) I'm delighted to meet you.

Orpheus (*with an embarrassed gesture*) Thank you.

M. Henri You must be wondering why I'm so interested in you.

Orpheus *makes a gesture.*

M. Henri I was at the back of the room when she came to you, as if summoned by your music. These brief moments when we surprise Destiny setting its scene are very disturbing, aren't they?

The **Waiter** *has entered.*

M. Henri Ah! Here's your brandy!

Waiter One brandy, sir.

Orpheus Thank you.

Waiter *goes out.*

M. Henri (*after watching him go out*) Did you notice how remarkably slowly that waiter left the room?

Orpheus No.

M. Henri (*going to listen at the door*) He's definitely taken up his position again behind the door. (*Returning to* **Orpheus**.) I'm sure he's come in here several times with some excuse or other. I'm sure he's tried to speak to you.

Orpheus He has, yes.

M. Henri You see, I'm not the only one to be interested in you today ... I'm prepared to bet that since yesterday tradesmen, railway staff, girls in the street have been smiling at you in an unusual way ...

Orpheus People are always kind to young lovers.

M. Henri It's not just kindness. Don't you think they stare at you rather?

Orpheus No. Why?

M. Henri (*smiling*) No reason. (*He dreams for a moment, then suddenly takes his arm.*) My dear fellow, there are two breeds of men. A numerous breed, prolific, happy, a great mass of dough to be kneaded into shape, eating their meals, producing their children, plying their trade, counting their cash, year in, year out, in spite of wars and epidemics, till the end of their allotted span; people for living, for everyday life, people one can't imagine dead. And there are the others, the aristocracy, the heroes. People one can easily imagine stretched out, pale with a red hole in their head, one minute triumphant with a guard of honour, or alternatively between two policemen. The cream. Has that never tempted you?

Orpheus Never. This evening less than ever.

M. Henri (*goes to him, puts his hand on his shoulder and looks at him; almost tenderly*) A pity. We mustn't believe too much in happiness. Especially if we belong to that special breed. We're merely storing up disappointments.

The **Waiter** *knocks and enters.*

Waiter Sir, there's a girl downstairs asking for the young lady who was here. I told her she's gone out, but she doesn't seem to believe me. She insists on seeing you. Shall I tell her to come up?

*The **Girl** enters, and pushes the **Waiter** aside.*

Girl I am up. Where's Eurydice?

Orpheus She's gone out. Who are you?

Girl A friend of hers in the company. I've got to talk to her right away.

Orpheus I tell you she's gone out. Anyway I don't think she's anything to say to you.

Girl You're wrong, she's a lot to say to me. How long is it since she went out? Did she take her suitcase with her?

Orpheus Suitcase? Why do you expect her to take her suitcase? She went out to buy our dinner.

Girl She may have gone out to buy your dinner, but she'd every reason to take her suitcase. She was due to join us at the station to catch the eight twelve train.

Orpheus (*shouting*) Join who?

Waiter (*having taken out his big copper watch*) It's eight ten and forty seconds.

Girl (*as if to herself*) She must be on the platform with him. Thank you.

*She wheels round. **Orpheus** catches her at the door.*

Orpheus On the platform with who?

Girl Let me go. You're hurting me. I'll miss my train!

Waiter (*still consulting his watch*) It's eleven past exactly.

Dulac *appears in the doorway.*

Dulac (*to the **Waiter***) Thirteen. You're slow. The train's gone. (*To **Orpheus**.*) Let the girl go. I can answer your question. On the platform with me.

Orpheus (*falling back*) Who are you?

Dulac Alfredo Dulac. Eurydice's manager. Where is she?

Orpheus What do you want with her?

Dulac (*advances peacefully into the room, chewing his old cigar*) And you?

Orpheus   Eurydice is my mistress.

Dulac   Since when?

Orpheus   Yesterday.

Dulac   She also happens to be mine. For the last year.

Orpheus   You're lying.

Dulac (*smiling*)   Because she forgot to tell you?

Orpheus   Eurydice told me everything before coming away with me. For the last three months she's been the mistress of the boy who jumped under the train yesterday.

Dulac   How stupid can you be! He was a tough young man, he played the heavy parts. Everyone in the company was afraid of him. The child tells him she's leaving him and he chucks himself under the train for Perpignan. What I can't understand, by the way, is why she told *him*. She flew off without a word to anyone else, like a bird . . .

Orpheus   He was probably the only person she felt she ought to tell.

Dulac   No. There was me. First as her manager. For the last two nights I've had to replace her at a moment's notice; that's never amusing. Secondly because two days ago, with all respect, she spent the night with me.

Orpheus (*looking at him*)   I don't know which you are most: odious or ridiculous.

Dulac (*advancing a little more*)   Is that so?

Orpheus   On the whole, in spite of your behaviour, I think you're ridiculous.

Dulac   Because the girl spent last night in this bed instead of mine? You're a child, my dear fellow. With a girl like Eurydice, you have to put up with her little whims. She also slept with the fool who killed himself yesterday. You at least I understand. You've nice eyes, you're young . . .

Orpheus (*shouting*)   I love Eurydice and she loves me!

Dulac   She told you so?

Orpheus   Yes.

Dulac (*goes and sits down peacefully in the armchair*) She's an extraordinary girl. Luckily I know her.

Orpheus Suppose I know her better than you?

Dulac Since yesterday?

Orpheus Yes, since yesterday.

Dulac Listen, I'm very good-natured. If it were a different matter, you look more intelligent than me, I might say 'All right'. But there are two things I know: first, my job.

Orpheus And secondly Eurydice?

Dulac No, I don't claim that. I was going to say something much more modest: women. I've been a manager for twenty years. I sell women, my dear fellow, by the dozen, to raise a leg in a provincial revue or bawl the big aria from *Tosca* in a casino. It's all the same to me. Besides, I love them. That at least is one of two good reasons to claim to know them. Eurydice may be an odd girl, I told you that, but from the way we've both of us seen she's constructed, you will grant me that at least she is a woman.

Orpheus No.

Dulac What do you mean, no? Did you think your Eurydice was an angel? Take a good look at me, my dear fellow, Eurydice has belonged to me for a year. Do I look capable of seducing an angel?

Orpheus You're lying. Eurydice can't have belonged to you!

Dulac You're her lover, so am I. Would you like me to describe her?

Orpheus (*falling back*) No.

Dulac (*approaching, vulgar*) What is your Eurydice like? You got her out of bed this morning? You snatched a thriller out of her hands? And cigarettes? In the first place have you seen her for a single moment without a cigarette end in the corner of her mouth like a street urchin? And her stockings? Did she find her stockings when she got up? Be frank with me. Anyway admit her blouse was hanging on the wardrobe door, her shoes in the bath, her hat under the chair and her handbag unfindable anywhere. I've bought her seven already.

Orpheus It's not true.

Dulac What do you mean, not true? You've seen a tidy Eurydice? I don't believe in miracles. Anyway I hope she's already made you stop in front of shop windows. How many dresses has she asked you to buy her since yesterday? How many hats? Between ourselves . . .

Orpheus Eurydice came away with me with one dress. One tiny suitcase.

Dulac I'm beginning to think we're not talking about the same girl. Or else she thought it wasn't for long . . . She told you it was for life? I'm sure she meant it. She thought: 'It'll be for life, if he's strong enough to keep me, if Papa Dulac doesn't pick up the trail, if he doesn't come and take me back.' And deep down inside she knew Papa Dulac would find her again. That's typical of her too.

Orpheus No.

Dulac Oh yes, my dear fellow, yes . . . Eurydice's a rare being, I agree, but she has the same mentality as all the girls of that type.

Orpheus It's not true!

Dulac Nothing's true for you. You're a funny boy. How long ago did she go out?

Orpheus Twenty minutes.

Dulac All right. That's true?

Orpheus Yes.

Dulac She insisted on going alone, didn't she?

Orpheus Yes, it amused her to go and buy our dinner alone.

Dulac That's true too?

Orpheus Yes.

Dulac Well listen to me. I had a letter given to her five minutes before, asking her to meet me on the platform.

Orpheus No one could have given her a letter. I haven't left her for a moment since yesterday.

Dulac Are you quite sure?

Dulac *looks at the* **Waiter**, **Orpheus** *does so too, without knowing why.*

Waiter (*suddenly anxious*)   Excuse me, I think someone's calling me.

The **Waiter** *disappears.*

Orpheus   I did leave for a minute, yes. That man came and said I was wanted in the office.

Dulac   I told him to give Eurydice a note when she was alone. He gave it to her when you were downstairs.

Orpheus (*going towards him*)   What did you say in this note?

Dulac   I expected her on the eight twelve train. There was no need to say more ... As fate had just knocked at her door and told her it was finished, I was sure she'd obey. Some men, my dear fellow, jump out of the window ...

Orpheus   But you see, she didn't come and meet you.

Dulac   That happens to be true. She didn't. But my Eurydice's always late. I don't worry too much. You asked yours to do a lot of shopping?

Orpheus   Bread, fruit.

Dulac   And you say she's been gone for twenty minutes? Surely that's rather a long time to buy bread and fruit. The street's full of shops. Isn't your Eurydice equally late? (*To the* **Girl**.) She must be at the station looking for us. Go and see.

Orpheus   I'll go too.

Dulac   You're beginning to believe she might have wanted to meet us? I'm staying here.

Orpheus (*stops and calls to* **Girl**)   If you see her, tell her I ...

Dulac   There's no point. If she finds her at the station, it means I was right; it means your faithful tidy Eurydice was a dream. In that case you've nothing more to say to her.

Orpheus (*calling to* **Girl**)   Tell her I love her!

Dulac   That might raise a tear; she is sensitive. But that's all.

Orpheus (*still calling*)   Tell her she's not like other people think, she's like I know she is.

Dulac   That's too complicated to explain in a railway station. (*To* **Girl**.) Hurry up and look, I'm a good sport, bring her back. It won't take her a minute to tell us herself what she is.

The **Girl** *begins to go out and bumps into the* **Waiter**, *who appears in the doorway.*

Waiter   Sir . . .

Orpheus   What is it?

Waiter   It's a policeman with the police van . . .

Orpheus   What does he want?

Waiter   He's come to ask if anyone here's related to the girl, because she's had an accident, sir, in the Toulon bus . . .

Orpheus (*shouting like a madman*)   She's hurt? She's downstairs?

Orpheus *rushes into the corridor.* **Dulac** *follows him, throwing away his cigar with a stifled oath. The* **Girl** *also disappears.*

Dulac (*as he goes out*)   What on earth was she doing in the Toulon bus?

The **Waiter** *has remained alone, facing* **M. Henri**, *who has not moved.*

Waiter   They'll never know what she was doing there . . . She's not hurt, she's dead. As the bus left Marseilles, it hit a tanker lorry. The other passengers were just struck by flying glass. Only she . . . I saw her, they've put her in the back of the van. She's one tiny wound in her forehead. She looks as though she's asleep.

M. Henri *does not seem to hear him. With his hands buried in his raincoat pockets, he passes in front of him. In the doorway he turns round.*

M. Henri   Tell them to prepare my bill. I'm leaving this evening.

M. Henri *goes out.*

The curtain falls.

Act Three

The station buffet, in darkness. It is night. Nothing but a dim light from the platform, where only the signals are shining. The indistinct tinkle of a bell can be heard in the distance.

The buffet is empty. The chairs are piled on the tables. The stage remains empty for a moment. Then one of the doors onto the platform opens a little; **M. Henri** *enters and makes* **Orpheus** *enter too, hatless, wearing a raincoat. He is haggard, tired.*

Orpheus (*looks about him, not understanding*)   Where are we?

M. Henri   You don't recognise it?

Orpheus   I can't walk another step.

M. Henri   You'll be able to rest now. (*Taking a chair from a table.*) Here's a chair.

Orpheus (*sitting*)   Where are we? What did I drink? Everything's spinning round me. What's happened since yesterday?

M. Henri   It's still yesterday.

Orpheus (*suddenly realises and shouts, wanting to get up*)   You promised . . .

M. Henri (*putting a hand on his shoulder*)   Yes, I promised. Don't get up. Have a rest. Would you like to smoke? (*He offers him a cigarette.*)

Orpheus (*takes it automatically and looks around him while the match goes on burning*)   Where are we?

M. Henri   Guess.

Orpheus   I want to know where we are.

M. Henri   You said you wouldn't be afraid.

Orpheus   I'm not. I only want to know if we've finally arrived.

M. Henri   Yes, we've arrived.

Orpheus   Where?

M. Henri   Be patient for a moment.

He strikes another match, follows the walls, goes to a light switch. A slight noise in the darkness and a wall bracket lights up on the rear wall, transmitting a miserly light.

You recognise it now?

Orpheus   It's the station buffet . . .

M. Henri   Yes.

Orpheus (*getting up*)   You lied to me, didn't you.

M. Henri (*making him sit*)   No, I never lie. Don't get up. Keep quiet.

Orpheus   Why did you come into my room just now? I was lying on that unmade bed. I was in agony. I was almost happy, luxuriating in my agony.

M. Henri (*dully*)   I hadn't the courage to go on listening to you suffer.

Orpheus   What could my suffering matter to you?

M. Henri   I don't know. It's the first time. Something strange began to make me weaken. If you wept, if you went on suffering, it would bleed like a wound . . . I was just going to leave the hotel. I put down my bags and came in to calm you. As nothing would calm you, I made this promise, to keep you quiet.

Orpheus   I'm quiet now. I'm suffering in silence. If you're sensitive, that should be enough for you.

M. Henri   You still don't believe me?

Orpheus (*putting his head in his hands*)   With all my strength I want to believe you, but I don't, no.

M. Henri (*after a little silent laugh, pulling* **Orpheus**'*s hair*) Stubborn little man! You weep, you moan, you suffer, but you won't believe. I like you. I had to yesterday or I'd have left immediately as usual. I had to, to go into that room where you were sobbing. I hate pain. (*He pulls his hair again with a sort of strange tenderness.*) Soon you'll stop weeping, little man, soon you'll stop wondering whether to believe or not to believe.

Orpheus   She'll come?

M. Henri   She's already here.

Orpheus   In this station? (*Shouting.*) She's dead. I saw her being taken away.

M. Henri You want to understand, little man? You're not satisfied with fate making an enormous exception for you. You put your hand in mine without trembling, you followed me till the end of the night without asking who I was, without slowing your step, but you still want to understand . . .

Orpheus No, I want to see her again, that's all.

M. Henri Aren't you more curious than that? I bring you to the gates of death and all you think about, little man, is your girlfriend . . . You're right, death deserves your contempt. It spreads its enormous nets, cuts down at random, grotesque, terrifying, gigantic. An idiot, capable of cutting off one of its own limbs with all the rest. To anyone who has seen a man getting out of a tight corner, standing firm at the butt of a machine-gun or the helm of a ship, using every last resort and killing his enemy with precision, men are formidable in a different way. Poor death . . . what a clumsy fool it is! (*He has sat down next to* **Orpheus**, *a little wearily*.) I'm going to tell you a secret, only you, because I like you. Death has a single quality which no one knows about. It is good, terrifyingly good. It's afraid of tears, pain. Every time it can, every time life allows it to, it acts quickly . . . it unlaces, unties, undoes. But life is obstinate, clings like a beggar even if the game is lost, even if a man can't move, is disfigured, even if he must suffer for the rest of his life. Only death is a friend. With the tip of its finger it gives a monster back his face, it appeases a soul in torment, it provides a release.

Orpheus (*suddenly shouting*) I'd rather have had Eurydice disfigured, suffering, old.

M. Henri (*lowering his head, suddenly overwhelmed*) Of course, little man, you're all the same.

Orpheus Death stole Eurydice from me, this friend. With its finger it destroyed Eurydice, young, happy, smiling . . .

M. Henri (*rising suddenly as if impatient; sharply*) It will give her back to you.

Orpheus (*having also risen*) When?

M. Henri Right away. But listen carefully. Your happiness was finished in any event. These twenty-four hours, this poor day, was all that life, your beloved life, had allotted little Orpheus and Eurydice. Today you wouldn't perhaps be weeping for a dead Eurydice, but you'd be weeping for a

Eurydice who had vanished . . .

Orpheus   It's not true. She didn't go to meet that man!

M. Henri   No. But she didn't return to you either. She took the Toulon bus on her own, with no money, no suitcase. Where was she running away to? Who exactly was this little Eurydice you thought you were able to love?

Orpheus   Whoever she is, I still love her. I want to see her again. Oh, please, give her back to me, even if she's not perfect. I want to suffer and feel ashamed because of her. I want to lose her and find her again. I want to hate her and then cradle her in my arms like a child. I want to fight, I want to suffer. I want to accept . . . I want to live.

M. Henri (*annoyed*)   You're going to live.

Orpheus   With the blots and the erasures, the moments of despair and the new beginnings, with the shame . . .

M. Henri (*looking at him, contemptuously, but nevertheless affectionately, in a whisper*)   Little man . . . (*Going to him; in a different tone.*) Goodbye, she's being given back to you. She's there on the platform, in the same place where you saw her yesterday for the first time – waiting for you, for eternity. You remember the condition?

Orpheus (*already looking at the door*)   Yes.

M. Henri   Repeat it. If you forget this condition, there's nothing more I can do for you.

Orpheus   I mustn't look her in the face.

M. Henri   That won't be easy.

Orpheus   If I look her in the face, once, before morning, I shall lose her again.

M. Henri (*stops smiling*)   You don't ask why any more, or how, stubborn little man?

Orpheus (*still looking at the door*)   No.

M. Henri (*still smiling*)   Good . . . Goodbye. You can start all over again from the beginning. Don't thank me. I'll see you again soon.

M. Henri *goes out.* **Orpheus** *remains for a moment without moving, then he goes to the door and opens it onto the empty platform. At first he says nothing.*

Orpheus (*dully questions, without looking*) You're there?

Eurydice (*off*) Yes, darling. How long you've been!

Orpheus They've allowed me to come and take you back
... Only I mustn't look at you before daylight.

Eurydice *appears.*

Eurydice Yes darling, I know. They told me.

Orpheus *takes her by the hand and brings her forward without looking
at her. They cross the stage in silence to a banquette.*

Orpheus Come, we'll wait for dawn here. When the waiter
arrives for the first train, when we see the daylight, we'll be
free. We'll ask for hot coffee and something to eat. You'll be
alive. You haven't been too cold?

Eurydice Yes. That worst of all. A terrible cold. But I've
been forbidden to talk about anything. I can only tell you up
to the moment when the driver smiled into the rear mirror
and the tanker lorry leapt on us like a mad beast.

Orpheus The driver looked back in the mirror and smiled?

Eurydice Yes. You know these boys in the South, they think
every woman's looking at them. But I didn't want to be looked
at.

Orpheus He was smiling at *you*?

Eurydice Yes. I'll explain later, darling. He grabbed the
steering wheel and everybody shouted at the same time. I saw
the tanker lorry loom up and the boy's smile turn to a
grimace. That's all. (*A pause; adding in a tiny voice.*) After that
I'm not allowed to.

Orpheus Are you all right?

Eurydice Oh yes, against you.

Orpheus Put my coat round your shoulders.

He puts his coat round her. A pause; they are happy.

Eurydice You remember the waiter from the Comédie
Française?

Orpheus We'll see him again tomorrow morning.

Eurydice And the beautiful silent cashier. Perhaps we'll
know at last what she was thinking about us. It's convenient

coming back to life ... It's as if we'd just met. (*Asking, as she did the first time.*) Are you good, are you bad, what's your name?

Orpheus (*joins in the game, smiling*) Orpheus, and yours?

Eurydice Eurydice. (*Adding quietly.*) But this time we're warned. (*She lowers her head; then, after a short pause.*) I'm sorry. You must have been so frightened ...

Orpheus Yes. To start with, you're aware of a dull presence staring at you from behind, listening to you talk. Then suddenly it leaps on you like a wild beast. At first it's a weight you carry on your shoulders, growing heavier and heavier, then it moves, it begins to plough into your neck and strangle you. You look at other people, calm, with no wild beast on their backs, who aren't frightened, who say: 'No, it's normal, she may have missed the tram or stopped to gossip on the way ...' But the beast goes on ploughing into your shoulder blades, screaming now: 'Do people miss the tram?' No, they fall underneath when they get off while it's moving, or crash into it when they cross the road. 'Do people stop to gossip on the way?' No! They go suddenly mad, they're kidnapped, they run away ... Luckily the waiter came in to release me, with disaster written all over his face. When I saw you downstairs, lying in that van, it stopped, I wasn't frightened any more.

Eurydice They'd put me in a van?

Orpheus The police van. They'd stretched you out on the back seat with a policeman next to you. Like a little thief they'd arrested.

Eurydice Did I look dreadful?

Orpheus You just had a spot of blood on your forehead. You looked as though you were asleep.

Eurydice Asleep? If you knew how I was running! I ran straight ahead like a lunatic. (*She stops; a slight pause, asking.*) You must have suffered?

Orpheus Yes.

Eurydice I'm sorry.

Orpheus (*dully*) Don't say that.

Eurydice They must have brought me back to the hotel because I was still holding a letter. I wrote to you in the bus, while we were waiting to start. Did they give it to you?

Orpheus   No. They must have kept it at the police station.

Eurydice   Oh! (*Suddenly anxious.*) Do you think they'll read it?

Orpheus   They might.

Eurydice   Can't we stop them, do you think? Can't we do something right away? Send someone, telephone, tell them they've no right to?

Orpheus   It's too late.

Eurydice   I wrote that letter to you. I said it all for you. How can someone else read it? Someone else whisper those words? A fat man with beastly thoughts maybe, a fat ugly self-satisfied man? He'll laugh at my misery, of course he will ... Oh, stop him, please, stop him reading it, you must! I feel completely naked in front of him ...

Orpheus   They may not have opened the envelope.

Eurydice   I didn't stick it down! I was going to, when the lorry hit us. That must be why the driver looked at me in the mirror. I was sticking my tongue out, that made him smile, I smiled too ...

Orpheus   You smiled too. You could smile?

Eurydice   No, I couldn't, you don't understand anything! I'd just written you this letter, saying I love you, I'm miserable, but I have to go ... I stuck my tongue out to lick the envelope; he made some joke, the way these boys do ... Everyone round me was smiling ... (*She stops, disheartened.*) Oh, it's not the same when I tell it. It's difficult. You see, it's all too difficult ...

Orpheus (*starting dully*)   What were you doing in the Toulon bus?

Eurydice   Escaping.

Orpheus   You got Dulac's letter?

Eurydice   Yes, that's why I was going.

Orpheus   Why didn't you show me that letter when I came back?

Eurydice   I couldn't.

Orpheus   What did he say?

Eurydice   I'd to meet him on the eight twelve train or he'd come and get me.

Orpheus   That's why you ran away?

Eurydice   Yes. I didn't want you to meet him.

Orpheus   You didn't think he'd come, so I'd meet him anyway?

Eurydice   Yes, but I was a coward, I didn't want to be there.

Orpheus   You were his mistress?

Eurydice (*shouting*)   No! He said that? I knew he would and you'd believe him! He's been chasing me for ages, he hates me. I knew he'd talk about me. I was afraid.

Orpheus   Yesterday when I asked you to tell me everything, why didn't you admit you'd been his mistress too?

Eurydice   I wasn't!

Orpheus   Eurydice, it's better to say everything now. We're two poor wounded creatures sitting on this bench, two poor creatures talking without seeing each other . . .

Eurydice   What must I say to make you believe me?

Orpheus   I don't know. You see, that's what's so dreadful . . . I don't know how I'll ever be able to believe you now . . . (*A pause; asking gently, humbly.*) Eurydice, so I won't have to worry afterwards when you tell me the simplest things, if you've been out, if it was fine, if you've been singing, tell me the truth now, even if it's terrible, even if it must hurt me. It won't hurt me more than my struggle to breathe, since I know you've lied to me . . . if it's too difficult to say, better not answer at all, but don't lie to me. Did this man tell the truth?

Eurydice (*after an imperceptible pause*)   No. He lied.

Orpheus   You've never belonged to him?

Eurydice   No.

There is a silence.

Orpheus (*dully, looking straight in front of him*)   If you're telling the truth now, it's very easy to know, you eyes are clear like a pool of water at night. If you're lying or you're not sure of yourself, there's a darker circle of green contracting round the pupil . . .

Eurydice   It will soon be dawn, darling, you'll be able to look at me.

Orpheus (*suddenly shouting*)   Yes. Deep into your eyes, suddenly, like water. Head first, deep into your eyes, where I can stay and drown . . .

Eurydice   Yes darling.

Orpheus   Because it's unbearable being two people! Two skins, two completely waterproof envelopes round us, one for each of us, with its oxygen, its own blood, whatever we do, completely enclosed, completely alone in our bag of skin. We snuggle up against each other, we rub shoulders to escape a little from this terrible solitude. A little pleasure, a little illusion, but we quickly find ourselves alone again, with our tripe and lights and liver as our only friends.

Eurydice   Shut up!

Orpheus   So we talk. We've discovered that too. This noise of air in our throat and against our teeth. This improvised morse code. Two prisoners tapping on the wall of their cell. Two prisoners who'll never see each other. Oh, we're alone; don't you think we're too alone?

Eurydice   Keep tight up against me.

Orpheus (*holding her*)   A warmth, yes. A warmth that's not our own. That's something almost certain. A resistance, too, an obstacle. A warm obstacle. So there is someone! I'm not completely alone. We mustn't ask too much!

Eurydice   Tomorrow you'll be able to turn round. You'll take me in your arms.

Orpheus   Yes. For a moment I'll be part of you. For one minute I'll believe we're two entwined stalks from the same root. Then we'll separate and become two people again. Two mysteries, two lies. Two. (*He caresses her; dreaming.*) One day you ought to breathe me in with your air, swallow me up. It would be wonderful. I'd be tiny within you, I'd be warm, I'd be all right.

Eurydice (*quietly*)   Don't talk any more. Don't think any more. Let your hand wander over me. Leave it there, happy, on its own. Everything would become so simple again, if you'd let just your hand love me. Without saying another word.

Orpheus   Do you think this is what they call happiness?

Eurydice   Yes. Your hand is happy now. All your hand asks is for me to be there, warm and gentle, beneath it. Don't *you* ask anything. We're in love, we're young, we're going to live. Accept being happy, please . . .

Orpheus (*rising*)   I can't.

Eurydice   Accept, if you love me . . .

Orpheus   I can't.

Eurydice   Then just be quiet.

Orpheus   I can't do that either! Every word's not been said. And we must say every word, one after the other. We must go on to the end now, word by word. There are so many words, you'll see!

Eurydice   Darling, be quiet, please.

Orpheus   Can't you hear them? Since yesterday there's been a swarm around us. Dulac's words, mine, yours, other people's, all the words which have led us here. And the words of all the people who watched us as if we were two dogs on a lead, and the words that are still unspoken but are there, attracted by the smell of the rest: the most conventional, the most vulgar, the ones we hate the most. We're going to speak them, of course we are. We always do.

Eurydice (*having risen, shouting*)   Darling!

Orpheus   Oh! No, I don't want any more words! Enough! Since yesterday we've been trapped by words. Now I've got to look at you.

Eurydice (*having thrown herself against him; holds him with her arms round his waist*)   Wait, wait, please. What we must do, is get through the night. It will soon be morning. Wait. It will all become simple again. They'll bring us coffee, rolls . . .

Orpheus   It's too long to wait till morning. It's too long to wait to be old . . .

Eurydice (*holds him in her arms, her head in his back: pleads*)   Oh, please, darling, don't turn round, don't look at me. What's the point? Let me live! You're terrible, you know, like the angels. You believe everyone goes forward, strong and clear like you, banishing the shadows from each side of the road. Some people have only a little hesitant light, whipped by the wind. And the shadows increase, they push us, pull us, make us fall

... Oh please, darling, don't look at me, don't look at me yet
... Perhaps I'm not the girl you wanted me to be. The one
you invented in the happiness of our first day ... You feel me
against you, don't you? I'm here, I'm warm, I'm kind, I love
you. I'll give you all the happiness I can. Don't ask for more
than that, be content ... Don't look at me. Let me live ...
Please, please ... I do so want to live ...

Orpheus (*shouting*)   Live, live! Like your mother and her lover
perhaps, with their whispers and smiles and indulgences:
followed by a good meal, then a little love and everything's
okay. Oh, no! I love you too much to live!

*He has turned round. He looks at her; they are face to face now,
separated by a dreadful silence.*

(*Asking dully.*) That fat man held you in his arms? He touched
you with those hands covered in rings?

Eurydice   Yes.

Orpheus   How long have you been his mistress?

Eurydice (*answering now with the same eagerness to tear herself in
pieces*)   A year.

Orpheus   Is it true you were with him the day before
yesterday?

Eurydice   Yes, the day before I met you, he came to find
me at night after the show. He blackmailed me. He
blackmailed me every time.

Dulac *enters suddenly.*

Dulac   Admit you followed me that night of your own free
will, little liar.

Eurydice (*tears herself from* **Orpheus**'s *arms and runs towards
him*)   Free will? Free will? I spat every time you kissed me.

Dulac (*peacefully*)   Yes, my dove.

Eurydice   As soon as you let me go, I ran away, I stripped
naked· in my room, I washed, I changed every stitch. You
never knew that?

Dulac (*to* **Orpheus**)   She's mad.

Eurydice   You can laugh, darling. I know you, not much
mirth there!

Orpheus Why did you call him darling?

Eurydice (*shouting, sincerely*) I didn't!

Dulac (*laughing*) You see. Everything else is on the same lines. I tell you, you made a mistake.

Eurydice Don't start playing the bully, don't pretend to be the strong man. (*To* **Orpheus**.) I'm sorry, everyone says darling in the theatre. Vincent calls him darling, mother does; that's why I said I didn't. I don't call him darling because I was his mistress, I do it because everyone does. (*She stops disheartened.*) Oh, it's so difficult, it's so difficult always explaining everything!

Orpheus You must explain everything now. You said he blackmailed you that night like every night. What blackmail?

Eurydice Always the same.

Dulac Are you going to tell us you believed in this blackmail for a year, little liar?

Eurydice You see, you admit you did it for a year?

Dulac Don't pretend to be stupid, Eurydice, you're not. I'm asking if you believed in this blackmail for a year?

Eurydice Then why did you do it each time if you thought I didn't believe it?

Dulac The threat became a formality. I did it so that in your dirty proud little mind you'd have a reason to go with me without admitting you enjoyed it. You can't be more gallant than that with the ladies, can you?

Eurydice You mean that when you threatened me, you didn't believe in the blackmail yourself? You deceived me every time? You took me every time and it wasn't true, you wouldn't really have sacked him?

Dulac Of course not, you little fool.

Orpheus What did he threaten you with?

The little **Stage Manager** *appears, sickly, clumsy.*

Stage Manager (*taking off his hat*) He threatened to sack me every time, from my job as stage manager.

Dulac (*exploding at the sight of him*) He's a fool! He's always losing everything! I won't have a fool like that in my company!

Eurydice   You see, darling, this poor man's all alone with his ten-year-old brother; they've only his pay to live on. Besides it's too unfair, everyone hates him, they're always thinking about sacking him.

Stage Manager (*to* **Orpheus**)   You see, I have to look after all the trunks, the scenery, and I'm on my own. (*He falls onto a banquette, in tears.*) I'll never manage! Never!

Dulac   He's a half-wit, I tell you, a half-wit!

Eurydice   You've made him a half-wit, by always yelling in his ears. I'm sure if you spoke to him quietly, he'd understand. Listen to me, Louis, darling...

Stage Manager   Yes, Eurydice, I'm listening.

Eurydice (*to* **Orpheus**)   You see I called him darling, too. Everyone does. (*She goes back to the* **Stage Manager**.) Listen, Louis, it's really very simple. You arrive at the station where we have to change. You hurry off the train. You run to the luggage van. You were careful to get in the back of the train to be there when they start unloading. You count the trunks to make sure not one is forgotten...

Stage Manager   Yes, but everyone's in such a hurry to get into town. They bring me their suitcases...

Eurydice   You must tell them to wait, you have to see to the trunks first.

Stage Manager   Yes, but they put their suitcases down on the platform next to me and tell me to look after them, then they disappear. The platform's full of people...

Eurydice   You mustn't let them go! Run after them!

Stage Manager   If I run after them, I'll lose sight of the trunks! Oh, I'll never manage; I tell you I'll never manage. You'd better leave me...

Dulac (*exploding*)   He's a fool! I tell you he's a fool! This time I've made up my mind! Over and done with! I'll get rid of him at Châtellerault!

Eurydice   Don't shout the whole time! How do you expect him to understand if you shout?

Dulac   He'll never understand! I tell you he's a minus quantity. At Châtellerault you'll get your cards, you bloody fool!

Stage Manager If you sack me, I don't know where I'll go. My brother and I will be finished, both of us . . . I promise I'll be careful.

Dulac You'll get your cards! It's settled!

Eurydice I'll help him! I promise I'll see he never loses anything again.

Dulac We know your promises! No, no, his head's solid wood! Dismissed! I can't stand any more!

Eurydice (*hangs onto him; pleading*) I promise he'll be careful. I promise . . .

Dulac (*looking at her*) Oh, you always make promises, but you don't often keep them.

Eurydice (*more quietly*) Yes . . .

Dulac (*approaches, dropping his voice*) If I keep him on, you'll be nice to me?

Eurydice (*lowering her eyes*) Yes. (*Returning to* **Orpheus**.) That's how it happened every time. I'm sorry, darling, I was a coward, but I didn't love you then. I didn't love anyone. And I was the only person who could stand up for him. (*A pause, whispering.*) I know you won't be able to look at me again now . . .

Orpheus (*having fallen back; dully*) I'll always see you with this man's hands on you. I'll always see you the way he described you in that room.

Eurydice (*humbly*) Yes, darling.

Orpheus He wasn't even jealous when he came back for you. He laughed: 'With a girl like Eurydice, you have to put up with her little whims.'

Eurydice (*moving back a little*) He said that?

Orpheus 'What is your Eurydice like? You got her out of bed this morning? You snatched a thriller out of her hands? And cigarettes?' He even knew you're a coward. He knew if he came back for you, you wouldn't stay with me. Because you are a coward, aren't you? He knows you better than me.

Eurydice Yes, darling.

Orpheus Do at least defend yourself. Why don't you?

Eurydice (*moving back*) How do you expect me to? By lying: I'm untidy, it's true, I'm lazy, I'm a coward . . .

Stage Manager (*shouting suddenly*) It's not true!

Eurydice (*gently*) What do you know about that?

Stage Manager You weren't a coward when you defended me. I know. You weren't lazy when you got up at six to help me in secret before the others came down . . .

Dulac (*thunderstruck*) What? You got up early to help this little fool send off the trunks?

Eurydice Yes.

Stage Manager I know she never finds anything, muddles everything, but she sorted out my notices, she stopped me making mistakes . . .

Dulac It's unbelievable!

Orpheus Well, if this man's telling the truth, say something! Stand up for yourself!

Eurydice (*quietly*) He is telling the truth, but so is Dulac. It's too difficult.

While she was speaking, all the characters in the play have entered; they are massed in the darkness upstage behind **Eurydice**.

Orpheus It's true. It is too difficult. All the people who've known you are around you; all the hands that have touched you are there, touching you again. And all the words you've spoken are on your lips.

Eurydice (*moving back a little, with a poor smile*) So you see, it's better if I do die again.

Bus Driver (*breaks away from the group and comes forward*) Don't you understand the poor girl's tired? And she's ashamed to stand up for herself? I chase after women, okay, there are some kids like that, you have them because they're tired out or disgusted. They return to nature, they don't resist. It's like that business in the bus I heard her muddling up just now . . .

Orpheus Who on earth are you?

Eurydice He's the bus driver, darling. (*To the* **Driver**.) It was nice of you to come.

Bus Driver He imagines you smiled at me. In the first place have I the sort of face this kid would smile at? He imagines you left him with that smile. And in the state he's in, it's only a tiny step to believe you don't love him. Well, I was there. I saw her.

Stage Manager Oh, I'm glad he's going to defend you. (*To the* **Driver**.) You are going to tell him, aren't you?

Bus Driver Of course I am! That's why I'm here!

Orpheus What do you want to tell me?

Bus Driver Why she smiled. I'd been watching her out of the corner of my eye. She was in the front, writing with a stub of a pencil, waiting for us to start. She was writing, writing and crying at the same time ... When she'd finished writing, she dried her eyes with her scrap of a handkerchief rolled into a ball and stuck out her tongue to lick the envelope. Then to say something, I said to her: 'At least I hope the fellow you're writing to is worth the trouble!'

Eurydice Then I smiled because I was thinking of you.

Bus Driver There you are!

There is a pause. **Orpheus** *raises his head. He looks at* **Eurydice**, *who is standing humbly in front of him.*

Orpheus If you loved me, why did you go?

Eurydice I thought I'd never manage to ...

Orpheus What?

Eurydice Make you understand.

They are facing each other, silent.

Mother (*suddenly exclaiming*) What I don't understand is why these children think everything's so sad! I mean, we were passionate lovers, pussy, but did that make us sad?

Vincent Not in the slightest! Never! In the first place I've always said: 'A little love, a little money, a little success, and life's beautiful!'

Mother A little love? Lots of love! This child thinks she and her darling violinist invented the whole thing. We adored each other too! We wanted to kill ourselves too. You remember Biarritz in 1913, when I wanted to throw myself off the cliffs?

Vincent Luckily I grabbed hold of your cape, my beloved.

Mother (*after a little shout at the memory, beginning to explain to* **Orpheus**) It was enchanting. That year we all wore tiny little capes trimmed with silk, the same material as the jacket. Why did I want to kill myself that time?

Vincent Because Princess Bosco had kept me in her room all night reciting poetry . . .

Mother No, no! Princess Bosco was when I wanted to swallow vinegar. I took the wrong bottle. It was wine. I made such a face!

Vincent Oh, we're out of our minds! That time it was the skating teacher!

Mother No, the skating teacher was during the war, in Lausanne. No. No. In Biarritz *you'd* been unfaithful to me, I'm certain. Anyway the exact details don't matter. The fact is we were so passionately in love, we wanted to die . . . Well, are we dead?

Eurydice (*moving back*) No, mother.

Mother You see, you little fool, if you'd listened to your mother! But you never do . . .

Eurydice (*moving away from her*) Don't go on, mother, we've no time left.

Orpheus *is standing motionless, watching her moving away.*

Eurydice (*to* **Orpheus**) You mustn't be too sorry about us. You were right, through trying to be happy, we might have become like them. How dreadful!

Mother What do you mean, dreadful?

Vincent Why dreadful?

Orpheus Why didn't you admit everything the first day? The first day I might have been able to understand . . .

Eurydice You think it's because I was a coward? Well, it wasn't because of that . . .

Orpheus Why, then, why?

Eurydice It's too difficult, darling, I'd muddle it up again. Besides I've no time now. I'm sorry. Don't move . . .

She moves further away, then stops before someone.

Oh, it's you, the beautiful cashier who never said a word! I always thought you had something to say to us.

Cashier How beautiful you both were when you advanced towards each other, with the music playing! You were beautiful, innocent and terrible, like love . . .

Eurydice (*smiles at her and moves a little further off*) Thank you. (*Stopping before someone else.*) Oh, the waiter from the Comédie Française. Our first character. Hullo!

Waiter (*with a gesture that is too noble*) Goodbye.

Eurydice (*smiling in spite of herself*) You know, you're very noble, very charming. Goodbye, goodbye.

She moves further back and stops in front of a young man in black. She looks him up and down, surprised.

Who are you? You must have made a mistake. I don't remember you.

Secretary I'm the police superintendent's secretary. You've never seen me.

Eurydice Ah, then *you*'ve got my letter. Give it back to me please. Give it back . . .

Secretary I can't.

Eurydice I don't want that fat, dirty, self-satisfied man to read it!

Secretary I can promise you the superintendent won't read it. I too felt it was impossible for a man like the superintendent to read that letter. I removed it from the file. The case is closed, no one will ever notice. I have it here. I read it every day . . . With me it's not the same thing.

He bows, noble and sad, takes the letter from his pocket and, after putting on his pince-nez, begins to read in a rather colourless voice.

'Darling, I'm in this bus and you're waiting for me in the room and I know I'm not coming back. And though I tell myself you don't yet know, I'm sad, sad for you. I should have been able to take all the pain upon myself. But how? It's pointless being full of pain, so full you have to bite your lips to stop it leaving your mouth as a moan, so full, you can't help the tears leaving your eyes. No one's ever borne all the pain; there's always enough left for two. People in this bus are looking at me. They think it's sad because of my tears. I hate tears. They're too stupid. You cry when you hurt yourself or peel onions. You cry when you're angry or when you've some other pain. For the pain I have now, I'd rather not cry. I'm much too unhappy to cry.' (*He steadies his voice, turns the page and continues.*) 'I'm going away, darling. Since yesterday I've been afraid, and when I was asleep, you heard, I was already saying "it's difficult". You thought I was so beautiful, darling. I mean morally beautiful, because I know, physically, you've never thought me very, very beautiful. You thought I was so strong, so pure, completely your little sister . . . I'd never manage that. Especially now another man is coming. He sent me a letter. Another man I haven't mentioned. He's been my lover too. Don't think I loved him; you'll see him, no one could love him. Don't think either that I surrendered to him because I was frightened of him, as he may tell you. You won't be able to understand, I know. But I felt so strong: besides I thought so little of myself. I didn't love you, darling; that's the whole secret; I didn't love you. I didn't know. The modesty of well-brought up girls made me laugh. This idea of preserving something, from pride or for a selected beneficiary is so hideous . . . Since yesterday, darling, I'm more modest than they are. Since yesterday I blush if I'm looked at, I tremble if I'm touched. I cry because someone's dared to desire me . . . That's why I'm going away, darling, on my own . . . Not just because I'm afraid he'll tell you he's known me, not just because I'm afraid you'll begin to stop loving me . . . I don't know if you'll really understand, but I'm going because I'm quite red with shame. I'm going, captain, and I'm leaving you precisely because you've taught me I'm a good little soldier . . .'

Throughout this letter **Eurydice** *has moved away. She is now right at the back of the stage.*

Orpheus I apologise, Eurydice.

Eurydice (*upstage. Gently*) You mustn't darling. I apologise to you. (*To the others.*) I'm sorry, I have to go.

Orpheus (*shouting*) Eurydice!

He runs upstage like a madman. She has disappeared. All the other characters have also vanished. **Orpheus** *remains alone. He doesn't move. Dawn rises. A train whistles in the distance. A bell tinkles. When it is almost completely light, the* **Waiter** *enters, clearly very much alive.*

Waiter Good morning, sir. Not very warm this morning. Can I get you something?

Orpheus (*collapsed onto a seat*) Yes. Anything. A coffee.

Waiter Very good, sir.

The **Waiter** *begins to take the chairs off the tables. The* **Cashier** *enters and goes to her till, humming a sentimental pre-War song. A traveller passes on the platform, hesitates, then enters timidly. He's loaded with suitcases and musical instruments. It is* **Orpheus' Father**.

Father There you are, my boy! I didn't take the train to Palavas after all. Full. To bursting! And the brutes tried to make me pay extra for second class. I got out. I'll complain to the company. A passenger's entitled to a seat in any class. They should have upgraded me for nothing. Will you have some coffee?

Orpheus (*apparently not seeing him*) Yes.

Father (*sitting down next to him*) I'd welcome it. I've spent the night in the waiting room. It wasn't warm. (*Whispering in his ear.*) To tell the truth I crept into the first-class one. An excellent leather bench, dear boy, I slept like a prince. (*He sees the* **Cashier**, *looks her up and down; she looks away, he does too.*) You see, in the light of day that woman loses a lot. Her breasts are good, but she looks extremely common ... So what have you decided, my boy? Sleeping on an idea's usually for the best. You'll come with me after all?

Orpheus Yes, father.

Father I knew you wouldn't abandon your old father! We'll celebrate with a good little dinner in Perpignan. You won't believe it, dear boy, but I know a little fixed price meal there for fifteen francs seventy-five, including wine, coffee and brandy! And for four francs extra, you get lobster instead of the hors d'oeuvres. The good life, eh, my boy, the good life ...

Orpheus Yes, father.

The curtain has fallen.

Act Four

The hotel room.

Orpheus, *half lying on the bed.* **M. Henri** *standing, leaning against the wall near him. The* **Father**, *looking important, in the only armchair. He is smoking an enormous cigar.*

Father (*to M. Henri*) This is a 'merveillitas'?

M. Henri Yes.

Father A cigar like this must be worth something?

M. Henri Yes.

Father You don't smoke?

M. Henri No.

Father If you don't smoke, I can't understand why you carry around these expensive cigars. You're a commercial traveller, perhaps?

M. Henri That's right.

Father Big business, I suppose?

M. Henri Yes.

Father Then I do understand. You have to be able to work on a customer. At the right moment you bring a merveillitas out of your pocket. Do you smoke? He says yes; too delighted. And, bang, the deal's done. All you have to do is deduct the cost of the merveillitas from the sale price, which you'd added it on to anyway. You're full of tricks, the lot of you! I'd have loved to be in business, wouldn't you, my boy?

Orpheus *doesn't answer.*

Father (*looking at him*) You must pull yourself together, dear boy, pull yourself together. Look, give him a merveillitas. If you don't finish it, I will. When I'm miserable, a good cigar . . .

Orpheus *and* **M. Henri** *ignore this new remark.*

Father (*sighs and adds more timidly*) Well, each to his own taste.

He begins to smoke unostentatiously, with occasional glances at the two silent men.

M. Henri (*quietly, after a pause*) You must get up, Orpheus.

Father That's right. I'm fed up telling him . . .

Orpheus No.

Father But he never listens to his father.

M. Henri You must get up and carry on with your life where you left it . . .

Father Yes, they're expecting us in Perpignan.

Orpheus (*half gets up, shouting at him*) Shut up!

Father (*making himself very small*) I said they're expecting us in Perpignan. There's no harm in that.

Orpheus I'll never go back with you!

M. Henri (*quietly*) Your life's there, waiting for you, like an old coat you have to put on in the morning.

Orpheus Well, I won't put it on.

M. Henri Have you another?

Orpheus *does not answer. His* **Father** *is smoking.*

M. Henri Why don't you go back with him? I think your father's charming.

Father I didn't make him say it . . .

M. Henri Besides you know him. That's enormous for a start. You can tell him to shut up, walk at his side without talking. Have you thought of the torture that's waiting for you without him? The dinner companion who tells you at length about his tastes, the old lady who questions you with an interest that's a little too affectionate? Every girl you meet will insist you talk about her. If you're unwilling to pay your tribute of useless conversation, you'll be terribly alone.

Orpheus I'll be alone. I'm used to it.

M. Henri I warn you against those words: 'I'll be alone'. They immediately evoke a cool shade, tranquillity. What a vulgar error! You won't be alone, no one ever is. You're alone with yourself, that's quite different, as you know . . . Take up your life again with your father. Every day he'll make his usual remarks about fixed price menus and how hard life is. It will occupy your mind. You'll be lonelier than entirely alone.

Father (*lost in his cigar*) Talking about fixed price menus, there's a little one I know in Perpignan, the Restaurant Jeanne

Hachette. You may know it? Your competitors use it a lot.

M. Henri No.

Father For fifteen francs seventy-five, wine included, they give you hors d'oeuvres, or lobster for four francs extra, meat dish with vegetables, large helping, separate vegetable course, cheese, dessert, fruit or pastry, and, wait for it, coffee and brandy or a liqueur for the ladies. Ah, that menu at the Jeanne Hachette, with a good cigar like this! . . . I'm almost sorry I smoked it right away. (*His remark not having the desired effect, he sighs.*) Ah, well! You're coming to Perpignan, my boy? I'll pay.

Orpheus No, father.

Father You're wrong, my boy, you're wrong.

M. Henri It's true, Orpheus. You are wrong. You should listen to your father. At the Restaurant Jeanne Hachette you'll find it easier to forget Eurydice.

Father Oh, I'm not saying they produce a banquet. But you do eat well.

M. Henri The only place in the world where Eurydice's ghost does not exist is the Restaurant Jeanne Hachette in Perpignan. You ought to rush there.

Orpheus You think I want to forget her?

M. Henri (*tapping him on the shoulder*) You must, my dear fellow. As quickly as possible. You've been a hero for a day. In those few hours you exhausted your share of the pathos in life. It's over now, you're at peace. Forget, Orpheus, forget even Eurydice's name. Take your father's arm, go back to his restaurants. Life can assume its reassuring face again, death its usual percentage of chances, despair a form you can bear. Come on, get up, go with your father. Ahead of you there's still a fine career as a living being.

He has said this more sharply, leaning over **Orpheus**, *who raises his head and looks at him.*

Father (*after a pause, into his cigar*) You know, my boy, I've been in love too.

M. Henri You see, he's been in love too. Look at him.

Father That's right, look at me. I know it's sad. I've suffered, I have too. I'm not talking about your mother; when she died, we hadn't been in love for years. I lost a woman I adored. From Toulouse, a fiery creature. Dead in a week. Bronchitis. I wept like a dog, as I followed the coffin. They had to take me into a café. Look at me.

M. Henri (*quietly*) That's right. Look at him.

Father I must say, when I happen to sit down in the Grand Comptoir in Toulouse where we used to go together, I get a little pang in my heart, as I unfold my napkin. But enough of that! Life exists! You've got to live it! (*Pulls dreamily at his cigar and whispers with a sigh.*) Ah, the Grand Comptoir in Toulouse ... when I went there with her before the war, you could eat for one franc seventy-five!

M. Henri (*leaning over* **Orpheus**) Life exists. Life exists, Orpheus. Listen to your father.

Father (*made important by* **M. Henri**'s *words*) I'm going to be tough, my dear boy, and you're going to be angry, but I'm tougher than you and when you get to my age you'll admit I was right. You suffer at first, agreed. But soon, you'll see, without wanting to, you feel a new happiness ... One fine morning, it happened to me in the morning, you wash your face, you tie your tie, the sun's shining, you're out in the street and, suddenly, psst, you realise women have become pretty again. We're terrible, my dear fellow, all of us the same, rascals.

M. Henri Listen to him, Orpheus.

Father I'm not saying you make a dead set at the first one. No. After all we're not animals, and the first words seem odd ... It's funny, but all you can start talking about is the other woman. You say how lonely and helpless you are on your own. And it's true! You mean it! Oh, dear boy, you can't imagine how that kind of conversation softens a woman's heart. I know, you'll say I'm shameless. I used the same trick again ten years later.

Orpheus Shut up, father.

M. Henri Why do you want him to shut up? He's talking to you the way life will talk to you from every mouth; he's telling you what you'll read tomorrow in every eye, if you get up and try to live ...

Father (*off the leash now*) Life! Life's magnificent, dear boy ...

M. Henri Listen to him.

Father You mustn't forget you're an inexperienced lad and the man addressing you now has lived. God, how he's lived! Terrible we were at the Conservatoire in Niort! Such dogs! Gilded youth! Always a cane in our hand, a pipe in our mouth, up to some escapade or other. At that time I hadn't dreamt of the harp. I was studying the bassoon and the French horn. Every evening I walked seven kilometres to play under a lady's windows. Oh, we were merry, mad, extraordinary. We'd shrink at nothing. Once in the woodwind class we challenged the brass. We bet we'd drink thirty beers. Oh, how sick we were! But we were young! We understood life, we did!

M. Henri You see, Orpheus.

Father When you've health, muscle, a spark in you, all you have to do is forge ahead. I don't understand you, dear boy. First of all, good humour. Good humour's a question of balance. A single secret: daily exercise. The reason I've the shape you see I have is I've never stopped doing my exercises. Ten minutes every morning. That's all you need, it's ten minutes that count. (*Rises and, the remains of his cigar in his mouth, starts making ridiculous gym movements.*) One, two, three, four; one, two, three, four; breathe deeply. One, two, three, four, five. One, two, three, four, five. One, two. One, two. One, two. One, two. One, two. With this, no stomach, no varicose veins. Health from cheerfulness, cheerfulness from health and vice versa. One, two, three, four. Breathe deeply. One, two, three, four. That's my only secret.

M. Henri You see, Orpheus, it's really very simple!

Father (*having sat down, puffing like a seal*) It's a question of will-power. Everything in life's a question of will-power. What has helped me get out of the most difficult situations is my will-power. A will of iron! Of course there's the way you do it too ... I've always been considered a most amiable man. Velvet, but steel underneath. I walked straight. I knew no obstacle. Enormous ambition. Money, power. But careful! I'd a strong technical base. First prize for bassoon at the Niort Conservatoire. Second prize for French horn, honourable mention for harmony. I could proceed, I had baggage. (*To* **M. Henri**.) You see, I like youth to be ambitious. (*To* **Orpheus**.) Damn it all, don't you like the idea of being a millionaire?

M. Henri Answer your father, Orpheus.

Father Ah, money, money! That's what life's about, dear boy! You're unhappy, but you're young. Think, you might one day be rich. Luxury, elegance, food, women! Think about the women, my boy, think about love! Blondes, brunettes, redheads, hair dyed any colour! What variety, what a choice! It's there for you! You're the sultan, you take a stroll, you raise your finger. That one! You're rich, young, handsome, she falls into your arms. Then those nights of madness ... Shouts, bites, passion, hot kisses, the warm half-light, a touch of Spain! Or in a locked boudoir between five and seven, on a sofa swathed in mink, with a young girl, blonde, depraved. The light of a log fire plays on her bare skin, as she invents unimaginable games. There's no need to tell you more, dear boy. The excitement. Every possible excitement. A life of excitement. Where's your misery now? Vanished in smoke. (*He makes a gesture; becoming serious.*) But there are other things in life. Respectability, a social life. You're strong, powerful, a tycoon. You've given up music. The hard, impenetrable mask. Board meetings with wily operators, where the fate of the European economy's at stake. You lick the lot of them. Then the strike, the workforce up in arms, violence. You appear alone at the factory gate. A shot rings out; it misses you. But you don't flinch. In a voice of steel you talk to them. They were expecting promises, a climb-down. They don't know you. You are terrible. You lash them. They bow their heads, they return to work. Beaten. It's magnificent ... Then on your friends' advice you take up politics. Honoured, powerful, decorated, a senator. Always in the forefront. A great figure of a great Frenchman. A national funeral, flowers, vast quantities of flowers, muffled drums, speeches. And I, modest in a corner, they insisted on my presence at the ceremony, a handsome old man, ah yes, dear boy, my hair will be white! But nevertheless mastering my sorrow at the salute. (*Declaiming.*) 'Let us render homage to a father's grief ... !' (*It's too beautiful, he collapses.*) Oh, my boy, my boy, life's wonderful!

M. Henri You see, Orpheus.

Father The man before you has suffered. He has drunk from every chalice. He has often been silent, his teeth biting his lips till they drew blood, to avoid complaining. His boon companions have never suspected the torture he was suffering and yet ... treason, contempt, injustice ... Do you sometimes wonder why my body's bent, my hair prematurely white? If you knew the weight of life on a man's shoulders ...

He pulls in vain on the remains of his cigar, looks at it, irritated, and throws it away with a sigh.

M. Henri (*goes to him and holds out his cigar case*)   Another cigar?

Father   Thank you. I'm embarrassed. Yes, yes, embarrassed. What an aroma! The band's a little jewel. Tell me, my dear fellow, do you know, I've heard the girls who make them roll them completely naked on their thighs. (*He breathes it in.*) On their thighs ... (*He stops.*) What was I saying?

M. Henri   The weight of life ...

Father (*having lost his lyrical flow*)   What's that, the weight of life?

M. Henri   If you knew the weight of life on a man's shoulders ...

Father (*biting off the end of his cigar*)   Ah, yes, yes. If you knew, young fellow, the weight of life on a man's shoulders ... (*He stops, lights his cigar at length, and concludes simply.*) It's very heavy, my boy, it's extremely heavy. (*Taking a large puff appreciatively.*) Marvellous!! (*With a wink at* **M. Henri**.) I've the impression I'm smoking her thigh. (*He wants to laugh and chokes on the smoke.*)

M. Henri (*going to* **Orpheus**)   Were you listening to your father, Orpheus? Everyone should listen to his father. Fathers are always right.

Orpheus *raises his eyes and looks at him.*

M. Henri (*smiling; adds quietly*)   Even if they're fools. The way life is constructed, foolish fathers know as much about it as intelligent fathers, sometimes more. Life doesn't need intelligence. In fact it's the most embarrassing thing it meets in its happy progress.

Orpheus (*whispering*)   Life ...

M. Henri   Don't malign it. Yesterday evening you were defending it.

Orpheus   Yesterday's a long way off.

M. Henri (*quietly*)   I did tell you life would make you lose Eurydice.

Orpheus   Don't start accusing life ... 'Life' means nothing. It was me, just me.

M. Henri (*smiling*) Just you. How proud you are!

Orpheus Exactly ... my pride.

M. Henri Your pride! Really, little man? You want pride to belong to you too? Your love, your pride, now your despair I expect ... Why do you have to put a possessive pronoun before each of your little emotions? You are extraordinary! Why not my oxygen, my nitrogen? You must simply say Pride, Love, Despair. They're the names of rivers, little man. A stream breaks away and waters you among a thousand others. That's all. The river Pride does not belong to you.

Orpheus The river Jealousy doesn't either. I know that. And I suppose the pain that's drowning me comes from the same river Pain that at this moment's drowning millions of other men. It's the same icy water, the same anonymous current, so what? I'm not the sort of man who consoles himself by saying: 'That's life'. Why should I care if that's life ... if a million grains of sand are pulverised at the same time as me?

M. Henri They're your brothers, so it's said.

Orpheus I hate the lot of them, every one ... So don't let anyone try to provide a great affectionate sister for me out of the crowd. We're alone. We're better alone. That's the one thing that's certain.

M. Henri (*having leant towards him*) And you're alone because you've lost Eurydice. Remember that what life, your beloved life, was holding in store for you was being alone one day, with Eurydice still living.

Orpheus No.

M. Henri Yes. Some day or other, in one year, five years, ten years, if you like, without ceasing to love her maybe, you'd have realised you didn't desire Eurydice any more, she didn't desire you.

Orpheus No.

M. Henri Yes. It would be as stupid as that. You'd have been the man who was unfaithful to Eurydice.

Orpheus (*shouting*) Never!

M. Henri Why do you shout like that, for me or for yourself? If you'd rather, let's say you'd have been the man who wanted to be unfaithful to Eurydice; it's no better.

Orpheus I'd have been faithful to her for ever.

M. Henri Perhaps, in a sense for a long time. Never daring to cast a look at other women. With a slow, sure hatred beginning to grow between you because of all the girls you wouldn't have gone off with for her sake.

Orpheus It's not true.

M. Henri Yes. Till the day one of them passed in front of you, young and firm, without a hint of unhappiness, without a hint of a thought; a brand new woman, in contrast to your weariness. Then you'd be able to see death, treachery, a lie suddenly become the simplest things, to see injustice take another name, fidelity another face . . .

Orpheus No. I'd have closed my eyes. I'd have run away.

M. Henri The first time perhaps, and for a while you'd have gone on walking beside Eurydice, with the eyes of a man trying to lose his dog in the street. But the hundredth time . . . (*He makes a gesture.*) Anyway Eurydice might have left you first.

Orpheus (*this time plaintively*) No.

M. Henri Why not? Because she loved you yesterday? A little bird, able to fly away without knowing why, ready to die as a result, she too.

Orpheus We couldn't have stopped loving each other.

M. Henri She might not have stopped loving you, poor girl. It's not so easy to stop loving. Affection has a hard life, you know. She might have found a way of giving herself to you before going to meet her lover, so humble, so sweet, you could almost have gone on being a little happy. That's true.

Orpheus No, not us, not us!

M. Henri You, like everyone else. You, more than everyone else. With your way of being affectionate you'd have torn each other to shreds.

Orpheus No.

M. Henri Yes. Or else one day, tired, smiling, weak, you might have tacitly decided to kill the pathos between you and finally become happy and sweet to each other. And there would be Orpheus and Eurydice, accommodating . . .

Orpheus No! It would have lasted forever, till she was old and white at my side, till I was old with her!

M. Henri   Life, your beloved life, would never have let you reach that point. The love of Orpheus and Eurydice would not have escaped it.

Orpheus   Yes.

M. Henri   No, little man. You're all the same. You thirst for eternity and from the first kiss you're green with fright because of a vague feeling it can't last. Promises are soon exhausted. So you build houses, because stones last; you have a child, as in other days people cut their children's throats, to remain loved. You cheerfully gamble the happiness of this innocent little recruit in your dubious struggle over the most fragile thing in the world, the love of a man and a woman ... And that dissolves, crumbles, shatters, as it does for the ones who made no promises at all.

Father (*half asleep*)   When I say life's wonderful ... (*He turns over in his armchair, the hand holding the cigar falls: whispering blissfully.*) On their thighs ...

Orpheus *and* **M. Henri** *have been looking at him in silence.*

M. Henri (*abruptly in a whisper*)   Life would not have left you Eurydice, little man. But Eurydice can be given back to you for ever. The Eurydice of the first day, eternally pure and young, eternally like herself ...

Orpheus (*looks at him, then, after a pause, shakes his head*)   No.

M. Henri (*smiling*)   Why not, little man?

Orpheus   No, I don't want to die. I hate death.

M. Henri (*quietly*)   You're not being fair. Why do you hate death? Death is beautiful. Only death provides the real climate for love. You listened to your father talking about life just now. It was grotesque, wasn't it, deplorable? Well, that's what it is ... This farce, this absurd melodrama, is life. This awkwardness, these theatrical effects, are precisely it. Take a walk through life with your beloved Eurydice; you'll find her at the exit with the marks of hands all over her dress, you'll find her strangely decrepit. If you find her, if you find her! I'm offering you an intact Eurydice, a Eurydice with the real face life would never have given her. Do you want her?

The **Father** *begins to snore terribly.*

Your father's snoring. Look at him. He's ugly. Pitiful. He has
lived. Who knows? He may not have been as silly as he said
he was. There may have been one moment when he was
touched by love or beauty. Look at him now, clinging to life,
with his poor snoring carcass slumped in that chair. Have a
good look. People think the wear and tear of life on a face is
the fear of death. What a mistake! The fear is of once again
finding the insipidity, the softness of fifteen-year-old faces,
caricatured but intact, under these beards and glasses and
dignified airs. It's the fear of life. These wrinkled adolescents,
always laughing, always impotent, always weak, and more and
more sure of themselves. That's what men are ... Have a
good look at your young father, Orpheus, and remember that
Eurydice is waiting for you.

Orpheus (*suddenly, after a pause*) Where?

M. Henri (*goes towards him, smiling*) You always want to know
everything, little man ... I like you. I was distressed by your
suffering. It will be over now. You'll see how everything
becomes pure, limpid, luminous ... A world for you, my dear
Orpheus ...

Orpheus What must I do?

M. Henri Take your overcoat, the night is cool. Leave town
by the road that lies in front of you. When the houses thin
out, you'll reach a hill, by a grove of olive trees. It's there.

Orpheus What is?

M. Henri Your appointment with death. At nine o'clock. It's
almost time. Don't keep it waiting.

Orpheus I'll see Eurydice again?

M. Henri Right away.

Orpheus (*taking his coat*) Fine. Goodbye.

M. Henri Goodbye little man. But not for long.

*The **Father**'s snoring increases until it becomes a sort of continuous roll
of drums that does not cease till the end of the scene.*

The lighting changes imperceptibly. **M. Henri** *has stayed where he was,
motionless, his hands in his pockets.*

M. Henri (*suddenly, quietly*) Come in.

The door opens slowly. **Eurydice** *enters and remains upstage.*

Eurydice   He accepts?

M. Henri   Yes, he accepts.

Eurydice (*clasping her hands*)   Darling, please, come quickly.

M. Henri   He's coming.

Eurydice   At least he won't suffer?

M. Henri (*quietly*)   Did you?

The **Waiter** *knocks and enters.*

Waiter   If you don't mind, sir, I'll turn down the bed.

He draws the curtains and starts on the bed. He passes several times in front of **Eurydice** *without seeing her. He looks at the* **Father** *and smiles.*

Waiter   The gentleman's snoring, apparently that's a sign of good health. My mother always said only people who live well snore. I heard you talking, sir, I was afraid I'd disturb you.

M. Henri   I was talking to myself.

Waiter   That happens to me too. You sometimes tell yourself extraordinary things other people would never have told you. How's the young man, sir?

M. Henri   Fine.

Waiter   It must have been a terrible shock.

M. Henri   Yes.

Waiter   Do you think he'll ever get over it?

M. Henri   Yes. What time do you make it?

Waiter   Two minutes to nine, sir. (*He does the bed in silence.*)

We can only hear the **Father**'s *snoring. It increases.*

M. Henri (*suddenly calling*)   Waiter!

Waiter   Sir?

M. Henri   Tell them to prepare my bill, I'm leaving this evening.

Waiter   Yesterday you said . . .

M. Henri   I've changed my mind; this time I am going.

Waiter   Very good, sir. You've finished with Marseilles?

M. Henri Yes.

The **Waiter** *is about to go out.*

What time is it now?

Waiter Exactly nine, sir.

The **Waiter** *goes out, leaving the door wide open.*

M. Henri (*to* **Eurydice**, *who has not moved*) Here he is.

Eurydice (*quietly*) He can look at me?

M. Henri Yes, now, without fear of losing you.

Orpheus *enters, hesitating in the doorway, as if dazzled by the light.* **Eurydice** *runs to him and takes him in her arms.*

Eurydice Darling, how long you've been!

Nine o'clock strikes in the distance. The **Father** *suddenly stops snoring and wakes up with great rumbles.*

Father (*drawing on his cigar which has gone out*) Oh, I've been asleep? Where's Orpheus?

M. Henri *does not answer.*

Father (*looking around him, worried*) He's gone out? Well, answer me, dammit! Where is Orpheus?

M. Henri (*points to the embracing couple, but the* **Father** *does not see them*) Orpheus is with Eurydice at last!

The **Father** *has risen, dumbfounded. He has dropped his cigar.*

The curtain falls.

The Orchestra

A Play within a Concert

translated by Jeremy Sams

In the orchestra:

Patricia, *first violin*
Paméla, *second violin*
Madame Hortense, *double-bass and orchestra leader*
Suzanne Délicias, *cello*
Ermeline, *viola*
Léona, *flute*
M. Léon, *piano*

M. Lebonze, *manager of the brasserie*
A Waiter }
A Doctor } *non-speaking roles*

On the programme:

1   *Gay Reverie*
2   *Impressions of Autumn*
3   *Cockades and Cockcrows*
4   *Rapture in Havana*
5   *Gavotte of the Little Marquis*

Lively music. Curtain up on an all-female orchestra on a bandstand, in the restaurant in a spa-town, invisible to the audience. The ladies are dressed in rather revealing concert-gowns, indicative of thorough research in the realm of bad taste. At the back of the stage, a rather pinched, insignificant-looking individual – the **Pianist** *at his piano. At the side, an easel bearing a placard with the number three. The piece ends shortly after the curtain rises. As soon as they have finished, the musicians start chatting.*

Patricia   Anyway – then I put in the shallots and leave the whole thing to simmer – low heat – ten minutes maximum. And that's your sauce – so then I dice the veal . . .

Paméla   I normally add bacon.

Patricia   Well that's not *timbale de Poitiers* then is it – you never use bacon.

Paméla   Well I do.

Patricia   Then it's not the real thing. Not proper *timbale de Poitiers*. Sounds more like pig swill to me. When you're from Loudon, like me, then you know.

They give their parts to **Mme. Hortense** *(double-bass, leader of the orchestra).*

Paméla   So what, nothing to boast about – I'm from Batignolles.

Patricia *(sourly)*   Oh, very metropolitan.

Mme. Hortense, *still collecting parts, comes round to* **Suzanne Délicias**, *who is knitting discreetly behind her cello. They continue an interrupted conversation.*

Mme. Hortense   No, it's knit three, purl two, slip three, start again and Bob's your uncle.

Suzanne   Oh, that's Japan stitch.

Mme. Hortense   Hardly, my dear. Japan stitch has got a wrong side, my personal stitch has got two right sides.

Suzanne *(bitter laugh)*   Well, as I see it, if you're going to loop it round like that, that's going to be more like two wrong sides – for a man's pullover it must look ghastly.

Mme. Hortense   Have it your way, my dear. Anyway, Japan stitch is *so* vulgar.

Ermeline *(viola) is finishing a conversation with* **Léona** *(flute) who* *is slightly hunchbacked.*

Ermeline   So I told him straight out. Edmond, you cannot make a woman suffer like that with impunity.

Léona   What did he say?

Ermeline   Something unrepeatable.

Mme. Hortense (*continuing her rounds; jokily, to the* **Pianist**)   Monsieur Léon – miles away as usual, head in the clouds. Come on, chop chop. Let's have your *Gay Reverie* out smartish, or we'll get our parts all mixed up again. Can't have that. Dreaming as usual – and your dandruff's getting worse.

Pianist   All artists have dandruff.

Mme. Hortense   In moderation perhaps. Why didn't you try the lotion I recommended? Papal Pomade – just the job.

Pianist   I thought the scent a trifle louche. A touch oriental. Not exactly manly.

Mme. Hortense   Well it was manly enough for Monsieur Hortense, whom God preserve. And I think I may say that in our twelve years of marriage, he was most attentive. Regular as clockwork, three performances a day, including a matinée, which says something. Oh yes, happy days – much loved I was – and thoroughly attended to. What woman could ask for more.

Pianist   Well he was a violinist – and you know violinists . . .

Mme. Hortense (*meaningfully*)   I have also known pianists with hot blood in their veins.

Pianist (*modestly*)   Yes – but that's rarer.

Mme. Hortense *parts the scores she's collected on a table at the back of the bandstand.* **Suzanne Délicias** *leaves her knitting and goes to the piano.*

Suzanne   Never stops, does she.

Pianist   We were just chatting. This and that.

Suzanne   If you don't shut her up, then I will.

Pianist   That's tricky when we're working, she is the leader.

Suzanne   You're a coward. Pathetic.

Patricia (*continuing a conversation, most of which we've missed*)   No,

I give a good rub-down with a spot of Eezikleen on a nice dry rag.

Paméla   Oh, I prefer a drop of ammonia.

Patricia   Use ammonia and you don't get rid of the stain, you get rid of the varnish.

Paméla   Well, we all have our methods.

Patricia   Yours sound particularly unsuitable, I must say. Interior decoration – you have to have a feel for it.

Paméla   My interior's every bit as good as yours. (*She giggles.*) Perhaps fewer knick-knacks and whatnots.

Patricia   Well we can't all have flair can we? My home's my little nest, warm, cosy, rather feminine – it's my little touches make all the difference.

Paméla   Sounds like a dust-trap. My décor's absolutely bang up to date. Nice tubular furniture, formica tops. Everything neat and spic and span. No nonsense.

Patricia   Sounds more like a clinic. Not for me thank you very much. I'm not ill.

Paméla   You're implying I am?

Patricia   Well your eyes do look a bit ... you know, haggard.

Paméla   Well if I do have circles under my eyes it's because I have a lover who adores me and can't leave me alone. Which is certainly not so in your case. And at least my eyes both look in the same direction.

Patricia (*squinting nervously*)   That's right, make fun of other people's physical imperfections. Imperceptible ones to boot. That's as low as low. And as for your lover – he's not that much to boast about – a washer-up in a café.

Paméla (*giggling*)   Well at least he works. And works hard. Yes, I like a man who enjoys hard work – who likes to see a job well done. Who puts his back into it!

Patricia (*recoiling*)   You are so cheap – I am surprised they let a woman like you into a respectable orchestra like this!

Mme. Hortense (*who has changed the number on the easel, handing out music*)   Ladies. No tiffs, please. Not on stage. Even when we're not playing, we're on display. Grace, manners, deportment, please. You can still speak your minds – but with a smile. Point taken? Paméla – your bloom.

Paméla   What about it?

Mme. Hortense   It's drooping – I want to see perky blooms in my orchestra.

Patricia (*sarcastic*)   It's all washed up!

Paméla *furious at this allusion, stamps on her foot.*

Patricia   Ow!

Mme. Hortense   Ladies, please.

Patricia   She's a bitch. She just trod on my foot.

Mme. Hortense   Ladies, conduct, please. You owe it to your public. That's what the manager said when he gave us this job, in preference I may say to Mag's All Stars and the Symphonic Syncopators – both respectable bands – 'I choose you, because I want femininity, I want grace, I want to let my customers dream a bit.'

Paméla   Dream? Some hope. They've all come here for their constipation. That's all they talk about. They're probably not even listening to us. They're adding up their bills, as well as they may!

Mme. Hortense   It is none of our concern what the customers are thinking of, or whether they are constipated or not. Style, posture, elegance – those are the key-notes. That is what they want. And bags of femininity. Now we will play *Impressions of Autumn* – by Chandoisy, in a lovely arrangement by Goldenstein. Lots of emotion, lots of *vibrato*, if you please.

As she passes him, she slides her finger round M. Léon, the **Pianist***'s collar.*

I say, you're jolly hot, Monsieur Léon. Your collar is quite moist.

Pianist   I keep two. I'll change in the break, after we've done the march from *Tannhäuser*.

Suzanne   That's *it*! That does it! I'm leaving!

Pianist   Please, Suzanne, no scenes, no scandal. She merely pointed out that I was too hot. I could hardly deny it.

Suzanne   You're a monster. A cruel vicious monster.

Mme. Hortense We'd better watch out for the accidentals on your solo on the *da capo*, hadn't we, Mademoiselle Délicias? They do sometimes take us by surprise, don't they?

Ermeline (*finishing a conversation with* **Léona**) So I went mad. I told him everything. The lot. Couldn't stop. About my mortgage, about my mother, about my period being late, you know . . .

Léona Heavens, what did he say?

Ermeline Nothing. He was asleep.

Léona Insensitive beast. I'd never have put up with that from André.

Mme. Hortense *discreetly taps her bow against a music stand. The piece starts. Very tender and melodious. While they play, the musicians talk.*

Patricia I'm still a woman. To my fingertips. More than you are – even though I don't get on my back for just anybody. I'm waiting for the man who can look me deep in the eyes.

Paméla Could be tricky with yours.

Patricia (*sobbing*) Oh!

Paméla He'd have to make a round trip.

Patricia How dare you!

Mme. Hortense *gives her a discreet tap on the hand with her bow.* **Patricia** *swallows her anguish, plays on with feverish abandon.*

Ermeline Anyway, we'd gone to this restaurant, posh place, nice, we were meeting friends there. I said, 'Edmond, my love, where shall I sit?'

Léona And he said?

Ermeline 'Where do you think? On your fat ar . . .'

Another tap from the bow and a big chord from the orchestra drown the rude word. The piece ends, brilliantly, but with much pathos. **Mme. Hortense** *sets out to recover the parts, changes the placard.*

Patricia Where's the waiter with our drinks! I'm dying of thirst here. It is in our contract.

Paméla There's punters to serve first. They couldn't care less about our little glass of beer.

Patricia   Typical. The artists always come last.

Mme. Hortense (*changing the number*)   At the break, ladies, you know the rules. We get one drink per session – at the break.

Patricia   Yesterday it arrived at midnight. But he's quick enough off the mark on Saturdays, when he gets his tips. Last week I gave 20 centimes ... provincials – there's some as don't mind though, don't care. Happy to entertain them, in bed even. But I was brought up differently, that's all. My father was an army man. Officer. Fancy me ending up in a dump like this.

Mme. Hortense   The Brasserie du Globe et du Portugal is a first-rate establishment, as you well know. You were happy to take the job in the first place. Don't rock the boat.

Patricia   And with my talent. I've given concert after concert. As a soloist too. One time, at a charity do, Massenet, yes, *the* Massenet was in the hall. Afterwards, backstage, he kissed my hand. We'd done an arrangement of *Mignon*, and I'd given it my all. The Master had tears in his eyes. In fact he was so moved, he couldn't say a word. And he was famously so garrulous ... Obviously, you wouldn't understand.

Mme. Hortense   We've all had our little triumphs. Monsieur Hortense was first violin at the Brasserie Zurki in St Petersburg, as was. Obviously this was before the revolution: he played before the crowned heads of Europe. But there's downs as well as ups. Which never stopped him being a conscientious artist. He used to say, 'Zelia, Zelia, music's like soup – it comes in all forms, but it's always good stuff.'

Patricia   But playing for the constipated; I mean, really.

Mme. Hortense   Constipation never stopped anyone from appreciating good music. Quite the opposite, I would have thought. There are many, many music lovers here. Only yesterday a fat Belgian industrialist came up to congratulate me. He even mentioned you.

Patricia (*transformed*)   Oh really? How super. What did he say?

Mme. Hortense   He wanted to know if you were from Ghent. Seems you reminded him of someone there. At the Kursaal. A cloakroom attendant.

Ermeline (*to* **Léona**) So I said, 'Edmond, please. It may not be your cup of tea – but don't go upsetting everyone else.'

Léona *Touché.*

Ermeline *Touché* indeed. That showed him. I went on: 'I'm a woman – and you can't prevent a woman from thinking and feeling like a woman.' Well, my dear, I could see that hit the spot.

Léona What did he say?

Ermeline Nothing. He just kept on brushing his teeth.

Léona So what did you do?

Ermeline I put down my clippers – I was just doing my toenails at the time – and I walked out of the bathroom.

Léona Just like that?

Ermeline Just like that. I wasn't going to let him get away with it. So I put my girdle back on, stockings. Still not a dicky-bird. So I put my dress on and thought, right, that's it – you know me – and I left, giving the door a good, hard slam. I was furious. I thought, the first man who has a kind word for me, that's it, I'm his. Except there was no one about but the night doorman, an old chap, black, and you know what Moulin's like at the best of times. But one o'clock in the morning! Not a soul. I was round by the cathedral. Apparently it's quite pretty – but of course it was dark so I couldn't really see. So at half past two I went back up. I was done in. I had my pink shoes on – you know, the ones I gave you because they were too tight. And my girdle was killing me. And because I'd shouted on the way out that I was going to finish it once and for all, I was afraid he was going to call the police because of the Beaune. And I didn't want any trouble, or awkward questions, you know, because . . .

Léona What bone?

Ermeline Don't be dim. It's the river that runs through Moulins. Moulins-sur-Beaune. A woman in a bit of a state, you know, like I was, I mean it's well known, she might do anything. And actually I did go to the bank – of the river I mean, but it was so dark. So I came back.

Léona Oh I see. He thought you might be dead. So what did he say when he saw you?

Ermeline Nothing. He didn't see me. He'd gone out as well.

Léona To contact the police?

Ermeline No, to play cards with his mates in the all-night café opposite the station.

Suzanne (*standing by the piano, to the* **Pianist**) I've put up with so much. Our secret meetings, our sporadic couplings in that sordid little hotel, where the manager talks to me like I'm a tart. To me! The dreams I've had – of walking round this town with my head held high, with my best boy on my arm. But there are some things I will not put up with. And one is the shameful advances of that woman to the man I have chosen. And given myself to. Your wife, fine, she's not a well woman – I understand your concern for her, although all these precautions are so humiliating, but even so . . . I understand. But here, under my very nose, so shameless, rampant. And on stage.

Pianist We only talk about work, my love.

Suzanne Oh yes. Her finger in your collar, is that work? Stroking your hair, is that work?

Pianist She merely pointed out that I had dandruff on my DJ which is perfectly within her rights as orchestral manager.

Suzanne Your collar, is mine, Léon. Your hair's mine – your dandruff's mine. That fine, soft snowfall, the right to brush your shoulders, mine, all mine! I've given you all of myself, my cherished virginity, all my illusions, the good name of my family, irreproachable in every regard, all the way down to my sister the nun whom it would kill if she heard about it. So every part of you is now mine. And I'll scratch like a lioness if . . .

Pianist Lionesses bite. It's tigresses scratch – I told you that before.

Suzanne Fine. So be it. I'll bite then.

As **Mme. Hortense** *passes,* **Suzanne** *suddenly bares her teeth and roars like a lion.*

Rrrrrraaaa!

Mme. Hortense Are you all right?

Suzanne *bursts into tears.*

Pianist It's her nerves. Her nerves.

Mme. Hortense Have your nerves by all means, my dear, but not at work. Not in the orchestra. We are the focal point of the entire establishment. (*To* **Léon.**) Slap her on the back, will you, go on, quick. They'll think something's gone down the wrong way. No scandal in the orchestra.

Pianist (*hitting her on the back*) My love, my bunny rabbit, my kitten, my little mousey, my . . .

Mme. Hortense Please. Spare us La Fontaine's fables, at least till after work. You're here to do one thing only, will you please do it.

Suzanne Stop hitting me. You're hurting me. (*She rises. To* **Mme. Hortense.**) He is my lover, he loves me and I love him. I want you to know that.

Mme. Hortense No Mademoiselle Délicias. I have no desire to know any such thing; sordid details. You are desecrating the Temple of Music!

Suzanne Oh, that's right, shut me up in the name of Art. I am not ashamed. I hold my head high, as you see, high and proud. (*She promenades absurdly.*)

Mme. Hortense (*removing the score which* **Suzanne** *is waving about in an aristocratic fashion*) All I ask is don't damage your parts! Have you any idea what this library costs? Look at that *Cockades and Cockcrows*, all crumpled up. And such a charming piece!

Suzanne Charming, that? Ha! Your taste in music, if you don't mind me saying so, is execrable. Charming? Third-rate. By, who, Duverger?

Mme. Hortense Yes, arranged by Benoiseau, my dear, a professional who knew his job, I'm here to tell you. I worked with him in Royan at the casino, in the good old days. A real musician.

Suzanne I'm sorry, but I was brought up on the classics. They are my life-blood. Oh Beethoven. Oh – Saint-Saëns.

Mme. Hortense In an establishment of this sort, the customers play cards, or dominoes, anything to distract them from his or her health problems. And what he or she requires is a nice comfortable cushion of sound. Something they can rely on. This piece is gay, exciting, uplifting. And French.

Which is just what is needed in a café.

Suzanne Oh God, that I should have fallen so low. This humiliation is killing me, this mediocrity is suffocating me. No, I will not be singing the grand aria from *La Vestale*. My voice is in tatters. I cannot, I will not sing.

Mme. Hortense My dear, the aria from *La Vestale* is on the programme. The printed programme. And to change the programme creates a most unfortunate impression. Monsieur Lebonze has expressly forbidden it. It unsettles the customers. You will sing.

Suzanne No, no. I can't. My nerves. I can't stand it. Help me, Léon. She's a slave driver.

Mme. Hortense You have a small spirit and a small mind. Monsieur Léon is an artist and a man – he has learned to adapt, to fit in. As I have.

She sweeps on, grandly, distributing music.

Ermeline None of my business. I'm not getting involved. Although I have to say that if she was making a fraction of the advances to my Edmond that she's making to that poor boy, I'd hit the roof. Once, we were working in the casino at Palaras. I went out in the break, came back and he'd gone, left the stage. You know where I found him?

Léona No.

Ermeline With the lavatory attendant!

Léona Never!

Ermeline You bet. A big brassy blonde – the stories we'd heard about her! I mean, can you imagine? The lav lady!

Léona What was he doing?

Ermeline Well afterwards he claimed he was after some change. Didn't fool me for a minute. Know what I did?

Léona No, what?

Ermeline Nothing. I just gave them a look, like that, and went into the ladies, asking 'sorry, is there any paper?'

Léona *Touché*! What did *he* do?

Ermeline He went into the gents – he didn't say a word. But he'd gone a very funny colour, believe you me. He knew he'd been caught out, I could tell.

Léona   Quite right too. Some people have to be put in their place.

Mme. Hortense (*suddenly from the back*)   Men! Listen, I've had dozens of them. Dozens. Big ones, handsome ones, rich ones ... but since Monsieur Hortense died – I've been in voluntary retirement. But I'll have you know that if I needed a man, I would ...

Suzanne   You would what, madame?

Mme. Hortense   I'd pick someone a bit better built. So there!

Suzanne   This is outrageous.

Pianist   Ladies!

Suzanne   Léon is beautiful – he has a Greek nose.

Mme. Hortense   Forget the nose. I believe in the pectorals.

Pianist   Ladies!

Mme. Hortense   Monsieur Hortense was built like a refrigerator. He could really do a girl some damage. Now that's what I call love.

Suzanne   You are so vulgar, madame.

Pianist   Ladies!!

Suzanne   You with your stevedores, your stagehands, your barmen. They are anathema to me. I refuse them. I vomit them up. I'd rather die than be pawed by their horny hands. Léon has the body of a sylph, not a suspicion of a tum. Léon – show her your body. Who could deny that you are beautiful?

Pianist   Suzanne! Not at work!

Suzanne   Why not? I'm not ashamed of our love. Let the whole world know, let them look, let them talk. I am proud of it.

Mme. Hortense (*terrified look into the café*)   Suzanne Délicias – pull yourself together. The manager's looking this way. You know he doesn't like us gossiping in the orchestra. And you also know our contract is renewable fortnightly. (*Shouts, obsequiously.*) Straightaway Monsieur Lebonze, straightaway. On we go. Ready, ladies; *Cockades and Cockcrows*. Up tempo. Bags of verve. Here we go. Bar for nothing. One, two, three, four.

And they play a genre piece, heroic, lively. **Suzanne Délicias** *whispers to the* **Pianist***, playing passionately the while.*

Suzanne   I'll kill myself.

Pianist   Suzanne!

Suzanne   Laudanum!

Pianist (*different tone, this time, and subsequently*)   Suzanne!

Suzanne   I'll throw myself in the river.

Pianist   Suzanne!

Suzanne   Or under a train.

Pianist   Suzanne!

Suzanne   No, no. That's just what she wants. She'd have no competition. No, I know what I'll do. Tomorrow, I'll buy a new dress. Whatever's most expensive at 'Le Petit Paris'. Two weeks' salary I'll spend. I'll look as slim as a wasp in it, and show her up with her great fat bottom.

Pianist   Suzanne!

Suzanne   Do you love me, Léon?

Pianist   I adore you, my love, you know that, no one but you.

Suzanne   You're not afraid of death, are you?

Pianist   With you?

Suzanne   Yes!

Pianist   No!

Suzanne   So if life is too miserable for us we'll die in each other's arms. That'll show them!

Pianist   Yes it would, I suppose.

Suzanne (*darkly, in spite of the piece of music which is getting progressively jollier*)   Death must be wonderful!

Pianist (*lukewarm*)   Yes, I suppose so . . .

Big splashy chords – end of number. Sporadic applause – **Mme. Hortense** *radiant, takes a discreet bow, indicates orchestra. Then turns to gather up the scores.*

Mme. Hortense Did you hear that applause? You see, *Cockades and Cockcrows* arranged by Benoiseau still weaves its magic spell. And what did you call it, third-rate? Well, my dear, you see the effect. It gets people somewhere deep inside – in their guts. A true Frenchman recognises it straightaway as *his* music. For him, and about him. Those who don't appreciate it, firstly do not love their country and then have cabbage water in their veins rather than true French blood!

Suzanne I won't honour that with a reply…

Mme. Hortense I have patriotism in my blood and in my soul. During the war, when work was really thin on the ground, I wouldn't go and play in Vichy. I said no. There are others I could mention who didn't share my scruples – some, even, who entertained the enemy.

Suzanne Your insinuations mean nothing to me. Sticks and stones … Very well, I did play in a brasserie in Paris in 1940, but we were a Resistance orchestra. When there were German officers in the audience, we put the word around and we played out of tune. Which took some courage, actually, because the Bosch were all considerable musicians.

Mme. Hortense Playing out of tune on purpose, eh? I'm surprised they noticed.

Suzanne Right, that's it – you attack me, you attack my talent: I'm not wanted, plainly. I'm leaving.

She starts to leave the stage, stopped by the **Pianist**.

Patricia That's a bit much, attacking her on that score. Pots and kettles. Maybe she didn't play in Vichy, but I'm sure she did some radio work.

Pianist This argument is ridiculous – pointless. We're not discussing your talent, Suzanne.

Suzanne Talent? What talent? I plainly have no talent at all any more. Funny that, when I was a bit of a prodigy in my day. Don't you think that's funny? So I've given nothing to my Art, nor to my country, nor to you.

Pianist No, I mean yes, you have. Please Suzanne, don't make a scene, no scandal, not here, Suzanne!

Suzanne Hang scandal! I am steeped in it. I have given myself to you, regularly in degrading circumstances in furnished rooms. (*She shouts, a madwoman.*) *Furnished*, do you hear!

Pianist   Calm down, Suzanne, calm down. Hotel rooms are
always furnished. At least in Europe they are, mostly. And
anyway, when we were on the road . . .

Suzanne (*long nervous laugh*)   Oh yes, on the road; the road to
the other side of town. Travelling light, weren't we. No luggage
– the way the manager looked at me – so embarrassing, when
we'd ask for our room. Looking me up and down, sharing me
with you, carving me up.

Pianist   You're exaggerating, Suzanne. He's a respectable
married man . . .

Suzanne   So are you, that's what I'm saying – both of you
sharing me, checking me in, checking me out . . . travelling
light! We made love with one eye on the clock. So your pitiful
sick wife shouldn't be incommoded by your coming home late
again. But what about me? Wasn't I sick? Wasn't I pitiful?

Pianist   That's different Suzanne . . .

Suzanne (*exalted*)   No luggage perhaps but we were weighed
down with timepieces, weren't we – clocks, watches. On our
bedside tables. Some lovers lie in bed and listen to the beating
of their hearts. For us it was the ticking of our watches.
Together, apart, together. Always wondering whether one of
them was slow, or both. That watch! I hate it – I stamp on it.
(*She tears it off, stamps on it.*) Give me yours too. (*She tries to tear it
off.*)

Pianist (*pitiful, trying to pick up her watch, defending his own*)   My
love, everyone's looking . . . please . . . The glass isn't cracked,
thank God. You're going too far Suzanne. This is silly.
Everyone checks their watch nowadays. That's the pace of
modern life.

Suzanne   Don't give me modern life. I'm a modern woman
– a liberated woman as they say. Emancipated. I've thrown off
my chains – except, ha! my watch chains, they bind me still.
Isn't that ironic – isn't that funny.

Pianist   I told you at the beginning that I would not risk
killing my poor sick wife. And you said that our love was big
enough to survive.

Suzanne   Well it wasn't, and it didn't. It's been throttled, our
love, by the hands of your watch. It's been flushed down the
lavatory, along with the children I could have had. Time after
time I've said we should die, Léon – together, which would be

seemly. Everyone drowned together, the father, the mother, our children, instead of just the children like normal. So simple!

Pianist It only seems simple, my love, to you ... I didn't have the right to just abandon her.

Suzanne You had the right to abandon me when my time was up, three-quarters of an hour sessions, once a day. I didn't preserve my honour all those years only to be allowed to be a real woman for forty-five minutes a day. Each one counted off, on two watches, if you please.

Pianist No, no. An hour, sometimes an hour and a half. I always told her I was working late, you know that.

Suzanne Yes, but there's travelling to be taken into account. *And* porterage. I could only be your wife on the other side of town. Otherwise people might see us. Walking stiffly side by side as if we were strangers.

Pianist (*trying to be romantic*) But what of that? What does time matter, when you're in love?

Suzanne I think it matters a great deal. I've worked that much out. Because what else is life made of but time? And I've wasted mine. Funny expression that – wasted – what have I done, poured it down the sink, mislaid it somewhere? Can't exactly pray to St Anthony, can I, to return it? (*Suddenly bursts out.*) What time do you have, Léon? Have we got the same time? Mine says quarter to eleven.

Pianist Twelve minutes to, actually, which means we're still 'on'. Get back on stage, my love. We'll have a nice long talk about it at the break. Fifteen lovely long minutes.

Suzanne (*haughty*) No thank you. I've finished work for tonight.

Mme. Hortense (*has come over to them, voice low, with suppressed fury*) Have you *quite* finished? This is disgraceful – the manager is staring at us. Do you want to get us all the sack? Is that what you want, you grumpy cow?

Suzanne (*nobly*) No, madame. But who cares? It's all over for me, anyhow. No more playing out of tune. Farewell madame, he's all yours. I wish you joy of him. You're right, he's a scrawny runt. I only hope you've got a decent watch.

Laughs, exits.

Mme. Hortense (*shouting after her*) Right, that's 500 francs' fine. On the spot and I'll have you replaced by Saturday.

Pianist She's not happy, Madame Hortense. Do not abuse your power. (*He goes back to his piano.*) You should be ashamed of yourself.

Mme. Hortense No, you should, Monsieur Léon, with your poor sick wife. That hysteric will tell her everything, you mark my words, just to make herself feel better.

Pianist (*dumbfounded*) Oh no, oh no . . .

Mme. Hortense I know all about men, Monsieur Léon, I've tamed a few in my time, not just you. A man needs comfort and love, that's only human. But demand it from a real woman who understands life and has something to offer, for God's sake. And yes, I was lying just now. I don't find you skinny at all. A little slight perhaps, but for the motherly type, like myself, well, it's just another attraction. (*Finger round the collar.*) Oh, who's a naughty boy? Aren't we getting hot and sweaty. Oh, doesn't he like being petted? He does so need someone to make a big fuss of him.

Pianist (*weeping now, head in his arms*) I can't take any more of these scenes. My nerves won't stand it. I'm not strong enough for this life.

Mme. Hortense You want someone to help, don't you, you know you do. Who needs all these unsavoury episodes? No one. A little discreet pleasure on the side, that's all one needs to be happy. You're dripping, you're sopping. Go on, put on a clean collar, my little love.

Pianist (*a broken man, yet still dignified*) After the March from *Tannhäuser*. Before would be pointless. (*He sobs.*) You mustn't think I no longer love my wife. Twelve years, unforgettable years. Of course I could have put her away in hospital. She is incurable. No one would have thought the worse of me. I kept her at home where she belongs, in spite of her nagging and her petty jealousy. I took a housekeeper, someone I can rely on. But it all costs money! Sometimes I feel so alone.

Mme. Hortense You need someone to help you – instead of torturing yourself like this. Someone with feelings like yourself. Someone sensitive.

Pianist (*groan*) Sensitive. I'm *too* sensitive, I'm fragile; like a harp.

Mme. Hortense You're an artist, that's all. And artists, apart from in their art, can't afford to be sensitive, to have *feelings*. A little discreet pleasure, yes of course – but all the rest must go into the music. You notice that that madwoman was the only one we had problems with?

Pianist She's a harp too, like me.

Mme. Hortense Well she needs tuning. And she's got half her strings missing. Really, waltzing off the platform like that, for *nothing*! Just as we were going to do *Rapture in Havana*. Léona, be a poppet will you and have a look in the toilets, see if she's in there snivelling.

Exit **Léona**.

Feelings, you see, are fine and well and good but work comes first. And we'll get the sack if we're not careful. The manager's on the warpath. I don't know what's got into him tonight – he's really suspicious.

She hands out parts.

Patricia (*continuing a conversation with* **Paméla** – *surprisingly amicable*) Well I don't know, I still think she's horrible to her. Talking about the war like that – it's a subject to avoid, isn't it. I mean I did my bit, resisted – we all did. I listened to the broadcasts from London every day. I did what I could, naturally. But you see, there was always my mother. Poor thing. I had to get her the odd treat, didn't I?

Paméla Do you still look after her, your old lady?

Patricia 'Course. Poor baby. Tootsie. That's what I call her now. She's not much more than a baby, is she, not now; my Tootsie Wootsie. I've devoted my life to her – her and my Art – and my little flat of course.

Paméla Well, that's you isn't it? I mean, I couldn't do what you do. When I go and see mine – in Batignolles – she's quite happy, she's a concierge. It's fine at first. Hello mummy, yes mummy. It's like when I was tiny. She makes me mutton stew, with beans – she's obsessed with beans for some reason – silly old bat. After a couple of mouthfuls off we go – major rows – we turn the table, crockery flies all over the place and I go home in a huff.

Patricia Well, to be honest, we have our altercations too, my Tootsie and I, silly tiffs. She's more like a little girl the older she gets. Silly whims. I have to be awfully strict. If she tries to steal a sweetie – then it's whack! Right on her thieving paws. She goes 'Ow, ow!' Then tries tears and snivels but after that she's as good as gold. The real worry of course is toilet training. I try and get her to ask. But often she doesn't – she just goes, there, on the spot.

Paméla   It's probably a phase. I'm sure she'll get better, I'm sure she will.

Patricia   She's almost eighty so it's hardly likely. But I'm absolutely inflexible with her. I change her three times a day – and if she's had an accident in between, she has to put up with it. Sometimes I think she does it out of spite. The way she times it. I'm all dolled up ready to go off to work, and that's when she asks to go.

Paméla   You have to be firm. When my little girl was at home . . .

Patricia   (*interrupts*)   You'll never guess what the latest thing is. She's started sucking her thumb.

Paméla   My mother smeared mustard on mine. But I don't know if it would work for old people.

Patricia   Mustard! She'd be thrilled. She adores mustard. Everything that's bad for her, she loves. God, if I let her eat what she wanted! And when I catch her, a good sharp whack. And no pudding! Which really hurts. Oh yes, puddings, chocolates, sweets, if I gave in then that'd be half my income down the drain. No. I'm very strict about that. We won't have any sweeties in the house. If any are smuggled in – a visitor, say – I hide the bag and it's one a week. Sunday. If she's been good. You should hear her snivelling in front of the cupboard, begging, 'Sweetie, sweetie, Tootsie want a sweetie'. Pathetic. As I said, a real baby.

Paméla   It's for her own good. They're so bad for the teeth.

Patricia   It would be if she had any. But it's the principle of the thing. If you give in once, well . . .

Paméla   It must be a funny old life, though, yours.

Patricia   Well there is one great satisfaction – one is doing one's duty. Mummy is everything to me, apart from my Art of course. She is my sacrifice – one I'm happy to make. I'm not one to boast as you know – but I do think I am a model daughter. It's just that she has to toe the line.

Paméla I sent my kid off to the country. When work drove my husband and I apart, I couldn't cope. Plus I'm a woman, and a woman needs a man. And men never really get used to children. And if one turns up who isn't put off, you can be sure that sooner or later he'll change his mind. But every penny goes on her clothes. I know it's . . . but I want my little Mouquette to be just perfect. Just gorgeous. A real little lady. For her fifth birthday I bought a party dress, a little crinoline with paniers, ribbons, the lot. Set me back 12,000 – you see I won't scrimp on her. Oh no. I sent her a postal order, as well, to pay for her first perm and a perfect little case of assorted lipsticks, nail varnish, everything. It was such a hit. You should have seen her – done up to the nines – fingernails, lips, gorgeous. Like me – only tiny. A miniature me. That's why I love that kid. Unfortunately on that occasion I couldn't stop long. I'd had a row with Fernand – he wouldn't even get out of the car. Just sat there – started tooting the horn. 'Mummy, mummy,' she said, 'You haven't even given me a kiss.' (*She sighs.*) Of course you'd love to see them more often. But what can you do – you've got your own life to live and that's that. Anyway, she got her party dress. And that's what they *remember* isn't it?

Patricia But that's us all over isn't it, artists? Big hearts. Friends say to me, 'Put her in a home – she'll have everything done for her there.' And they're right, she would be better off – I'm always away, I'm always working. But – I just couldn't do it – I really couldn't. I'm happier at home – punishing her when she has one of her little accidents and knowing that I'm doing my duty. Much happier. I mean, she is my mother. Friends say to me 'Patricia, you're a saint.' I say yes, I know, but that's the way I am, I can't change now.

Paméla And even if you could change – or had done things differently – would it be for the better, necessarily? I could have stayed with her father, I could have taken care of her. All right, I know he walked in on me and Georges, but I convinced him it was the first time! These things happen – you work them out, especially if there's a child involved. But then Georges said, 'I'm going to Nice.' And I was crazy about him – I couldn't just lose him. So I left the kid. I was only off with Georges for two months for God's sake – but I suppose I wasn't to know that at the time. But there we go. *C'est la vie.*

Patricia   Wouldn't your husband have had you back?

Paméla   Well I thought about it, of course I did, you know, for the sake of the kid. The divorce hadn't actually come through. And he was so – well I could easily have made things up – in bed, I mean. So I packed my things and set off home. Only I met this chap in the train. I was feeling quite rich at the time, so I'd gone 'first'. And it was just the two of us in the compartment. Well you know how these things happen. (*She sighs.*) Silly. I'd bought her this gorgeous little outfit from Nice – matching hat and skirt, everything. Which was stupid of me. But anyway I sent it on by post . . . and she was over the moon, little Mouquette. Apparently all the girls at school were green with envy. They were saying 'Lucky you, having a mum like that.' Because it was the very very best – little silk apron, everything. I know I spoil that kid, but there's nothing I wouldn't do for her.

Patricia   Just like me and my mother. I make so many sacrifices, give her everything – and all she has to do is behave. Otherwise it's a sharp whack and no pudding. We devote our lives to them. But do we expect gratitude? We don't.

Léona (*returns*)   I've looked everywhere – she's not in the toilets. At least I don't think so – there's one cubicle engaged but I didn't want to bash on the door. It might be a customer.

Mme. Hortense   Silly bitch. Ah well. Right, ladies, quickly into *Rapture in Havana*. Monsieur Lebonze is rather ostentatiously checking his watch. He must be thinking we're taking our break early. Ermeline, look sharp, back to your place. Hats, everybody. We'll say she's got food poisoning – happened last week, didn't it? Somebody got a dodgy mushroom.

Mme. Hortense *is handing out parts.*

Ermeline (*putting her hat on, helped by* **Léona**)   Poor girl, she's suffering I can tell. I understand. Love hurts. Love kills. Once I said to Edmond, right to his face, 'Feelings do not forgive. I catch you with someone else, I'll shut my eyes and just pull the trigger. When a woman's suffered what I've suffered – there are laws in this country – and they'd let me off.'

Pianist   What did he say?

Ermeline   Nothing. He was yawning at the time. But he